Cracking the
CAHSEE

Mathematics

Third Edition

James Flynn and Matthew McIver

PrincetonReview.com

Random House, Inc. New York

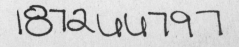

The Princeton Review, Inc.
2315 Broadway
New York, NY 10024
E-mail: editorialsupport@review.com

Reprinted, *Mathematics Content Standards for California Public Schools
K–12*, © 2005, California Department of Education,
P.O. Box 271, Sacramento, CA 95812-0271

ISBN 978-0-375-42868-5

Editors: Heather Brady
Production Editors: Meave Shelton
Production Artist: Kim Howie
Manufactured in the United States of America.

10 9 8 7 6 5 4 3 2 1

Third Edition

John Katzman, Chairman, Founder
Michael J. Perik, President, CEO
Stephen Richards, COO, CFO
John Marshall, President, Test Preparation Services
Rob Franek, VP Test Prep Books, Publisher

Editorial
Seamus Mullarkey, Editorial Director
Rebecca Lessem, Senior Editor
Selena Coppock, Editor
Heather Brady, Editor

Production Services
Scott Harris, Executive Director, Production Services
Suzanne Barker, Director, Production Services
Kim Howie, Senior Graphic Designer

Production Editorial
Meave Shelton, Production Editor
Emma Parker, Production Editor

Research & Development
Tricia McCloskey, Managing Editor
Ed Carroll, Agent for National Content Directors
Briana Gordon, Senior Project Editor
Liz Rutzel, Project Editor

Random House Publishing Team
Tom Russell, Publisher
Nicole Benhabib, Publishing Manager
Ellen L. Reed, Production Manager
Alison Skrabek, Associate Managing Editor
Elham Shabahat, Publishing Assistant

Contents

What Is The Princeton Review?

The Princeton Review is a test-preparation company that has spent more than 20 years helping students achieve higher scores on standardized tests. We offer test-preparation courses in more than 500 locations in 12 different countries, as well as online. We also publish over 200 books ranging from test-preparation guides like the one you have in your hand, to books on getting into college, applying for financial aid, and getting on the right career track.

Our phenomenal success improving students' scores on standardized tests is due to a simple, innovative, and radically effective philosophy: Study the test, not what the test claims to test. This approach has led to the development of techniques for taking standardized tests based on the principles the test writers themselves use to write the tests.

The Princeton Review has found that its methods work not just for cracking the CAHSEE, but for any standardized test. We've already successfully applied our system to the GMAT, LSAT, MCAT, and GRE, to name just a few. Although in some ways the CAHSEE is a very different test from those mentioned above, in the end a standardized test is a standardized test. This book uses our time-tested principle: Crack the system based on how the test is written.

You are about to unlock a vast collection of powerful strategies that have one and only one purpose: to help you pass the CAHSEE exam. Our techniques work. We developed them after spending countless hours scrutinizing real tests. Our methods have been widely imitated, but no one else can achieve our rates of success. Read this book to find out how our techniques can help you crack the CAHSEE exam.

Part I:
Orientation

Chapter 1
Tips on How to
Use This Book

WHAT DO I DO WITH THIS BOOK?

You've got a hefty amount of information in your hands. The key to getting through it all is to plan ahead. You are already in good shape by looking at this book.

Instead of worrying about how dense this book is, focus on starting your preparation early. We know that it may be easier said than done. That's why we've organized this book into easily digestible topics. (Wait! Don't eat the book!) Having trouble identifying the difference between an exponent and an expression? Turn to Chapter 7. Want extra practice with charts and graphs? Turn to Chapter 12. Studying for the CAHSEE doesn't have to be overwhelming. This book will help you focus your CAHSEE practice and provide you with solid preparation in all the subject areas tested on the CAHSEE. If you know you are weaker in one of the subjects covered by the test, you should begin with that subject so you can practice it throughout your preparation.

Our best advice for you is to start working through this book about three months before the test. Do you already have a good sense of your strengths and weaknesses? If not, make it a point to speak with your teacher after class about topics you should practice. You can also take a practice test in the back of the book to see how you do on different types of questions.

Then buckle down and set a study schedule. It is important that you stick to this study schedule. There are a lot of things than can distract you from studying: sports, work, friends, TV; you can probably add ten more to that list right now. So it is important that you make yourself a plan that you can and will stick to. Be realistic and allow yourself some fun time, but don't blow off your CAHSEE work completely!

Look at the schedule below to see an example of a realistic study plan that will help you stay on track.

	Sunday	Monday	Tuesday	Wednesday	Thursday	Friday	Saturday
School Work		After Dinner	After Dinner—CAHSEE first	After Dinner	After Dinner	First Thing	Write Report
Activities		Practice until 5:30	Practice until 5:30	Practice until 5:30			
Job	Work 12–4			Work 7–10			
Social Life						Big Date!	Movie
CAHSEE Prep	After Dinner		Right After Dinner		Do It Right After School— No Practice		Take Stuff To The Park

At Each Study Session

At each practice session, make sure you have sharpened pencils, scratch paper, blank index cards, and a dictionary. Each chapter is interactive; to fully understand the strategies we present, you need to be ready to try them out.

As you read each chapter, practice the strategies and complete all the exercises. Check your answers in the Answer Key as you do each set of problems, and try to figure out what types of errors you made to correct them. Review all of the strategies that give you trouble.

As you begin each session, review the chapter you did during the previous session before moving on to a new chapter.

When You Take a Practice Test

We recommend that you take the first practice test in the back of the book before you start your CAHSEE prep. This will give you a good idea of the concepts and question-types you need the most practice with. You can take the second practice test later, after you have reviewed the concepts in each chapter. When you are taking the practice tests remember to do the following:

Timing Your Study Sessions

Don't spend more than 2 hours studying in one sitting. This will help you stay fresh and alert and avoid study fatigue. You may want to cram four or five study sessions into one week, but we suggest that you give yourself at least a day or two between each session to absorb the information you've learned. Too much studying at once can be overwhelming, and we don't want you to stare at these pages like a zombie or burn out and quit.

- Time yourself strictly. Use a timer, watch, or set the alarm on your cell phone and do not allow yourself to go over time for any section.
- Take practice tests in one sitting. Allow yourself breaks of no more than 10 minutes between sections. This will help you build up your endurance for the real test and it will also provide an accurate picture of how you will do.
- Always take a practice test using an answer sheet with bubbles to fill in, just as you will for the real test. For the practice tests in this book, use the attached answer sheets.
- Each bubble you choose should be filled in thoroughly, and no other marks should be made in the answer area.
- As you fill in the bubble for a question, check to make sure you are on the correct number on the answer sheet. If you fill in the wrong bubble on the answer sheet, it won't matter if you've worked out the problem correctly in your test booklet. All that matters to the machine scoring your test is the No. 2 pencil mark—wherever it may happen to land.

MORE PRACTICE

If you complete the lessons in this book and take both practice tests and you still want more practice, you can ask your teacher for more homework. More homework? Are you crazy!? Actually, more homework could be good for you! Your teacher will most likely be more than willing to point you in the direction of more problems to practice on. It makes teachers feel prouder than an *American Idol* winner when you ask them for more work, so go ahead and make their day.

Study Tip: Staying Focused

Do you find it hard to stay focused when taking a standardized exam? If so, you're not alone. The good news is that there is a really easy thing you can do to improve your concentration: chew a piece of gum. That's right. Studies show that chewing gum can relieve stress and help increase focus, alertness, and concentration. Let's break out the Wrigley's!

WHAT TO DO ON EXAM DAY

The following chapters will go into a great bit of detail about what you should be doing to prepare for the CAHSEE exam. Below is a checklist of the things you should do on test day to make sure the cards are stacked in your favor:

- Get those zzzs! I know you're juggling school with other commitments, but it's important that you be fully rested on the day of the test. Try to get at least 8 hours of sleep the night before the exam
- Eat a good breakfast (and not just one that tastes good). Doughnuts are great for a sugar rush but the name of the game here is stamina, so eat something that will boost your energy as well as fill your stomach. Oatmeal, fruit and granola, and high-fiber cereals are all great options.
- Have with you all the necessary identification, and make sure to bring four No. 2 pencils with erasers. You may also want to bring juice and water and a small snack like a granola bar.
- Above all, pace yourself. You do not have to answer every question to pass the test. Don't let yourself become rushed.

Things to Bring

- Your ID or necessary information
- Four #2 pencils
- Eraser
- Drink (water or juice)
- Snack

ABOUT THIS BOOK

Cracking the CAHSEE Mathematics is designed to help you do two things.

- Improve your math skills
- Perform well on the Mathematics section of the California High School Exit Exam (CAHSEE)

This book is made up of two major parts: the lessons and the practice tests. The lessons review all the skills you need to pass the exam. The practice tests give you the chance to try out your refreshed skills in a format similar to the actual CAHSEE. Throughout the book you will also see these sidebars:

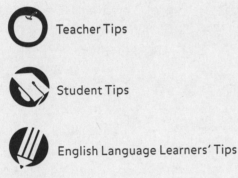 Teacher Tips

Student Tips

English Language Learners' Tips

Fun Facts

Before we get started, turn to the next chapter for a detailed overview of what is on the CAHSEE exam. By learning as much about the test and its purpose beforehand, you will be better prepared to master the test-taking strategies that will help improve your overall performance. At the end of the day, the CAHSEE exam is just a small hurdle that can be overcome with the right preparation. We'll show you how. Let's get started!

Chapter 2:
Introduction to
the CAHSEE

AN OVERVIEW OF THE TEST

CAHSEE stands for the California High School Exit Exam. It is a standardized test that aims to assess students' proficiency in the following subjects: reading, writing, and mathematics. A passing score on the CAHSEE exam first became a high school exit requirement for the graduating class of 2006.

There are two separate CAHSEE exams, one in Mathematics and one in English-Language Arts (ELA). The ELA exam also contains a Writing component. In order to attain your high school diploma in the state of California, you must pass both portions of the CAHSEE exam. The CAHSEE exam will first be offered in your 10th grade year, during either February or March. You will have several opportunities to take and pass the test.

Once you pass one of the exams (Mathematics or ELA), there is no need for you to take that portion of the test again. For example, if you pass the Mathematics part in your 10th grade year but not the ELA part, then you will only need to retake the ELA in your 11th grade year.

You may be nervous about trying to pass the CAHSEE exam the first time around. While this book will prepare you to earn a passing score the first time out of the gate, the good news is that you'll have six tries to pass the test. And since you're already studying, the odds are favorable that you'll come out ahead.

Teacher Tip

Tell your students far in advance what the dates of the CAHSEE exams are. Let them know that they have more than one chance to pass.

What is on the CAHSEE?

As we already mentioned, the CAHSEE aims to find out if you are learning what you are supposed to be in reading, writing, and mathematics. Here is what the CAHSEE writers are looking for on each test.

- **Mathematics**: Number Sense, Algebra and Functions, Measurement and Geometry, Algebra I, Mathematical Reasoning, Statistics, Data Analysis, and Probability.
- **English-Language Arts**: Word Analysis, Reading Comprehension, Literary Response and Analysis, Writing Strategies, Writing Conventions, Writing Applications.

Let's start with the Mathematics exam. This portion of the CAHSEE is composed of 92 questions—80 count toward your score, and 12 are questions the test makers are trying out to see if they want to use them for real in a later test. It is an untimed test—that means you can take as long as you need to fill out the answers, up to one whole school day! (We'll discuss strategies for staying focused and energized in the next chapter.) Realistically, though, it probably won't take you more than about three hours. However long it takes you, the key is to not get discouraged! The concepts you will be tested on break down as follows:

Number Sense	17 questions
Algebra and Functions	20 questions
Measurement and Geometry	18 questions
Probability and Statistics	13 questions
Algebra I	12 questions
Experimental	12 questions
TOTAL	**92 questions**

The lessons in this book will take you through each of these concepts step by step. We will also show you how to strategize your CAHSEE prep to focus on problem areas and maximize your chances of getting a passing score.

Though this book does not go over specific strategies for passing the ELA portion of the CAHSEE exam, here is a brief overview of what you can expect to encounter on the ELA section of the CAHSEE:

Word Analysis	7 questions
Reading Comprehension	18 questions
Literary Responses and Analysis	20 questions
Writing Conventions	15 questions
Writing Strategies	12 questions
TOTAL	**72 questions**

Writing Applications (essay)	1 question

Like the Mathematics section, the ELA portion is untimed. For more information on this section, check out *Cracking the CAHSEE: English-Language Arts*, available at PrincetonReview.com.

Field Test Items

Both the ELA and Mathematics sections of the CAHSEE will have Field Test Items on them. This is a fancy term for test questions that do not count towards your score. These items are used as research by the test writers. BEWARE: You will not be able to tell what is a Field Test Item and what is a real CAHSEE question when you take the test. The number of Field Test Items that will appear on each administration of the CAHSEE is not disclosed. All we know is that there will be Field Test Items and that they will appear to be exactly the same as the real test questions. It is never worth your time to try to figure out what is a Field Test Item and what is a real test question. You should always treat each and every question as though it is a real test question and answer it to the best of your ability.

Who Writes the CAHSEE?

Close your eyes for a moment and try to picture what goes on at ETS headquarters during a question-writing session. If you imagined a room full of prizewinning mathematicians and literary professors, you'd be way off base. If you saw some stuffy-yet-brilliant college professors working hand in hand with the Department of Education, keep dreaming. How about a group of the best teachers and educators? Not even close.

The truth is the CAHSEE is written by a bunch of regular Joes whose jobs just happen to involve writing test questions. Why does this matter? Because you should always remember that the CAHSEE is nothing special—it's just a test. And while ETS has become quite good at writing standardized tests, to the point that they can predict how you'll attack certain questions and what sorts of mistakes you'll probably make, this strength can also be a weakness. Because the test is standardized, the CAHSEE has to ask the same types of questions over and over again. With enough practice, you can learn how to think like ETS.

What Is a Passing Score on the CAHSEE?

Your score on the CAHSEE exam is determined by looking at the total number of questions you answer correctly. Best of all, there is no guessing penalty! You should plan to answer every question since you will not be penalized for wrong answers.

Each question is worth one point. The number of questions you get right is called your "raw score." Your raw score is then converted into a "scaled score" between 250 and 450. For example, a Mathematics raw score of 32 (meaning you got 32 questions right) is approximately equivalent to a scaled score of 330. And an ELA raw score of 65 (meaning you got 65 questions right) is approximately equivalent to a scaled score of 420.

For the Mathematics portion of the CAHSEE, there are a total of 80 possible points to be earned. This makes sense, as there are 80 total questions. In order to achieve a passing score on the Math portion of the CAHSEE, you will need to answer approximately 53 percent (or 42) of the questions correctly. Not too shabby! A score that would earn you a D in school is plenty good enough for the CAHSEE. You can do it!

The English-Language Arts component of the CAHSEE is scored and scaled differently. For the English-Language Arts portion of the CAHSEE, there are a total of 90 possible points to be earned. You're probably wondering how this is possible, considering that there are only 72 questions on the ELA test. This is because the Essay portion of the exam is treated as an additional 18 questions in terms of the scoring guidelines. In order to achieve a passing score on the English-Language Arts component of the CAHSEE, you only need to earn a Raw Score of 57 (out of 90). When converted, that typically amounts to a Scaled Score of 351 (out of 450). That means answering approximately 63 percent of the questions correctly.

You can get all the details by picking up our book, *Cracking the CAHSEE: English-Language Arts* at PrincetonReview.com.

So How Do I Pass the CAHSEE?

Unless you're a classic overachiever, it may be helpful to know that taking the CAHSEE exam is not the same as taking, for example, the SAT. The objectives are quite different. While the SAT pretends to test your college-readiness (The Princeton Review has long held its own views on how effectively the test actually accomplishes that goal), the CAHSEE simply gauges your readiness to graduate high school by testing your proficiency in English, Writing, and Math. In other words, by the time you take the CAHSEE, the tested concepts should look familiar from your high school classes. Moreover, whether you get all the questions right on the CAHSEE or just enough to earn a passing score, the result is the same: You still get to walk across that stage come graduation day.

Moral of the story: Take a deep breath and relax! You do NOT need to get an "A" on the CAHSEE. In fact, when it comes to the CAHSEE, you should stop thinking in terms of the A-B-C grading scale altogether. Think instead in terms of the number of questions you need to answer correctly. As we just discussed, you need to get approximately 53 percent of your Mathematics questions correct and 63 percent of your ELA questions correct in order to pass the exam. So let's say you did not pass your Mathematics CAHSEE in your 10th grade year. Let's say your scaled score was a 330. This would mean that you got about 32 questions correct (assuming you got the maximum number of points on the essay). In order to achieve a passing score in your 11th grade year, you will need to achieve a score of 351. This would mean that you need to get about 42 questions right. The difference between passing and not passing is a matter of only 11 questions.

Student Tip

On the CAHSEE, a correct answer is the equivalent to one point. There is no guessing penalty so it makes no sense to leave anything blank

Student Tip

If you're retaking the CAHSEE, there's a really good chance that you're only 10 to 15 points away from passing (maybe even less). By thinking in terms of number of questions rather than scaled score, the test will become much more manageable.

HOW TO PREPARE FOR THE CAHSEE

At the end of the day, the CAHSEE is just another standardized test. As with any standardized test, it is important to think about how the test is constructed when strategizing your CAHSEE prep.

When a standardized test is created, the concepts (standards) being tested are predetermined. For the CAHSEE exam, the approved list of standards cover ELA and Mathematics fundamentals appropriate for a student at a 10th grade level. The CAHSEE cannot, for example, put Calculus on the Mathematics exam. Calculus is not in the approved list of standards. So, there is really very little in the content of the exams that you are not already familiar with.

This might make you wonder: *If all they're testing me on is what I already know, then why does the CAHSEE seem so difficult to me?*

That is a great question!

The exam seems difficult because the test writers built it that way. The test writers don't want everyone to pass, because that would defeat the purpose of the test. They need to make sure that there is an even spread of scores among test takers. In order to make this happen, test writers build tricks and traps into their tests that cause students to get questions wrong for reasons that have nothing whatsoever to do with their knowledge of the concepts being tested. For example, have you ever wondered why there are big, bulky word problems on mathematics tests? What does reading a big, long paragraph have to do with knowing how to add, subtract, multiply, or divide? Nothing!

ELL Tip

One out of every four California high school students is an English Language Learner. You are not alone and you CAN pass this test!

But by burying a math question deep within a twist and tangle of awkwardly worded sentences, the test writers increase the likelihood that you will make a mistake on the question because you misinterpreted the information. While the interpretation of information has nothing to do with whether or not you know how to add, subtract, multiply, or divide, it doesn't matter: You still won't get those points if you don't read carefully. As a CAHSEE test taker you need to know not only the concepts being tested but also how to be a smart and savvy test taker who can recognize tricks and traps and know how to avoid them.

This is important to remember:

> Standardized tests don't tell how smart you are; they only reveal how good you are at taking standardized tests.

It is a common misperception that if someone is smart, then he or she will do well on the CAHSEE. Conversely, some people may think that not doing well on the CAHSEE means that they are not as smart as their peers. This is absolutely not true, so if you are guilty of this kind of thinking, get it out of your head right now.

Knowing how standardized tests work and what the test writers expect from you can help you do better on the exam. We hope you have paid attention in class so that you are familiar with the subjects on the CAHSEE, but even if you haven't, the strategies in the next chapter will help you get a better score.

Teacher Tip

Encourage your students by showing them how attainable a passing score can be and how close they are to achieving it.

Chapter 3
CAHSEE
Strategies

This chapter will cover general strategies that you can use on both CAHSEE exams, and specific strategies to help you just with math problems.

You also need to know how to

- take advantage of the order in which questions are asked
- make better use of your time by scoring the easy points first
- find the traps that the test writers have laid out for you
- turn those traps into points

To show you how to do this, we first have to tell you something about the way the CAHSEE is arranged.

Teacher Tip
Go over how to read a question slowly and translate word problems into math symbols.

DEGREE OF DIFFICULTY

On the CAHSEE, the test writers assign the questions three degrees of difficulty: easy, medium, and difficult. You should expect to see roughly one-third easy questions, one-third medium questions, and one-third difficult questions. It would make sense if the test writers were to put all the easy questions first, followed by all the medium questions, and then all the difficult questions. This way it would be really clear where you should expect to run into trouble. But test writers will not do this. Knowing that most unskilled test takers will work through the test from beginning to end, the test writers will actually mix up all the easy, medium, and difficult questions. This causes people to achieve lower scores. How?

Well, let's say that the first question on your CAHSEE is an easy one. You work the problem, get it right, and you feel like you're rockin' the CAHSEE. Then the second problem is really difficult. What do you think is going to happen?

You're going to spend a lot of time and a lot of energy trying to get this problem right. Maybe you will get it right or maybe you won't, but now you're tired and frustrated. As a result, you probably won't get as far into the exam, and you'll probably make a lot more mistakes. But when you're spending all that time on question 2, you've forgotten that there are still many more easy and medium questions left. You could probably move on to one of the easy/medium questions and figure out the correct answer with nowhere near as much effort, and your overall score would be higher as a result.

Moral of the story: Make sure you SLOW DOWN and focus your energy on the easy and medium questions before trying your hand at the difficult ones. Don't rush through the questions that you're more likely to answer correctly. Get those points. Then move on to the difficult questions, using POE to eliminate wrong answers. After all that, fill in guesses for the ones that are too hard to solve. Remember, there is no guessing penalty!

Is It Difficult for You?

Remember that you have particular strengths and weaknesses when it comes to math. So, even if you're in a section of the test that is not your strong suit, there will still probably be a bunch of problems you can do. Look for the ones you know how to solve first, no matter where they are in the test!

THE TWO-PASS METHOD

You have two major advantages going into the CAHSEE: 1) the test is untimed and 2) there is no guessing penalty. The Two-Pass Method is a very useful strategy for test takers who are not worried about a time crunch, and who want to use what they know about order of difficulty to answer more questions correctly.

The idea behind the Two-Pass Method is very straightforward: It involves reordering the questions on the test to help make the test as efficient and straightforward as possible for you. Here's how it works: On your first pass through the test, you should put all of your questions into one of two categories:

(1)   I know how to do this problem (in which case you should stop and do the problem before moving on).
(2)   I DON'T know how to do this problem (in which case you should skip the problem and move on).

The idea is that on the first pass through the test, you will do only the questions that you know how to do and you will skip the rest.

Slow Down

Most students do much better when they slow down and spend more time working carefully on the easy questions. Don't let careless, hurried errors ruin your score!

Please Pass

Just using the Two-Pass Method might be enough to raise your score to a passing one!

Then, on your second pass through the test, you should look at the questions that you did NOT answer on your first pass. You will put these remaining questions into two different categories:

(1)   I sorta-kinda think I could do this (in which case you should stop and use the test-taking strategies you've already learned to answer the question).

(2)   I really DO NOT know how to do this question (in which case you should pick the "letter of the day"—that is, just fill in an answer choice and move on). Remember, there's no penalty for guessing.

You are looking to get about 53 percent of your math questions and 63 percent of your ELA questions right. If you do the math, 66 percent (two-thirds) of the questions on the CAHSEE Math and 66 percent of the questions on the CAHSEE ELA are either easy or medium questions. So even if you did not touch a single difficult question, you could probably get enough easy and medium questions right to pass the CAHSEE.

PROCESS OF ELIMINATION

What's the capital of Azerbaijan?

Give up? If you're like most high school students, if this question came up on a test, you'd probably skip it. Let's turn this question into a multiple-choice question—just like the majority of questions you'll find on the CAHSEE—and see if you can figure out the answer.

What is the capital of Azerbaijan?
A. Washington, D.C.
B. Paris
C. Tokyo
D. Baku

Does the question still seem hard? Probably not. Students who give up on questions just because they don't know the correct answer right off the top of their heads are making a huge mistake, especially when there is no harm in guessing. These students don't stop to think that they might be able to find the correct answer simply by eliminating all the answer choices they know are wrong.

Almost all of the questions on the CAHSEE are multiple-choice questions. On every single multiple-choice question one of those choices, and only one, will be the correct answer to the question. The right answer is on the page; all you have to do is identify it!

Look for the Wrong Answers—Not the Right Ones

You're probably wondering why in the world you would want to look for the wrong answer. Because wrong answers are usually easier to find than the right ones. Remember the question about Azerbaijan? Even though you didn't know the answer off the top of your head, you easily figured it out by eliminating the three wrong choices.

In other words, you used Process of Elimination, which we'll call POE for short. POE is an extremely important concept, and one that you will need to master in order to pass the CAHSEE. The idea behind Process of Elimination (POE) is that your job as a test taker is NOT to find the right answer. Your job is to get rid of the wrong answers. Again, this might seem obvious, but it's really quite profound. Test writers know that the first thing any test taker is going to do is go searching for what they think is the right answer. So test writers will bend this to their favor. How?

Have you ever noticed that most standardized tests use phrases such as "Credited Response" or "Best Available Answer Choice" when explaining why a certain answer choice is correct? Test writers use this language because they will often intentionally put answer choices down that are less than ideal but better than the other options.

They do this so that you will second-guess yourself. You will work a problem, solve a problem, and come up with your own answer. Then you will look at the available answer choices and... Surprise!... the answer you're looking for is not there.

This will make you believe that you've done something wrong. So you go back to the question and rework it, changing things that you actually had done right in the first place. If you approach the answer choices with the goal of getting rid of the wrong answer choices first and then working with what is left, you'll have much more success. Instead of looking for an answer that is identical to what is in your head, you should look at the options you're given and try to eliminate wrong answers. By simply eliminating available answer choices, you increase your probability of getting the question right.

Student Tip

The CAHSEE is a multiple-choice test. Use this to your advantage. By attempting to solve all questions before considering your answer choice options, you're actually making the test more difficult than it needs to be.

GET YOUR PENCIL IN THERE

Don't be shy about physically marking up your test booklet. This can help you narrow down choices, take the best possible guess, and save time!

 Put a check mark next to the answer you like.

 Put a squiggle next to an answer you kinda like.

 Put a question mark next to an answer you don't understand.

 Cross out the letter of any answer choice you KNOW is wrong.

Of course, you can always come up with your own system. Just remember to be consistent!

GUESS AND GO

Remember, there is no guessing penalty on the CAHSEE. That means your odds of picking the right answer are 1 out of 4. If you can eliminate two choices, your odds shoot up to fifty-fifty! You don't always have to be sure of the answer to make a guess and fill one in.

Review of Test-Taking Strategies

When working with strategies, it is important to use them in the proper fashion. This means that you will not only need to know how to use the different strategies, but you will also need to know when a particular strategy will be helpful on a question. It is very important that you practice each strategy when you're studying for the CAHSEE. Test strategies are best learned by repeating the strategy over and over again, working strings of questions. Fortunately you have plenty of material to practice with in this guide.

Let's review the order of the strategies:

1. Order of Difficulty

2. 2-Pass System

3. Process of Elimination

4. Get Your Pencil in There

5. Guess and Go!

A FEW LAST WORDS

Here are a few more tips before we begin the Math Strategies and lessons.

Don't Panic!

The CAHSEE is untimed. So relax! A lot of test takers make mistakes because they get so anxious that they do silly things. Remember: The CAHSEE is not testing your intelligence. As we've discussed, CAHSEE questions are designed to get you to make mistakes for reasons that have nothing to do with your knowledge. Stay calm and use your strategies! And don't go thinking that you have to be perfect to pass the CAHSEE—you don't!

Use Your Time Wisely

Even though the time on the CAHSEE is unlimited, your energy is not. Be sure to work through the test doing all the questions you know how to do first. This way you can be sure to maximize your score by making certain that you get all the points that your knowledge will allow you to get.

At the same time, be smart about how much time and effort you put into the hard questions. A lot of times the hard questions are losing battles. Sure, you might eventually get them right, but by that time you'll have driven yourself crazy and drained your energy. Be smart about what you choose to do and what you choose NOT to do. Sometimes, the question you guess on will prove just as, if not more, valuable than the questions you spend time working through.

Save your brain power for the questions you can get right quickly.

Read the Questions Carefully

There's nothing worse than having done everything perfectly... and then realizing you didn't follow the directions. A lot of the mistakes that are made on mathematics questions are made while reading (or misreading) the question. Think about it: How many times have you missed the word "remainder" in a fraction problem and gotten the whole question wrong as a result?

Moral of the story: Read the questions thoroughly the first time through. Don't skim. It is so much better to read a math question one time and really get it than to read it over and over without knowing what you should do.

Put Questions In Your Own Words

If a question is complicated and hard to understand, take the question out of the test writer's language and rephrase it for yourself. Using your own language can help to clarify what the question is really getting at.

Remember, your job is to pull the important information out of a question. Restating a question is a tool that helps isolate the information you need.

Bubble Carefully

Be careful with your answer sheet! Since you will be using Personal Order Of Difficulty (more on this later) to skip around throughout the test, it is very easy to accidentally put the answer for question #22 in question #23's row of bubbles. Be careful! This is an unfortunate way to lose points.

Try placing your test booklet on top of the answer sheet, placing the top edge of the booklet underneath the answer sheet row of the question number you are working. When you move on to the next question, shift the booklet down a row. If you get into a habit like this, it can help to keep everything in the right place.

Play Answer Choices Against One Another

Sometimes, just from looking at the spread of the answer choices, you can get rid of some of the choices. Frequently, just looking at the size of the numbers in the answer choices will allow you to eliminate something that is way too big or way too small.

Bite-Sized Pieces

Math questions frequently require many steps to be solved. This is why math questions can be so difficult to maneuver. The best way to fight back is to break the questions down into bite-sized pieces. Gather your information. Assess your information. Work with your information. But do these things one at a time. Otherwise your brain will get crisscrossed and you'll make mistakes.

Stay Calm and Collected

Do NOT panic! Treat each question as a new opportunity to pick up some points. Don't get hung up on previous questions that you weren't too sure about. Move forward, not backward. Answer each question to the best of your ability and move on.

Remember, no one is asking for you to be perfect. Just do what you can and apply the strategies from this book to the questions you can crack. That's all anyone expects from you: that you'll try and that you'll take a solid swing at the questions.

Good luck!

Chapter 4
Math Strategies
for the CAHSEE

You just learned test-taking strategies that can be applied to any CAHSEE question type. There are a number of additional strategies that may be useful when it comes to tackling CAHSEE Mathematics questions in particular. We'll go over them now.

BALLPARKING

The CAHSEE is a goofy high school exit exam, and because all of the math questions are multiple choice, you can afford to approximate numbers like 9.211111187. When you work with rounded numbers, you can approximate what your answer will be. Knowing the range your answer should fall into before you do any real math can help you eliminate some answer choices right off the bat.

If your friend stood next to a wall in your living room and asked you how high the ceiling was, what would you do? Would you break out your geometry textbook and try to measure the angle of the shadow cast by your pal? Of course not. You'd look at your friend and think something like this: "Miguel's about 6 feet tall. The ceiling's a couple of feet higher than he is. It must be about 8 feet high."

Your ballpark answer wouldn't be exact, but it would be close. If someone later claimed that the ceiling in the living room was 25 feet high, you'd be able to tell him with confidence that he was mistaken.

You can do the same thing on the CAHSEE math questions. Whenever possible, you should round the numbers given to you in a math question in order to permit easier calculations. Ballparking is a math-specific strategy that allows you to solve the question by rounding the numbers to easier values, then applying POE to the available answer choices. For example, let's look at this problem:

> **The unit for weight in the metric system is the newton. One pound equals about 4.45 newtons. If Jordan weighs 89 pounds, what is his approximate weight in newtons?**
>
> A   20 newtons
> B   85 newtons
> C   396 newtons
> D   404 newtons

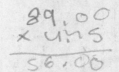

The information you have to work with is pretty clean: 4.45 newtons equals 1 pound, and Jordan weighs 89 pounds. So to solve this question, all you need to do is multiply 4.45 by 89. But this is going to take a good amount of time and some decimal places, both things that increase the likelihood that you're going to make a mistake.

So instead, you should Ballpark it. Round 4.45 down to 4. Round 89 up to 90. $90 \times 4 = 360$. So we know the answer is somewhere in the vicinity of 360. We can immediately eliminate answer choices A and B, because they're way too small.

Because C and D are so close together, now you might want to do some real math. Ballparking won't always take you all the way to the correct answer, but it will get you closer!

Ballparking is especially useful on the questions that would take you too long to figure out exactly. Use Ballparking to eliminate as many answers as you can, then Guess and Go!

Student Tip

How do you know when to Ballpark? Try it any time you see that the arithmetic is going to be difficult.

WRITE IT DOWN

Have you ever wondered why math problems have so many darn words in them? It's to get you to screw up. The more difficult the words and the sentences are to unpack, the greater the likelihood that you'll make a mistake.

Writing It Down is a great technique that can be used to solve long, bulky word problems. The first time you read a math question, you should do nothing more than simply remove the important pieces of information. Take these pieces, one by one, and write them down on your scratch paper. Once you have gathered all of the information, start to solve the problem.

Ballparking Helpers

Knowing the approximate values of some common square roots will help you ballpark more effectively. Be sure to memorize these:

$\sqrt{1}$ = 1
$\sqrt{2}$ = 1.4
$\sqrt{3}$ = 1.7

For example, let's look at a problem:

> **For his science class, Jamaar did a survey of the cars in the teachers' parking lot. Of the 92 cars parked there, 30 had four-cylinder engines. Approximately what percentage of the cars surveyed had four-cylinder engines?**
>
> **A**   3%
>
> **B**   30%
>
> **C**   33%
>
> **D**   92%

Now, do we really care who this dude is or what class he is in? And who cares that this takes place in the teachers' parking lot? This information is completely irrelevant.

It is your job to read through and transfer the important information to paper. As you read through you should write down the following things: 92 cars, 30 four-cylinder, % 4 cylinders. That's it. Nothing else is even close to be important. Now, working with these three pieces of information, this question becomes a lot easier.

What Was The Question?

Don't try to solve the question before you have gathered all of the information. One of the most common mistakes test takers make is to stop part way through a question and start solving. Read the whole question carefully, then write down the important information.

You're being asked to determine what percentage of the cars surveyed had four-cylinder engines? That means you have to divide 30 by 92. Nothing to it. And, if you use Ballparking, you don't even have to do the math to figure out what $30 \div 92$ will equal; you can tell right away that it is about one-third, or 33%. We know that it's not A) 3% or D) 92%. A is way too small and D is way too big. B and C are very close, so you might want to do the math now to figure out which one it is closer to. Did you get C? Good!

See, once you transferred the information to scratch paper, this was a very straightforward question. Approach word problems like a detective would approach a crime scene. A detective first gathers ALL the clues and then starts to connect them. He wouldn't worry about how everything fit together until he had all the information available to him. You should do the same thing. Get all the information available to you first, make sure it is clearly laid out in your own words, and then worry about problem solving.

DON'T SKIP THE GRAPHS!

When you see a chart, table, or graph question you should definitely try to solve it. Most of the time, the answers will be right there in the chart for you to grab!

First, look at the graph to see what information is being presented. Then, go straight to the question and read it carefully to find out what it is asking. Now go back to the chart, graph, or table and find the information you need. Then apply POE and move on to the next one!

Let's look at a problem.

1. **The graph below shows the number of spectators at a local sports team's home games from 1993 through 1998.**

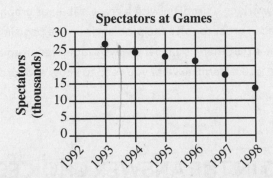

between

Based on these data, what was the most likely number of spectators at home games reported in 1992?

A   23,000

B   25,000

C   27,000

D   30,000

First, look at the graph. The axes are *Years* and *Spectators*. Next, go to the question. The question wants to know the approximate number of spectators in 1992. First of all, the word "approximate" immediately lets us know that we can Ballpark here.

Next, let's take a look at the graph very briefly. We can see that 1992 would be the first year on the graph. And we can see that each year, the dot gets a little bit lower. This means that each year there are fewer spectators. So, we can immediately eliminate answer choices (A) and (B) because the number of spectators was likely higher in 1992 than it was in 1993. And in 1993, the number of spectators was about 26,000 or so.

Next, when we look at answer choices (C) and (D), we can see they are both greater than 26,000. So the question now is really how much greater must the attendance be in 1992?

Again, look at the dots. See that they get gradually further apart from one another. The shift from 1993 to 1994 was around 2,000 spectators, so the shift from 1992 to 1993 should have been smaller than 2,000 spectators, according to the graph. Answer choice (C) shows a shift of about 1000, which is less than 2,000 and fits our rules. Choice (D), 30,000, would be a shift of 4,000 which is too large. The answer is (C).

Notice that we did not study the graph in all of its detail. We just want to deal with the information we need. Going to the question as soon as you have a sense of the graph allows you to focus on just the information that you need.

The advantage to working a problem with a chart, table, or graph is that all the information you need in order to solve the problem is on the page in front of you. The downside, though, is that there is almost always a lot more information than you really need. Your job is to determine what you need to know and forget the rest.

PLUGGING IN THE ANSWER CHOICES (PITA)

Plugging In the Answer Choices is a technique for solving word problems that helps you think through complicated algebraic and arithmetic relationships. When all of the answer choices are numbers (not variables), you can use PITA to see whether or not the numbers work out correctly. This strategy is also called "backsolving" because we are starting from the end (answers) and working backwards to see if they solve the problem. Let's look at a problem:

The Lopez family has three children. Ricky is the youngest. Lourdes is four times older than Ricky, and 9-year-old Maria is three years younger than Lourdes. How old is Ricky?

A   3 years old

B   4 years old

C   5 years old

D   6 years old

Trying to pull apart all of the relationships between the different children can be tricky and confusing. This problem would have you make an equation with variables, which can lead to a lot of mistakes. So let's try PITA instead.

Let's start with answer choice C. Plug the value 5 into the question for Ricky's age. So, if Ricky is 5 years old, then Lourdes is 20 years old. And if Lourdes is 20, then Maria (who is three years younger than Lourdes) would have to be 17. But, according to the question, Maria is 9. So Answer choice C is wrong. Eliminate it.

Pick another answer choice to Plug In. Since 5 was too big, we can also eliminate D, which is even bigger. Let's try a smaller number like answer choice A. Plug the value 3 in for Ricky's age. So, if Ricky is 3, then Lourdes is 12. And if Lourdes is 12, then subtract 3 to get Maria's age. So Maria would be 9, which is the age we wanted! So, we take answer choice A and we're done.

Only use PITA when your answer choices do NOT have variables in them. Next we will discuss a Plugging In technique you can use for variables.

PLUGGING IN FOR VARIABLES

Algebra and all those variables can bog you down and cause you to make mistakes. Isn't it easier when you can just make the calculations with real numbers? Well, that's what Plugging In is all about. We'll show you how to substitute real numbers and turn algebra problems into easier arithmetic.

Plugging In for variables is a multistep technique:

 Step 1 Plug In values for the variables in the question. For example, $x = 2, y = 5$.

 Step 2 Solve the question using the plugs to establish a target answer.

 Step 3 Plug the same values into the answer choices to see which answer choices give you your target answer.

PITA Chip... umm...Tip

When using PITA, start by plugging in one of the middle answers. If one doesn't work out, you can still eliminate the outer answers that will also be too big or too small.

PITA Everywhere

PITA works the same on difficult problems as it does on easy ones. This is truly a "one-size-fits-all" strategy. Use it with confidence!

You can get more than one answer choice that gives you your target answer. So be careful and check all of the choices. If you find yourself in such a situation, just go back, Plug In a new value for your variables to get a new target answer and Plug In again.

For example, let's look at a problem.

The expression $4(x - 3) - 2(x - 3)$ is equivalent to

A x

B $2x$

C $2x - 6$

D $2x - 18$

Step 1 Plug In values for the variables in question. In this example, we have only one variable: x. So, let's say that x is 5. You could pick any number you like, but it's best to pick a number that will allow easy calculations. Since 5 minus 3 is easy to work with, I'll choose 5.

Step 2 Solve the question using the plugs to establish a target answer.

So,

$$4(5 - 3) - 2(5 - 3) \text{ equals}$$
$$4(2) - 2(2), \text{ which equals}$$
$$8 - 4, \text{ which equals } 4.$$

Circle 4 on your scratch paper and write the word "TARGET" next to it. This is your Target Answer.

What Should I Plug In?

Although you can Plug In any number, you can make your life much easier by Plugging In "good" numbers—numbers that are simple to work with or that make the problem easier to manipulate. Picking a small number, such as 2, will usually make finding the answer easier. If the problem asks for a percentage, Plug In 10 or 100. If the problem has to do with minutes, try 60. Pick numbers that are manageable and work with the problem. -1.2 would not be a good choice.

Step 3 Plug the same value into the answer choices to see what gives you your target answer.

Answer Choice (A) is x. If I Plug In 5 for x, I will not get my target of 4. So eliminate answer choice (A).

Answer Choice (B) is $2x$. If I Plug In 5 for x, I will get 10. But my target is 4. So eliminate answer choice (B)

Answer Choice (C) is $2x - 6$. If I Plug In 5 for x, I will get $10 - 6$, which is 4. This matches my target answer, so set it aside as a possibility.

Answer Choice (D) is $2x - 18$. If I Plug In 5 for x, I will get $10 - 18$, which is -8. But my target is 4. so eliminate answer choice (D). The answer must be (C).

PLUGGING IN ON GRAPHS

A similar Plugging In strategy can be used on certain graph problems. This technique allows you to sidestep doing geometry by converting the problem to easy arithmetic.

Plugging In On Graphs means plugging in numbers for the x-coordinate and y-coordinate values and plotting the point you created on the graph provided. If the point lands on the line graphed, then keep that answer choice. If the point does not land on the line graphed, then eliminate that answer choice. Keep Plugging In different values for the x-coordinate and y-coordinates until you're left with only one answer choice. Let's take a look at a problem:

What Should I Plug In On Graphs?

Try some negative x-and y-coordinates after you try some positive ones. This will create a variety of results for you because it will place the point you are plotting into different quadrants of the graph.

2. **Which of these graphs could be the graph of the equation $y = 3x^2$?**

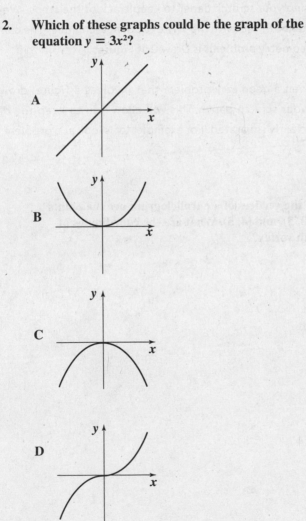

Start by Plugging In values for the *x*-coordinate and the *y*-coordinate. Let's say *x* is 1. So then, *y* must be 3. So, let's eliminate every graph whose line does not have a point (1, 3) on it. That will allow us to eliminate answer choices (C) and (D).

Now we Plug In new numbers. Let's Plug In –2 for *x*. So *y* must be 12. So, let's eliminate every graph whose line does not have a point (–2, 12) on it. This allows us to get rid of answer choice (A). And we're left with (B).

Use the Pictures

You can sometimes use the figures you are given to estimate values, if the figures are drawn to scale. This can be a useful shortcut!

DRAW OUT FIGURES

On any test, you should use your scratch paper to keep track of complicated information. Test writers love to give multistep problems because they know that the different steps can get jumbled up in your head and cause you to make mistakes. Counteract this by using your scratch paper to keep track of the steps. We have already seen the importance of this with the Write It Down technique. The companion for certain types of geometry problems is Draw Out Figures.

Whenever you are given a geometry problem that involves a figure, draw out as much as you can on your scratch paper. This will allow you to keep the different steps of the problem clearly separated. For example, let's look at a problem:

Three of the vertices of a parallelogram are the points (–2, 2), (0, 5), and (4, 5). What are the coordinates of the fourth vertex?

A (1, 2)

B (2, 2)

C (3, 2)

D (6, 2)

On a piece of scratch paper, or right in the margin of this book, draw an X axis and a Y axis. Now, one at a time, plot the three points you are given. It will become evident from this figure that we are looking for the bottom right corner of the parallelogram.

Now we can just use PITA and see what happens. For example, answer choice (D) will not create a parallelogram. The fourth vertex cannot be further out on the X axis than is point (4, 5), or we won't have a parallelogram. So eliminate (D).

When we Plug In answer choices (A), (B), and (C), we will see that answer choice (A) is too close to vertex (–2, 2) and answer choice (C) is too close to vertex (4, 5). Answer choice (B), however, is right in the middle.

Scratch It!

Nowadays, people use calculators all the time and it has made everyone a little bit lazy. Writing things down allows your brain to focus on navigating problems. Don't trust your tired brain to remember every piece of information. Use paper!

Review of Math Strategies

Ballparking

Ballpark when you're given difficult numbers to work with. Adjust the numbers you're given to easier numbers by rounding up or down. Work with the easier numbers to get an estimate of the answer. Then apply Process of Elimination.

Write It Down

Write It Down when you're given a problem with lots and lots of words. Read the problem one time through, thoroughly, and write down only the information you will need in order to solve the question.

Work the Charts, Tables, and Graphs

Skim the chart, table, or graph, and then go directly to the question. Use the chart, table, or graph to find the information you need to solve the problem.

PITA

PITA when the question has a lot of steps and your answer choices are numbers (not variables). Take each answer choice and drop it back into the question. Solve the question using the number. If everything works out right, then you've got the right answer. If the numbers don't quite work out, then eliminate that answer choice and move on to the next.

Plugging In For Variables

Plug In when the question involves variables and has variables in the answer choices. Plug In values for your variables and use them to solve the question and get a target answer. Plug In the same values into the answer choices to see what gives you your target answer.

Plugging In On Graphs

When the question involves graphs and there are variables given in the equation for the graph, Plug In values for the x- and y-coordinates. Then plot the point on your graph to see whether or not it falls on the line. Eliminate the answer choices that do not show an overlap of the line and the point you're plotting. Repeat this process until you have one answer choice left.

Draw Out Figures

Use your scratch paper to diagram the shapes and measurements that you are given. Do not leave anything floating around in your brain. Work it out on your scratch paper.

Part II
Math Review

Chapter 5
Arithmetic

The CAHSEE will cover a wide range of arithmetic problems. In this chapter we'll take you through what you need to know, step by step, with explanations and practice problems.

Standard NS 1.2

"Add, subtract, multiply, and divide rational numbers (integers, fractions, and terminating decimals) and take positive rational numbers to whole-number powers.

RATIONAL NUMBERS

Rational numbers can be integers (such as 3, –5 or 0), fractions (such as $\frac{1}{2}$), and decimals (such as 0.25 or 0.333333...). (Irrational numbers are basically numbers that cannot be represented as simple fractions. One of the most famous irrational numbers is π—irrational numbers really are crazy!) On the test, you will be asked to evaluate numerical expressions, combinations of numbers, and operation signs.

Let's take a look at an example.

Which of the following numerical expressions results in a positive number?

A   (3) + (–8) + (5)

B   (8) + (–3) = 5

C   (–3) + (–8) + (5)

D   (–8) + (3)

Negative Outlook

Another way to look at this is to let the negative sign take over the addition sign—which makes these subtraction problems.

Here's How to Crack It

Read the question carefully. Do you remember the rules that govern the addition of positive and negative numbers?

- When you add two positive numbers, the result is always a positive number.
- When you add two negative numbers, the result is always a negative number.
- When you add two numbers with *different* signs, the result is the difference between the two numbers and has the sign of the larger number.

Next, determine the value of each of the four answer choices and use Process of Elimination (POE) to arrive at the correct answer.

$$(3) + (-8) + (5) = (-5) + (5) = 0$$

0 is not a positive number, so you can rule out **A**.

$$(8) + (-3) = 5$$

5 is a positive number, so it seems that **B** might be the correct answer.

$$(-3) + (-8) + (5) = -6$$

−6 is not a positive number, so you can eliminate **C**.

$$(-8) + (3) = -5$$

−5 is not a positive number, so you can get rid of **D**.

Answer choice **B** is the correct answer.

Using a Number Line

You can visualize adding numbers on a number line. For example, consider choice **B** from the previous question.

$$(8) + (-3)$$

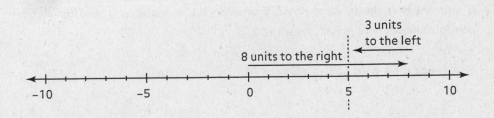

Some questions will give you a range of numbers and an operation (addition, subtraction, multiplication, and division are basic types of operations) and ask you to predict the possible range of answers.

An example might look like this:

―――――――――――――○―――――――――――――

1,000 is multiplied by a number between 0 and 1. The answer has to be

A   less than 0.

B   between 0 and 500, but not 250.

C   between 0 and 1,000, but not 500.

D   between 0 and 1,000.

Here's How to Crack It

Read the question carefully. First, remind yourself that all numbers between 0 and 1 are positive numbers. When you multiply two positive numbers, the answer has to be positive. Therefore, you can eliminate **A** right away, because an answer less than 0 would be negative.

Next, determine the smallest possible answer and the largest possible answer. (The following are not the absolute smallest and largest possible answers, but they are small *enough* and large *enough* to give you a hint regarding the correct answer.)

Pick a number close to 0—let's say 0.0001.

$$0.0001 \times 1,000 = 0.1$$

Now pick a number close to 1—let's say 0.9999

$$0.9999 \times 1,000 = 999.9$$

It appears that the smallest possible answer (0.1) is close to 0, and the largest possible answer (999.9) is close to 1,000.

Now check the answer choices. Choice **D** is the correct answer.

―――――――――――――○―――――――――――――

Now you try a few, and then we'll move on to the next topic. The answers are located at the end of this chapter, after the final quiz.

1. **Which of these sums is equal to a negative number?**

   A $(4) + (-7) + (6)$

   B $(-7) + (-4)$

   C $(-4) + (7)$

   D $(4) + (7)$

2. **One hundred is divided by a number between 10 and 100. The answer must be**

   A less than 0.

   B less than 1.

   C between 1 and 10 but not 5.

   D between 1 and 10.

3. **Which of these mathematical expressions has a negative value?**

   A $(3) - (9)$

   B $(-3) - (-9)$

   C $(9) - (3)$

   D $(3) - (-9)$

FRACTIONS, DECIMALS, AND PERCENTS

You will be asked to convert fractions to percents, and percents to fractions. Remember that both percents and fractions express parts out of the whole.

Standard NS 1.3

"Convert fractions to decimals and percents and use these representations in estimations, computations, and applications."

Let's look at an example.

Among all the baseball players currently playing in a league, 552 are not pitchers. Of these, 140 are left-handed batters. About what part of the non-pitchers are left-handed batters?

A   14%

B   25%

C   75%

D   140%

Here's How to Crack It

Read the question carefully and pay particular attention to the word "About". This tells you that your answer will be an approximation. You might notice that $\frac{140}{552}$ is close to $\frac{140}{560}$, which is exactly $\frac{1}{4}$ (or 25%). But to be safe, write a numerical expression that is equivalent to the information given in the question.

$$\frac{left \text{-} handed \; batters}{non \text{-} pitchers} = \frac{140}{552}$$

Next, notice that all the answer choices are percents. To determine the correct answer, you will need to convert the fraction above to a percent:

$$\frac{140}{552} = 552 \overline{)\begin{array}{r} 0.2536 \\ 140.0000 \\ \underline{1104} \\ 2960 \\ \underline{2760} \\ 2000 \\ \underline{1656} \\ 3440 \\ \underline{3312} \\ 128 \end{array}} = 25.4\% \; (rounded)$$

Left-handed batters account for a little more than 25% of the non-pitchers.

Now check the answer choices. Choice **B** is correct.

Another method you can use to change a fraction to a percent is to set up a proportion and make the denominator equal to 100:

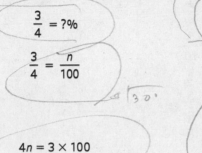

$$\frac{3}{4} = ?\%$$

$$\frac{3}{4} = \frac{n}{100}$$

Next, cross multiply:

$$4n = 3 \times 100$$

Now solve for n by dividing by 4:

$$\frac{4n}{4} = \frac{300}{4}$$

The 4s on the left side of the equation cancel each other out, leaving n. Divide 300 by 4 on the right side of the equation, and you are left with:

$$n = 75$$

The fraction $\frac{3}{4}$ is equivalent to 75%.

_____

The key to this next example is to remember that a percent is already a fraction: 20%, 20 out of 100, $\frac{20}{100}$. That same fraction, by the way, can also be expressed as the decimal 0.20.

Memorize These!

Some common decimal to fraction conversions are:

$0.1 \rightarrow \frac{1}{10}$

$0.2 \rightarrow \frac{1}{5}$

$0.5 \rightarrow \frac{1}{2}$

$0.25 \rightarrow \frac{1}{4}$

$0.50 \rightarrow \frac{1}{2}$

$0.75 \rightarrow \frac{3}{4}$

Let's try an example:

_____○_____

What is 30% expressed as a fraction?

A $\dfrac{1}{4}$

B $\dfrac{3}{10}$

C $\dfrac{2}{5}$

D $\dfrac{3}{8}$

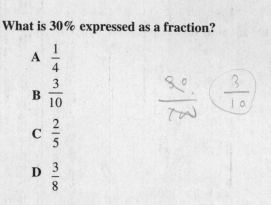

Here's How to Crack It

Read the question carefully. First, rewrite 30% as a fraction whose denominator is 100. The term "percent" literally means "per 100." Therefore, 30% equals $\dfrac{30}{100}$.

Next, reduce the fraction to its lowest terms. Divide both the numerator and denominator by the same number to get a simpler fraction. What number goes into both 30 and 100 evenly?

$$\frac{30 \div 10}{100 \div 10} = \frac{3}{10}$$

Therefore, 30% expressed as a fraction equals $\dfrac{3}{10}$.

Now check the answer choices. Answer choice **B** is correct.

_____○_____

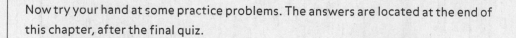

Now try your hand at some practice problems. The answers are located at the end of this chapter, after the final quiz.

1. For his science class, Jamaar did a survey of the cars in the teachers' parking lot. Of the 92 cars parked there, 30 had four-cylinder engines. About what percentage of the cars surveyed had four-cylinder engines?

   A   3%

   B   30%

   C   33%

   D   92%

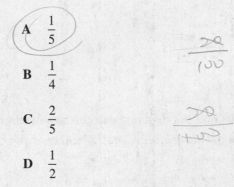

2. What is the fractional equivalent of 20%?

   A $\frac{1}{5}$

   B $\frac{1}{4}$

   C $\frac{2}{5}$

   D $\frac{1}{2}$

3. The student enrollment at Roosevelt High School is 689. Of these students, 340 live with one parent. About what percentage of the students lives with one parent?

   A   34%

   B   50%

   C   68%

   D   340%

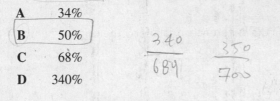

PERCENT INCREASE AND DECREASE

For some questions you will be given two numbers: an original number and a new number. Then you will be asked to determine what percent of the original number was added or subtracted to produce the new number. This is called the *percent increase* or *percent decrease*. To figure out the percent increase or decrease, take the difference between the two numbers and divide it by the original number. Multiply your answer by 100 to get the *percent change*.

Standard NS 1.6

"Calculate the percentage of increases and decreases of a quantity."

So the formula is $\dfrac{difference}{original} \times 100$. Let's look at an example.

Heather works part-time after school at a video store. She recently got a raise in salary from $6.00 an hour to $7.50 an hour. What is the percent of increase in her salary?

A   15%

B   20%

C   25%

D   75%

Here's How to Crack It

Read the question carefully. First, find the difference in the two numbers by subtracting the original number from the new number. The difference is also called the amount of increase, or amount of decrease.

$$\$7.50 \text{ (new)} - \$6.00 \text{ (original)} = \$1.50$$

$1.50 is the difference—the amount of increase—between Heather's old salary and her new salary.

Next, you want to divide the difference in salary by the original number:

$$\frac{\$1.50}{\$6.00} = 0.4$$

Now, multiply 0.4 by 100 to get the percent change:

$$0.4 \times 100 = .25 \text{ or } 25\%$$

The percent of increase is 25%.

Now check the answer choices. Choice **C** is correct.

So that was a percent increase. Now let's look at a percent *decrease*.

Attendance at a school play dropped from 1,280 last year to 1,088 this year. What is the percent of decrease?

A   10.9%

B   15%

C   17.6%

D   85%

(Here's How to Crack It)

Read the question carefully. First, determine the amount of decrease (the difference) by subtracting the new number from the original number.

$$1,280 - 1,088 = 192$$

Next, determine what percent of the original number is equal to the amount of decrease. Do this just like you solved the percent of increase equation: Divide the amount of decrease by the original number. Multiply the result by 100 to get the percent amount.

$$1280\overline{)192} = .15$$

$$.15 \times 100 = 15\%$$

The percent of decrease is 15%.

Now look at the answer choices. Choice **B** is correct.

Positive Outcome

You always want to subtract the smaller number from the larger. Otherwise you will get a negative number!

Remember What You Are Dividing

It's easy to make a mistake in these kinds of problems and find the percent of the wrong number. In the previous example, you might mistakenly divide $1.50 by $7.50 to find the percent of increase. (You would incorrectly get $\frac{1}{5}$, or 20%.) You will always be looking for the percent of increase or decrease from the *original* number. You need to find out what percent of the original number is equal to the amount of increase or decrease. When determining a percent, make sure you always divide by the original number—not the new number.

Now try your hand at some practice problems. The answers are located at the end of this chapter, after the final quiz.

1. **At the start of this year's baseball season, the price of a hot dog increased from $2.50 to $3.25. What is the percent of price increase?**

   A 7.5%

   B 23%

   C 30%

   D 70%

2. **A DVD originally priced at $20.00 was reduced to $15.00. By what percent was the price decreased?**

   A 15%

   B 25%

   C 33%

   D 75%

3. **Central High School's varsity football team won 7 games this season, compared to 5 wins last season. What is the percent of increase?**

   A 2%

   B 20%

   C 28.6%

   D 40%

4. Last year there were 44,600 applicants to a university in California. This year that number dropped to 41,032. By what percent was the number of applicants to the university lowered?

A   3.6%

B   8%

C   41%

D   92%

ADDING AND SUBTRACTING FRACTIONS

Standard NS 2.2

"Add and subtract fractions by using factoring to find common denominators."

On the CAHSEE, you will be asked to add and subtract fractions with different denominators. In some cases, you'll be asked to show the factoring method used to find the least common denominator. (Remember that the least common denominator contains all the **prime factors** of the two denominators.) This means you need to be able to find the prime factors of numbers.

First, let's review how we get to those prime factors:

Factors are the numbers you multiply together to get another number:

$$2 \times 3 = 6$$

2 and 3 are factors of 6.

Prime Factorization is finding which prime numbers you need to multiply together to get the original number. In the example above, 2 and 3 are factors of 6. They are also prime numbers, which means they are prime factors of 6. They are also the least common multiples of 6 because are the smallest numbers that can be multiplied to equal 6. Basically, they are all the smallest possible numbers that you can multiply to get your original number.

Prime Time

A Prime Number is a whole number, greater than 1, that can be evenly divided only by 1 or itself. Some of the most common primes are 2, 3, 5, 7, 11, 13, 17, 19...and so on!

When you add and subtract fractions with different denominators, you will have to make the denominators the same—that is, find the least common denominator.

The **least common denominator** (LCD) of two fractions is the **least common multiple** (LCM) of their denominators. You will have to use prime factorization to find the LCM of two numbers. For example, the prime factorizations for $\frac{1}{24}$ and $\frac{1}{30}$ are:

$$24 = 2 \times 2 \times 2 \times 3$$

$$30 = 2 \times 3 \times 5$$

Next, find the greatest number of times a factor appears in either number and multiply:

$$2 \times 2 \times 2 \times 3 \times 5 = 120$$

The least common multiple of $\frac{1}{24}$ and $\frac{1}{30}$ is $\frac{1}{120}$.

Ready to try an example?

Which of the following is the prime factorization of the least common denominator of $\frac{7}{12} + \frac{2}{15}$?

A 3×1

B $2 \times 3 \times 5$

C $2 \times 2 \times 3 \times 5$

D 12×15

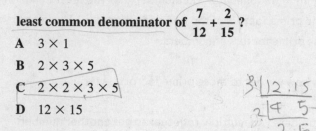

Here's How to Crack It

Read the question carefully. It's not asking you to add the fractions together. All you have to do is find the prime factors of the least common denominator of the two fractions. Remind yourself how to write a prime factorization of a number. You do this by writing the number as the product of prime numbers. So let's write the prime factorization of the two different denominators given in the question:

$$12 = 2 \times 6 = 2 \times 2 \times 3$$

$$15 = 3 \times 5$$

Next, find the greatest number of times a factor appears in either number and multiply them:

$$2 \times 2 \times 3 \times 5 = 60$$

The least common multiple of the denominators, also known as the least common denominator, is 60.

Now check the answer choices. Answer choice **C** is correct.

Let's try a slightly more complicated problem:

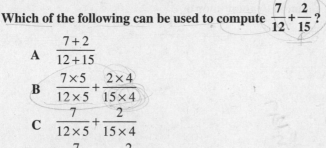

Which of the following can be used to compute $\dfrac{7}{12}+\dfrac{2}{15}$?

A $\quad\dfrac{7+2}{12+15}$

B $\quad\dfrac{7\times 5}{12\times 5}+\dfrac{2\times 4}{15\times 4}$

C $\quad\dfrac{7}{12\times 5}+\dfrac{2}{15\times 4}$

D $\quad\dfrac{7}{12\times 15}+\dfrac{2}{12\times 15}$

Here's How to Crack It

Again, read the question carefully. You have to choose which answer can be used to get to solve the equation $\dfrac{7}{12}+\dfrac{2}{15}$. To do that, you will need to need to find the least common denominator of the two fractions. Hey! You just did that, remember? It's in the question you just solved, so there's no need to do it again. You already know that the least common denominator is 60.

Now that you know that, you need to add the two fractions. What do you need to multiply each fraction by so that they both have a denominator of 60? This is pretty simple multiplication: 12 × 5 = 60, and 15 × 4 = 60. Now, multiply both the numerator and the denominator by that number:

$$\frac{7}{12} = \frac{7\times 5}{12\times 5} = \frac{35}{60}$$

$$\frac{2}{15} = \frac{2\times 4}{15\times 4} = \frac{8}{60}$$

This is all you have to do. The problem isn't actually asking you to solve $\dfrac{7}{12}+\dfrac{2}{15}$. All it's really asking you to do is choose which of the answer choices will get you the least common denominator (which you would need if you were really going to add the two fractions). So don't do any more math than you need to! Look at the answer choices and compare them to what you've got. Choice **B** is correct.

Save Yourself Some Time!

You don't always have to solve an equation to answer a test question correctly.

Now try a couple on your own. The answers are located at the end of this chapter, after the final quiz.

1. **Which of the following is the prime factorization of the least common denominator of $\dfrac{7}{8} - \dfrac{3}{10}$?**

   A $5 \times 2 \times 2$

   B $2 \times 4 \times 5$

   C $5 \times 2 \times 2 \times 2$

   D 8×10

2. **Cindy needs to find the sum of $\dfrac{1}{6} + \dfrac{5}{8}$. If she writes the least common denominator in prime factored form, the result will look like**

   A $3 \times 2 \times 2$

   B $3 \times 2 \times 2 \times 2$

   C $3 \times 2 \times 2 \times 2 \times 2$

   D 6×8

Standard NS 2.1

"Understand negative whole-number exponents. Multiply and divide expressions involving exponents with a common base."

UNDERSTANDING EXPONENTS

You will be asked to multiply and divide expressions that involve exponents with a common base. You'll also have to deal with negative exponents. Let's review the rules of multiplying and dividing exponents.

To *multiply* two numbers that have exponents with a common base, you *add* the exponents.

$$6^2 \times 6^3 = 6^{(2+3)} = 6^5$$

Why is this true? Let's write this out in long form:

$$6^2 = 6 \times 6 \qquad 6^3 = 6 \times 6 \times 6$$

$$\text{so, } 6^2 \times 6^3 = 6 \times 6 \times 6 \times 6 \times 6 \text{ or } 6^5$$

To *divide* two numbers that have exponents with a common base, you *subtract* the exponent of the number you are dividing by from the exponent of the number you are dividing into. Or, you could say you simply subtract the bottom exponent from the top exponent:

$$6^3 \div 6^2 = 6$$

$$\frac{6^3}{6^2} = 6$$

Why is this true? Let's write it out in long form:

$$6^{(3-2)} = 6^1 = 6$$

———————————◯———————————

$2^5 \times 2^3 =$

A 2^2

B 2^8

C 2^{15}

D 4^8

Here's How to Crack It

Read the question carefully. Remember the rule about multiplying exponents.

$$2^5 \times 2^3 = 2^{5+3} = 2^8$$

Now check the answer choices. Choice **B** is correct.

———————————◯———————————

The Power of One

Any number raised to the power of 1 will always be equal to itself. It's like multiplying that number by 1.

Let's try another one:

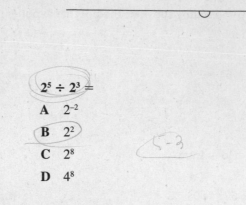

$2^5 \div 2^3 =$

A 2^{-2}

B 2^2

C 2^8

D 4^8

Here's How to Crack It

Okay, this one's not quite like the last problem. First, recall the rules about dividing expressions with exponents that have the same base. To <u>divide</u> two numbers that have exponents with a common base, you <u>subtract</u> the exponent of the number you are dividing by from the exponent of the number you are dividing into.

So $2^5 \div 2^3$ becomes 2^{5-3}, which is 2^2.

Now check the answer choices. Choice **B** is correct.

Negative Exponents

An easy way to understand numbers with negative exponents is to think of them as fractions. Any number with a negative exponent can be rewritten as 1 over that number. Rewrite the exponent in the denominator as positive:

$$9^{-4} = \frac{1}{9^4}$$

The rules for multiplying and dividing are the same. Just remember the rules for adding and subtracting negative numbers:

$$2^5 \times 2^{-3} = \frac{2^5}{2^3} = 2^{(5-3)} = 2^2$$

Now try a couple on your own. The answers are located at the end of this chapter, after the final quiz.

1. $4^4 \times 4^3 =$

   A 4^7

   B 4^{12}

   C 16^7

   D 16^{12}

2. $3^6 \div 3^2 =$

   A 3^3

   B 3^4

   C 3^8

   D 9^8

EXPONENT RULES

You will be asked to evaluate numerical expressions that contain exponents. Remember the rules we just covered, and be sure to reduce any common factors in the numerator and denominator of the expression—review the section on adding and subtracting fractions if you need to. If you reduce the fractions to common factors before you multiply out numbers, you'll make your arithmetic easier.

Standard NS 2.3

"Multiply, divide, and simplify rational numbers by using exponent rules."

$$\frac{2^3 \times 9^4}{3^3 \times 9^2} =$$

   A $1\frac{1}{3}$

   B $2\frac{2}{3}$

   C 24

   D 72

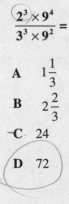

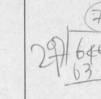

Here's How to Crack It

Read the question carefully. Remember the rules that govern the multiplication and division of numbers with exponents that have the same base. To multiply two numbers with exponents that have the same base, you add the exponents. To divide, you subtract the exponents.

First, simplify the expression given in the question:

$\dfrac{9^2}{9^4}$ can be reduced to $\dfrac{9^2}{1}$, which gives us $\dfrac{2^3 \times 9^2}{3^3}$

$\dfrac{2^3 \times 9^2}{3^3}$ becomes $\dfrac{8 \times 81}{27}$

Now find the value of what remains:

$$\frac{8 \times 81}{27} = \frac{8 \times 3}{1} = 24$$

Look at the answer choices. Choice **C** is correct.

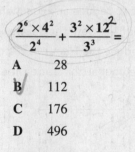

$$\frac{2^6 \times 4^2}{2^4} + \frac{3^2 \times 12^2}{3^3} =$$

A   28

B   112

C   176

D   496

Here's How to Crack It

Read the question carefully. First, remind yourself of the rules that govern the multiplication and division of numbers with exponents that have the same base.

Next, simplify and find the value of each expression.

$$\frac{2^6 \times 4^2}{2^4} = 22 \times 42 = 4 \times 16 = 64$$

$$\frac{3^2 \times 12^2}{3^3} \times \frac{12^2}{3} = \frac{144}{3} = 48$$

$$64 + 48 = 112$$

Check the answer choices. Choice **B** is correct.

———————————○———————————

Now try a couple on your own. The answers are located at the end of this chapter, after the final quiz.

1. $\dfrac{2^5 \times 3^2}{2^7 \times 3^1} =$

    A $\dfrac{3}{4}$

    B $1\dfrac{1}{2}$

    C 12

    D 36

2. $\dfrac{4^3 \times 2^3}{2^4} + \dfrac{5^5 \times 3^2}{5^3} =$

    A 19

    B $32\dfrac{9}{25}$

    C 257

    D 353

(handwritten margin notes: $\frac{64 \times 16}{16}$; $\frac{1024}{16}$; $64 + 48$; $\frac{1296}{27}$)

SQUARE ROOTS

You will be given a range of numbers and told that the square of a certain number falls within that range. Then, you will have to figure out roughly what the original number was. Remember, you can't use a calculator on the CAHSEE, so don't use one now when you practice. Instead, look at the squares of some common numbers to figure out roughly what the original number would have been.

Standard NS 2.4

"Use the inverse relationship between raising to a power and extracting the root of a perfect square integer; for an integer that is not square, determine without a calculator the two integers between which its square root lies and explain why."

When a <u>whole</u> number is squared, the result is a number between 400 and 500. The original whole number must be between

A   10 and 15.

B   15 and 20.

C   20 and 25.

D   25 and 30.

Here's How to Crack It

Read the question carefully. First, think of the squares of some common whole numbers. For example, $10^2 = 100$, $20^2 = 400$, $30^2 = 900$. Compare these known values to the range given in the question.

$$20^2 = 400 \qquad 30^2 = 900$$

Because the range given for the square of the unknown number is between 400 and 500, the number must be between 20 and 30. You can use POE to cross off **A** and **B**.

Next, narrow the range of your answer by computing the square of 25, a number in the middle of your range. You might not know this one off the top of your head, and it is okay to take some time and multiply it out on paper.

$$25^2 = 625$$

Because the range in the question is between 400 and 500, the unknown number must be between 20 and 25.

Now check the answer choices. Choice **C** is correct.

Similarly, you may be asked to figure out the range of the **square root** of a particular number. The process is similar.

The square root of 562 must be a number between

A 22 and 23.

B 23 and 24.

C 24 and 25.

D 25 and 26.

Here's How to Crack It

Read the question carefully. First, compute the squares of some common whole numbers.

For example, $10^2 = 100$, $15^2 = 225$, $20^2 = 400$, $25^2 = 625$. Compare these known values to the number given in the question.

> ### Ballparking a Square Root
> You can estimate the square root of a number by comparing it to perfect squares. For example, to estimate the square root of 250, you could write $15^2 = 225$, $x^2 = 250$, $16^2 = 256$. Therefore, $\sqrt{250}$ must be between 15 and 16. Because 250 is closer to 256 than it is to 225, the square root of 250 is closer to 16 (probably around 15.7–15.8).

$$20^2 = 400 \qquad 25^2 = 625$$

Because 562 falls between 400 and 625, its square root must be between 20 and 25. Therefore, you can eliminate answer choice **D**.

Next, narrow down your choices by computing the square of the whole numbers between 20 and 25, and eliminate as you go.

$$21^2 = 441 \qquad 22^2 = 484 \qquad 23^2 = 529 \qquad 24^2 = 576$$

Because 562 falls between 529 and 576, its square root must be between 23 and 24.

Now check the answer choices. Choice **B** is correct.

Now try a couple on your own. The answers are located at the end of this chapter, after the final quiz.

1. The square of an unknown positive integer falls between 1,000 and 1,100. The integer must be between

   A   30 and 35.

   B   35 and 40.

   C   40 and 45.

   D   45 and 50.

2. The square root of 387 must be a number between

   A   16 and 17.

   B   17 and 18.

   C   18 and 19.

   D   19 and 20.

ABSOLUTE VALUE

Standard NS 2.5

"Understand the meaning of the absolute value of a number; interpret the absolute value as the distance of the number from zero on a number line; and determine the absolute value of real numbers."

You can think of **absolute value** as the distance a particular number is from zero on a number line. So the absolute value of 5 and –5 is 5 for both, because 5 is 5 units away from 0 on the number line, and –5 is also 5 units away from 0 on the number line. Remember that absolute value is always written as a positive number.

$$|5| = 5 \qquad |-5| = 5$$

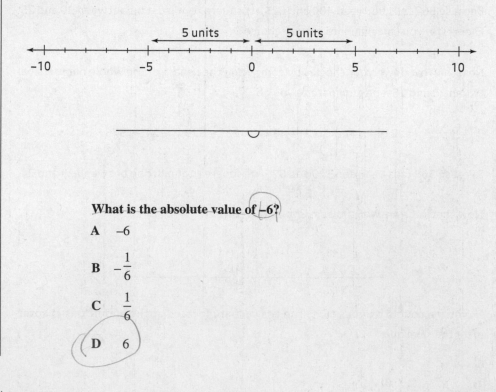

What is the absolute value of –6?

   A   –6

   B $-\dfrac{1}{6}$

   C $\dfrac{1}{6}$

   D   6

Here's How to Crack It

Remember, the absolute value of any number (other than zero) is its positive value regardless of whether the number is positive or negative.

So you can tell the absolute value of –6 by rewriting it without the negative sign.

$$|{-}6| = 6$$

Now look at the answer choices. Choice **D** is correct.

In some cases you'll actually be looking at a number line in the problem. See which number is literally furthest from zero.

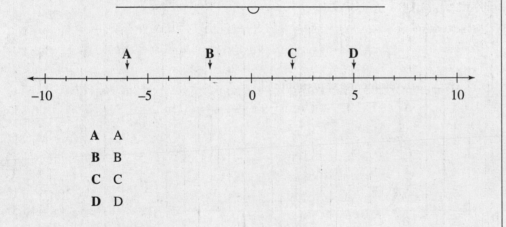

A	A
B	B
C	C
D	D

Here's How to Crack It

Read the question and study the diagram carefully. Remind yourself that absolute value can also be defined as the number of units a number is from zero on a number line.

Next, examine the numbers shown on the number line to determine which is the greatest number of units from zero:

A is 6 units from zero.
B is 2 units from zero.
C is 2 units from zero.
D is 5 units from zero.

Because the absolute value of a number is the number of units it is from zero, and A is the farthest number from zero, and choice **A** is the correct answer.

———————○———————

Now try a couple on your own. The answers are located at the end of this chapter, after the final quiz.

1. **What is the absolute value of –3?**

    A   –3

    B $-\dfrac{1}{3}$

    C $\dfrac{1}{3}$

    D   3

2. **Evaluate the expression: |7|**

    A   –7

    B $-\dfrac{1}{7}$

    C $\dfrac{1}{7}$

    D   7

CHAPTER 5: ARITHMETIC FINAL QUIZ

Answers to this quiz can be found on pages 270–272.

1. If a number between 1 and 10 is divided by 100, the answer must be

   A   less than 0.

   B   between 0 and 0.01.

   C   between 0.01 and 0.1.

   D   between 0.1 and 1.

2. Which of these expressions is equal to a negative number?

   A $(-5) \times (-5)$

   B $(-5) \div (-5)$

   C $(-5)^2$

   D $(-5)^3$

3. Ten is multiplied by a number between 0 and 1. The answer must be

   A   less than 0.

   B   between 0 and 1.

   C   between 0 and 10.

   D   between 10 and 100.

4. Which of the following fractions is the equivalent of 62.5%?

   A $\dfrac{9}{16}$

   B $\dfrac{3}{5}$

   C $\dfrac{2}{3}$

   D $\dfrac{5}{8}$

5. On the side of a box of pound cake, the nutrition label reads, "Per Serving: Calories—210; Calories from Fat—83." Approximately what percentage of the calories in one serving comes from fat?

   A   8.3%

   B   33%

   C   40%

   D   83%

6. What is 15% expressed as a fraction?

   A $\dfrac{3}{20}$

   B $\dfrac{1}{6}$

   C $\dfrac{1}{5}$

   D $\dfrac{3}{10}$

7. In 1990 total income from farms in California was $20 billion. In 1998 that number had risen to $26 billion. What is the percent of increase?

   A   6%

   B   23%

   C   30%

   D   77%

8. A high school had 1,020 enrolled students in 1998. By 2008 the student enrollment was 1,173. By what percent did the school's population increase?

   A   13%

   B   15%

   C   87%

   D   153%

9. The approximate population of California in 1990 was 29,800,000. In 2000 the population was reported to be around 33,972,000. What was the percent of increase in the population?

A   4%

B   12%

C   14%

D   88%

10. Mr. Torres bought a number of items at a pharmacy. The total price came to $35.00. After the senior citizen discount was taken off, the total price came to $31.50. What percent discount does the pharmacy give to senior citizens?

A   3.5%

B   10%

C   13%

D   35%

11. Which of the following can be used to compute $\frac{5}{7} - \frac{1}{4}$?

A $\frac{5-1}{7-4}$

B $\frac{5}{7 \times 4} - \frac{1}{4 \times 7}$

C $\frac{1 \times 7}{7 \times 4} - \frac{5 \times 4}{4 \times 7}$

D $\frac{5 \times 4}{7 \times 4} - \frac{1 \times 7}{4 \times 7}$

12. Which of the following is the lowest common denominator of $\frac{11}{12} - \frac{5}{16}$ written in prime factored form?

A $2^3 \times 3$

B $2^4 \times 3$

C $2^5 \times 3$

D $2^6 \times 3$

13. Which of the following is an appropriate middle step in finding the sum of $\frac{3}{8} + \frac{1}{6}$?

A $\frac{3 \times 3}{8 \times 3} + \frac{1 \times 4}{6 \times 4}$

B $\frac{3}{8 \times 3} + \frac{1}{6 \times 4}$

C $\frac{3}{8 \times 6} + \frac{1}{6 \times 8}$

D $\frac{3 + 1}{8 + 6}$

14. Which of these is the prime factorization of the least common denominator of $\frac{5}{6} - \frac{3}{4}$?

A 6×4

B $2 \times 2 \times 3$

C $2 \times 2 \times 2 \times 3$

D $2 \times 3 \times 2 \times 3$

15. Oona wants to find the sum of $\frac{3}{10} + \frac{1}{8}$. If she writes the prime factorization of the least common denominator, the result will be

A 5×8

B $2^2 \times 5$

C $2^3 \times 5$

D 10×8

16. $5^2 \times 5^5 =$

A 5^3

B 5^7

C 5^{10}

D 25^{10}

17. $4^3 \div 4^6 =$

   A 16^{-9}

   B 4^{-9}

   C 16^{-3}

   D 4^{-3}

18. $2^5 \times 2^{-3} =$

   A 2^{-8}

   B 2^{-2}

   C 2^2

   D 2^8

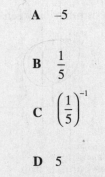

19. $5^3 \times 5^{-4} =$

   A -5

   B $\dfrac{1}{5}$

   C $\left(\dfrac{1}{5}\right)^{-1}$

   D 5

20. $3^{-5} \times 3^3 =$

   A 3^{-8}

   B 3^{-2}

   C 3^2

   D 3^8

21. $4^{-2} \div 4^4 =$

   A 4^{-8}

   B 4^{-6}

   C 4^{-2}

   D 4^2

22. $\dfrac{6^4}{2^3 \times 3^3} =$

   A $\dfrac{12}{27}$

   B 6

   C 18

   D 36

23. $\dfrac{2^4 \times 7^5}{7^3} - \dfrac{5^3 \times 3^4}{5^2} =$

   A -5

   B 257

   C 332

   D 379

24. $\dfrac{3^{-2} \times 2^{-3}}{6^{-1} \times 2^{-4}} =$

   A $-1\dfrac{1}{3}$

   B $-\dfrac{3}{4}$

   C $\dfrac{3}{4}$

   D $1\dfrac{1}{3}$

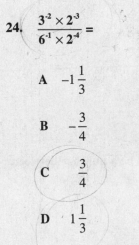

25. $\dfrac{4^2 \times 2^3}{2^4} - \dfrac{6^2 \times 3^2}{3^4} =$

   A 0

   B 4

   C 12

   D 28

26. $\dfrac{2^4 \times 3^3}{9^1 \times 2^2} =$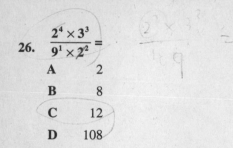

A   2

B   8

C   12

D   108

27. $\dfrac{4^{-1} \times 7^0}{2^{-3}} + \dfrac{2^5 \times 8^4}{8^5} =$

A   6

B   7

C   9

D   10

28. When a <u>whole</u> number is squared, the result is a number between 650 and 700. The original whole number must be between

A   15 and 20.

B   20 and 25.

C   25 and 30.

D   30 and 35.

29. The square root of 1,492 must be a number between

A   36 and 37.

B   37 and 38.

C   38 and 39.

D   39 and 40.

30. The square of a positive integer falls between 1,300 and 1,400. The integer must be between

A   30 and 35.

B   35 and 40.

C   40 and 45.

D   45 and 50.

31. The square root of 829 must be a number between

A   26 and 27.

B   27 and 28.

C   28 and 29.

D   29 and 30.

32. The square of a whole number is a number between 230 and 300. The original whole number must be between

A   15 and 20.

B   20 and 25.

C   25 and 30.

D   30 and 35.

33. The square root of 1,000 must be a number between

A   30 and 31.

B   31 and 32.

C   32 and 33.

D   33 and 34.

34. Which of the numbers shown on the number line below has the <u>greatest</u> absolute value?

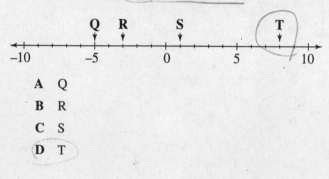

A   Q

B   R

C   S

D   T

35. What is the absolute value of –10?

A   –10

B $-\dfrac{1}{10}$

C $\dfrac{1}{10}$

D   10

36. Evaluate the expression: $|-1| \times |2|$

A   –2

B $-\dfrac{1}{2}$

C $\dfrac{1}{2}$

D   2

37. What is the absolute value of $-\dfrac{2}{5}$?

A $-\dfrac{5}{2}$

B $-\dfrac{2}{5}$

C $\dfrac{2}{5}$

D $\dfrac{5}{2}$

38. Which of the numbers shown on the number line below has the smallest absolute value?

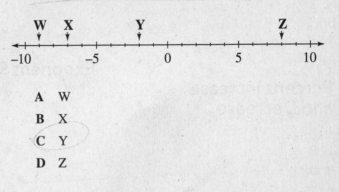

A   W

B   X

C   Y

D   Z

ANSWERS TO PRACTICE PROBLEMS

Rational Numbers
1. B
2. D
3. A

Fractions, Decimals and Percents
1. C
2. A
3. B

Percent Increase and Decrease
1. C
2. B
3. D
4. B

Adding and Subtracting Fractions
1. C
2. B

Understanding Exponents
1. A
2. B

Exponent Rules
1. A
2. C

Square Roots
1. A
2. B D

Absolute Value
1. D
2. D

Chapter 6
Applied Arithmetic

In addition to basic calculations, you will be asked to apply arithmetic to real-world situations such as sales, rates, interest, and commissions. Often, these will be word problems that require you to figure out which information is important and which is not. Your basic arithmetic skills, combined with your common sense, will be your best tools here.

MATH AND MONEY

These problems generally require you to use what you know about percents to figure out either a sale price or the amount of interest an investment earned. Keep your common sense with you at all times! If an item is on sale, it should be *cheaper* than the original price. All this talk of sales makes these math problems seem like a day at the mall! Or not...

Standard NS 1.7

"Solve problems that involve discounts, markups, commissions, and profit, and compute simple and compound interest.

Let's try an example:

A set of golf clubs that regularly sells for $350 is on sale for 40% off. What is the price of the set of golf clubs on sale?

A $140

B $210

C $310

D $490

Here's How to Crack It

Read the question carefully. First, ask yourself if the sale price of the set of golf clubs would be greater or less than the regular price. Common sense tells you that an item on sale would cost less. So you can eliminate answer choice **D** right off the bat.

Next, calculate the reduction in price. What is 40% of $350?

$$\$350 \times 40\% = \$350 \times 0.4 = \$140$$
$$\$140 \text{ is } 40\% \text{ of } \$350.$$

Finally, calculate the sale price by subtracting the reduction in price from the original price.

$$\$350 - \$140 = \$210$$

The price of the set of golf clubs on sale is $210.

Now check the answer choices. Choice **B** is correct.

How They Get Those Wrong Answers

If you look at the incorrect answer choices, you can get an idea of some of the common mistakes students make when solving this kind of problem. For example, a student might only multiply the regular price by the percent of the sale. He would get an answer of 40% × $350 = $140, and choose **A**. That would be wrong, since he didn't do the next step to get the sale price. Remember to read each question carefully!

Another student might simply subtract the percent from the regular price. In this case, she would get an answer of $350 – 40% = $310, and choose **C**. Percents are not "real" numbers—40 percent does not equal 40 dollars. In this case, if that were true, that wouldn't be much of a sale!

Finally, some students might make the mistake of *adding* the price reduction to the regular price instead of subtracting it. In this case, they would get an answer of $350 + $140 = $490, and choose **D**. This is where you need to use common sense. If an item is on sale, the price should be less, not more!

If you can spot answer choices from errors in calculation or in reading the problem, you can eliminate them!

Interest Problems

Another type of question you might see on the CAHSEE will ask you to compute interest earned on an account.

First, let's review how interest works.

Interest is a fee which is paid for the privilege of borrowing money. People pay interest on the amounts they charge on their credit cards; banks pay people interest on the amounts people deposit in savings or money market accounts. Interest is usually expressed as a percent of the original amount. The original amount is called the *principal*. Dealing with interest can get pretty complicated, but we're going to keep it simple, and just talk about **simple interest**.

You can compute simple interest using the formula below; each letter stands for a specific quantity.

<u>Simple Interest</u>:

$$A = P + (P \times i \times t)$$

A = amount in the account

P = principal

i = annual interest rate

t = time in years

Let's try an example:

Manuel deposited $1,000 in a money market account that pays 6% annual interest. If he leaves the money in the account, about how much will he have after 5 years?

A $1,060

B $1,300

C $1,350

D $5,000

Here's How to Crack It

Read the question carefully. Pay particular attention to the interest rate and the time in years. Now take your formula and plug in the information you've got:

$$A = P + (P \times i \times t)$$

A = the amount we're solving for

P = the original amount in the account, which is $1,000

i = the interest rate, which is 6%

t = the time in years, which is 5 years

A = $1,000 + ($1,000 × 6% × 5)

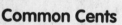
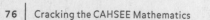

Remember to convert the percent to a decimal, in order to solve the equation.

$$A = \$1,000 + (\$1,000 \times 0.06 \times 5)$$
$$A = \$1,000 + \$300$$
$$A = \$1,300$$

After 5 years Manuel will have $1,300 in his account. Now check the answer choices. Choice **B** is correct.

Now try a few on your own. The answers are located after the final quiz for Chapter 6.

1. **A color scanner regularly sells for $150. It is on sale for 30% off. What is the sale price of the scanner?**

    A $45

    B $105

    C $120

    D $195

2. **A DVD player is on sale for 25% off. It regularly sells for $180. What is the sale price of the DVD player?**

    A $45

    B $80

    C $135

    D $225

3. **An encyclopedia on CD-ROM that normally sells for $50.00 is on sale at 35% off. What is the price of the encyclopedia on sale?**

    A $15.00

    B $17.50

    C $32.50

    D $67.50

RATE, SPEED, DISTANCE, AND TIME

On the test you will likely be given a word problem that involves a rate—that is, some measurement of speed. You will be asked to find the rate, or some other variable related to the rate (like distance or time). Remember that the basic formula for rate problems is *rate × time = distance*.

Rate and speed can sometimes be used interchangeably. So if you are looking for the speed of something, you can rewrite this formula as:

$$(\text{rate of}) \text{ speed} = \frac{distance}{time}$$

To find the average speed of an object, you will divide the total distance something has travelled by the total time it took to travel that distance:

$$\text{Average Speed} = \frac{Total\ Distance}{Total\ Time}$$

Now let's try an example:

Charisse and her family drove from Los Angeles to Las Vegas for a vacation. The 285-mile trip took them $4\frac{3}{4}$ hours. What was their average speed?

  A 57 miles per hour

  B 60 miles per hour

  C 63 miles per hour

  D 67 miles per hour

Here's How to Crack It

Read the question carefully. You want to find the average speed, so remember that formula:

$$\text{Average Speed} = \frac{Total\ Distance}{Total\ Time}$$

Now substitute the numbers from the problem into the proper location in the formula.

$$\text{Average Speed} = \frac{Total\ Distance}{Total\ Time} = \frac{285\ miles}{4\frac{3}{4}\ hours}$$

Standard AF 4.2

"Solve multistep problems involving rate, average speed, distance, and time or a direct variation."

Next, calculate the average speed by dividing 285 by $4\frac{3}{4}$. You might want to change $4\frac{3}{4}$ to 4.75 to make the calculation easier.

$$Average\ Speed = \frac{Total\ Distance}{Total\ Time} = \frac{285\ miles}{4.75\ hours} = 60\ miles\ per\ hour$$

Now check the answer choices. Choice **B** is correct. If you multiply 4.75 × 60, you will get 285, confirming the answer.

You might be solving for the rate, or the distance, or the time. If you remember the basic formula you can always solve for whatever piece is missing.

———————◯———————

Not all rate problems will ask you to find speed. Some problems will ask about time or distance.

———————◯———————

Planes, Trains, and Automobiles

One quick way to spot rate problems: They're usually about travel.

If an airplane averages 480 miles per hour, how long will it take to fly 2,160 miles from Chicago to San Francisco?

A 3 hours

B 3.5 hours

C 4 hours

D 4.5 hours

For this problem you are given the speed and the distance and are asked to find the time. You should use the formula $Speed = \frac{distance}{time}$, which we can simplify to $\frac{d}{t}$.

The speed in this problem is 480 miles per hour, the distance is 2,160 miles, and the time is the unknown. That makes our formula $480 = \frac{2,160\ miles}{t}$.

To get t out of the denominator, cross multiply, and you'll end up with

$$480t = 2,160.$$

Divide 2,160 by 480 to get t: $2,160 \div 480 = 4.5$.

That's answer choice **D**.

To check your answer, multiply the number of hours by the speed to see if it equals the distance. 4.5 hours × 480 miles per hour = 2,160 miles, so **D** is indeed correct.

———————◯———————

Now try a few on your own. The answers are located after the final quiz for this chapter.

1. A private jet flies from San Francisco to New Orleans in $4\frac{1}{2}$ hours. If the distance between the two cities is 1,944 miles, what is the jet's average speed?

   A   412 miles per hour

   B   422 miles per hour

   C   432 miles per hour

   D   442 miles per hour

2. Mr. Vargas is collating and stapling the pages of the final exam he plans to give. He is working at a rate of 2.5 exams per minute. At this rate, how long will it take him to collate and staple 90 copies of the exam?

   A   36 minutes

   B   87.5 minutes

   C   92.5 minutes

   D   225 minutes

3. A train covers the 380-mile distance from Los Angeles to Phoenix in 5 hours. What is the average speed of the train?

   A   72 miles per hour

   B   76 miles per hour

   C   78 miles per hour

   D   80 miles per hour

4. Rowena's bathtub can hold 210 gallons of water. If the faucet releases water at a rate of 15 gallons per minute, how long will it take to fill the bathtub?

   A   14 minutes

   B   195 minutes

   C   225 minutes

   D   3,150 minutes

RATE, WORK, AND PERCENT MIXTURE

The CAHSEE will ask you to use algebra to solve rate problems that involve work, as well as problems that involve a mixture of things, like percents. Remember, algebra uses **variables** (like *x, y, a, b*) to solve for unknown quantities in equations. You will need to set up equations to solve for the unknown variable. Relax—this isn't nearly as complicated as it sounds! Algebra can be incredibly useful in solving equations for rate and work.

Let's look at work first. Remember that if two people (or machines) are working together, you add their rates.

Shane runs a copying business out of his garage. He received an order for 2,520 copies. He has three printers that print at a rate of 12, 10, and 6 pages per minute respectively. How long would it take Shane to complete the order if all three printers were running simultaneously?

A   30 minutes

B   60 minutes

C   90 minutes

D   120 minutes

Here's How to Crack It

This is an example of a work problem. First, make sure you understand what the question is asking. The key words in the question are "How long..." You are looking for a *length of time* in minutes. You can use algebra to solve this. We'll choose *x* as our variable:

Let *x* = the number of minutes it takes to complete the order.

Next, set up an equation that shows the three printers running for *x* minutes each to produce 2,520 pages.

$$12x + 10x + 6x = 2,520$$

Combine like terms, so

$$(12 + 10 + 6)x = 28x$$
$$28x = 2,520$$

Standard A1 15.0

"Students apply algebraic techniques to solve rate problems, work problems, and percent mixture problems."

ELL Tip

A **variable** is a letter that stands in for a number. It's called a "variable" because the number it stands for can *vary*.

Divide both sides by 28.

$$\frac{28x}{28} = \frac{2,520}{28}$$

$$x = 90 \text{ minutes}$$

It will take Shane 90 minutes to complete the order. Check the answer choices. Choice **C** is correct.

You can check your answer by finding the number of pages each printer prints in 90 minutes and adding them together:

1st printer—12 pages per minute × 90 minutes = 1,080 pages
2nd printer—10 pages per minute × 90 minutes = 900 pages
3rd printer—6 pages per minute × 90 minutes = 540 pages

Total for all three printers = 1,080 + 900 + 540 = 2,520 pages

Other rate problems may have less to do with speed than with the rate at which something was charged. Let's look at an example.

Jackie just received her telephone bill for last month. The telephone company charges $27 per month for local service plus $0.20 per local call. If Jackie's bill was for $38.60, how many local calls did she make last month?

A   48
B   58
C   135
D   193

Here's How to Crack It

Read the question carefully. Let's have x equal the number of local calls Jackie made last month.

Next, set up an equation that shows how the bill was computed, then solve for x.

Monthly Fee + Local Calls @ $0.20 each = Total Bill

$$\$27.00 + \$0.20x = \$38.60$$

$$27.00 + 0.20x = 38.60$$

$$27.00 + 0.20x - 27.00 = 38.60 - 27.00$$

$$\frac{0.20x}{0.20} = \frac{11.60}{0.20} \text{ becomes } x = 58 \text{ calls}$$

Now check the answer choices. Choice **B** is correct.

───────○───────

Percent mixture problems are exactly what they sound like. You will have different substances, each with a different percentage, and you'll need to mix them to create a new mixture at a new percentage. Let's see what that looks like.

───────○───────

Selena wants to mix whole milk (4% fat) and low-fat milk (1% fat) to make a half-gallon (1.89 liters or 1,890 ml) of milk that is 2% fat. How many ml of each does she need to obtain 1,890 ml of 2% milk?

A   378 ml of 4% milk and 1,512 ml of 1% milk

B   472.5 ml of 4% milk and 1,417.5 ml of 1% milk

C   630 ml of 4% milk and 1,260 ml of 1% milk

D   945 ml of 4% milk and 945 ml of 1% milk

Here's How to Crack It

Read the question *and the answer choices* carefully. Notice that the answer choices give you amounts of both 4% milk and 1% milk. Here's the key to this kind of question:

You only need to find the amount of one kind of milk. You don't actually need to do all the math to find both. If you find the amount of one kind of milk, you'll have your answer. Let's find the amount of 4% milk. We'll use x to represent the amount of 4% milk needed.

First of all, the total amount of 2% milk needed is 1,890 ml. That means the amount of 1% milk needed is the difference between the total amount of 2% milk and the 4% milk (x). So, that means we can represent the 1% milk by the expression $1,890 - x$.

It might help to create a mental image of the situation.

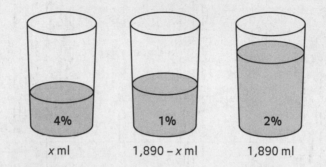

Now set up an equation to represent the three liquids and their containers, then solve for x.

$$x + (1,890 - x) = 1,890 \text{ ml}$$

$$0.04x + 0.01(1,890 - x) = 0.02(1,890)$$

$$0.04x + 18.9 - 0.01x = 37.8$$

$$0.04x + 18.9 - 0.01x - 18.9 = 37.8 - 18.9$$

$$\frac{0.03x}{0.03} = \frac{18.9}{0.03}$$

$$x = 630 \text{ ml}$$

Now that we've solved for x—that is, for the amount of 4% milk—let's look at the answer choices. Choice **C** is "630 ml of 4% milk and 1,260 ml of 1% milk," so **C** is correct.

You can check your work by plugging in the amount of 1% milk given in the answer choice—1,260 ml—and solving for x:

$$1,890 - x = 1,260 \text{ ml}$$

Selena needs to add 630 ml of 4% milk to 1,260 ml of 1% milk to get 1,890 ml of 2% milk.

Now try a few on your own. The answers are located after the final quiz for this chapter.

1. A computer store sells two different types of ink cartridges for a popular inkjet printer. The brand-name cartridge sells for $28 and the generic cartridge sells for $12. Last week they sold 82 cartridges for that printer. If the total collected from the sale of these cartridges was $1,512, how many of each type of cartridge were sold?

   A   13 brand-name and 69 generic

   B   22 brand-name and 60 generic

   C   33 brand-name and 49 generic

   D   41 brand-name and 41 generic

2. Kadeesha and her lab partners had an assignment for chemistry lab. They were supposed to make 400 ml of a 5% acid solution by combining different amounts of 2% acid and 10% acid solutions. How many ml of each do they need in order to obtain 400 ml of 5% acid solution?

   A   100 ml of 10% acid and 300 ml of 2% acid

   B   150 ml of 10% acid and 250 ml of 2% acid

   C   200 ml of 10% acid and 200 ml of 2% acid

   D   250 ml of 10% acid and 150 ml of 2% acid

ANALYZING PROBLEMS

These are often problems that are about spotting relationships or patterns among the numbers. You must read these carefully and decide what information is important and what is not. Let's try one.

Standard MR 1.1

"Analyze problems by identifying relationships, distinguishing relevant from irrelevant information, identifying missing information, sequencing and prioritizing information, and observing patterns."

**The combination to Nat's locker is a series of three
different numbers less than 40 in order from least
to greatest. Each number is a multiple of 3, 4, and 6.
What is Nat's combination?**

A 32-24-18

B 32-24-12

C 36-24-12

D 36-28-16

Here's How to Crack It

Consider the information in the problem and look for relationships among the numbers. All the numbers in Nat's combination are less than 40. They are also all multiples of 3, 4, and 6 and occur in order from least to greatest. List all the numbers less than 40 that are multiples of 3. Do the same for 4 and 6.

Step 1: Multiples of 3: 3 6 9 12 15 18 21 24 27 30 33 36 39

Multiples of 4: 4 8 12 16 20 24 28 32 36

Multiples of 6: 6 12 18 24 30 36

Now find all the numbers that are found in all three lists from Step 1.

Step 2: Multiples of 3, 4, and 6:

12 24 36

Step 3: Finally, list them in order from largest to smallest.

36 24 12

Now check the answer choices. Choice **C** is correct.

Sometimes the test writers will give you more information than you need to solve the problem. Yes, they are definitely trying to trip you up! The following example specifically asks which piece of information is NOT needed.

Yolanda just bought a satellite dish. With the dish, she gets 175 more channels than she got with cable and 245 more channels than she got with just a roof antenna. With cable she got 82 channels.

Which information is <u>not</u> needed to find out how many channels Yolanda gets with the satellite dish?

A With the dish she gets 175 more channels than she got with cable.

B With the dish she gets 245 more channels than she got with just a roof antenna.

C With cable she got 82 channels.

D All of the information given is needed to solve the problem.

Here's How to Crack It

First, figure out what you know for sure. You know that Yolanda got 82 channels with cable.

Next, re-read the passage. What information in the passage is given to us in terms of what we already know (that is, the number of cable channels)? The key is this part of the second sentence: *With the dish, she gets 175 more channels than she got with cable.* So now we know:

cable = 82 channels; dish = 175 more channels than cable

Can this tell us how many channels Yolanda gets with her satellite dish?

We can write a quick equation:

number of dish channels = numbers of cable channels + 175

or number of dish channels = 82 + 175

257 = 82 + 175

Now look at the answer choices and find the one that contains information we *didn't* need—the **irrelevant information**. Choice **B** is correct.

Now try a couple on your own. The answers are located after the final quiz for this chapter.

1. April, Gladys, Henry, and Tom had a contest to see who could collect the most state quarters. Henry collected 3 more quarters than April. Gladys collected half as many as Henry, and $\frac{1}{4}$ as many as Tom. Tom collected 24 quarters. How many quarters did April collect?

    A   3

    B   6

    C   9

    D   12

    The bus from Torrance to Laguna Beach makes three stops along the way: Long Beach (12 miles), Santa Ana (20 miles), and Costa Mesa (9 miles). The final leg to Laguna Beach is 11 miles. What is the average speed of the bus?

2. In order to answer this, what additional information is needed?

    A   The number of miles per gallon the bus gets

    B   The number of people that get on and off at each stop

    C   The traffic conditions on that day

    D   The time the bus takes for the entire trip

CHAPTER 6: APPLIED ARITHMETIC FINAL QUIZ

Answers to this quiz can be found on page 273–274.

1. A bathing suit has a regular price of $70. This weekend, it is on sale for 20% off. How much does the bathing suit cost on sale?

   A $14

   B $50

   C $56

   D $84

2. The regular price of a computer system is $1,100. The electronics store is running a special this weekend, and all computer systems are on sale for 25% off. What is the price of the computer system on sale?

   A $275

   B $825

   C $975

   D $1,375

3. A train in France can travel at a sustained speed of 225 kilometers per hour. At this speed, how long would it take the train to travel 300 kilometers?

   A $\frac{3}{4}$ of an hour

   B $1\frac{1}{4}$ hours

   C $1\frac{1}{3}$ hours

   D $1\frac{1}{2}$ hours

4. A truck driver is filling her tank with gas. The gas is being pumped at a rate of 4 gallons per minute. If it takes 12 minutes to fill up her tank, how many gallons of gas did she buy?

   A 3 gallons

   B 8 gallons

   C 16 gallons

   D 48 gallons

5. The Concorde flies at a rate of 1,440 miles per hour. At that speed, how far would it travel in 1.5 hours?

   A 960 miles

   B 1,441.5 miles

   C 2,160 miles

   D 2,720 miles

6. Thomas filled his 20-pound propane tank for an upcoming barbecue. However, the valve leaks, and propane gas is escaping at a rate of one-half pound per minute. How many minutes will it take for all of the propane gas to escape?

   A 10 minutes

   B 20 minutes

   C 30 minutes

   D 40 minutes

7. Migdalia's mother takes the bus to work every morning. It takes 20 minutes for the 8 mile trip. What is the average speed of the bus?

   A 2.5 miles per hour

   B 24 miles per hour

   C 28 miles per hour

   D 160 miles per hour

8. If the temperature remains constant, the mass of a substance that can be dissolved in water varies directly with the volume of the water. At room temperature, 36 grams of sodium chloride can be dissolved in 100 ml of water. How many grams can be dissolved in 250 ml of water at the same temperature?

A   54 grams

B   72 grams

C   90 grams

D   150 grams

9. A mountain cabin has snowmobiles for rent. The cost is $50.00 plus $8.75 per hour of rental time. If Jonathan was charged a total of $93.75, for how many hours did he rent a snowmobile?

A   3

B   4

C   5

D   6

48 ft

36 ft

10. Tracy, Kevin, and Irene work part-time for a landscaper. Today they have to install sod in a customer's backyard that measures 36 ft by 48 ft. Tracy can install 108 sq. ft of sod per hour, Kevin 96 sq. ft per hour, and Irene 84 sq. ft per hour. If they all work at the same time, how long will it take them to finish installing sod in the customer's backyard?

A   3 hours

B   4 hours

C   5 hours

D   6 hours

11. Ms. Worthington wanted to buy a new blend of coffee. She wanted the coffee merchant to mix different amounts of regular coffee that costs $4 per pound and special Arabican coffee that costs $10 per pound so she would end up with 6 pounds of the new blend at $6 per pound. How many pounds of each type of coffee should be blended into it?

A   2 lb. of Arabican and 4 lb. of regular

B   3 lb. of Arabican and 3 lb. of regular

C   4 lb. of Arabican and 2 lb. of regular

D   5 lb. of Arabican and 1 lb. of regular

12. A car leaves Los Angeles traveling at 40 mph. Two hours later, a second car leaves from the same location, following the same route, traveling at 60 mph. How many hours will the second car be traveling before it overtakes the first car?

A   1

B   2

C   3

D   4

13. The Lopez family has three children. Ricky is the youngest. Lourdes is four times older than Ricky, and 9-year-old Maria is three years younger than Lourdes. How old is Ricky?

A   3 years old

B   4 years old

C   5 years old

D   6 years old

14. The schedule below indicates departure and arrival times for domestic airline flights from Los Angeles (L.A.) to Chicago.

Departure L.A. Time	Arrival Chicago Time
7:45 A.M.	1:50 P.M.
9:30 A.M.	3:40 P.M.
10:45 A.M.	4:35 P.M.
11:55 A.M.	6:10 P.M.

Which flight has the longest travel-time?

A   The flight leaving at 7:45 A.M.

B   The flight leaving at 9:30 A.M.

C   The flight leaving at 10:45 A.M.

D   The flight leaving at 11:55 A.M.

15. A company makes tennis balls and ships them in boxes, 72 tennis balls per box. It originally shipped them in rectangular boxes, measuring 16 in by 9 in by 24 in. Recently, it changed the shape of its boxes to a cylinder with a diameter of 14 in. The height of the cylindrical boxes is 21 in. Which container takes up less space?

What information from the problem is not needed to find the answer?

A   It ships them in boxes, 72 tennis balls per box.

B   It originally shipped them in rectangular boxes, measuring 16 in by 9 in by 24 in.

C   It changed the shape of its boxes to a cylinder with a diameter of 14 in.

D   The height of the cylindrical boxes is 21 in.

16. Martin wanted to save money to buy a bicycle. He decided to increase the amount he saves each week according to a pattern. For the first 8 weeks, he saved the following amounts (in dollars): 1, 1, 2, 3, 5, 8, 13, 21, . . .

If the pattern continues, how much will he save in week 9?

A $29

B $21

C $34

D $39

ANSWERS TO PRACTICE PROBLEMS

Math and Money
1. B
2. C
3. C

Rate, Work and Percent Mixture
1. C
2. B

Analyzing Problems
1. C
2. D

Rate, Speed, Distance and Time
1. C
2. A
3. B
4. A

Chapter 7
Measurements and Scientific Math

Some questions on the CAHSEE deal with different ways of measuring or expressing the dimensions of an object. You will have to understand scientific notation, and be able to convert measurements from one kind of unit to another.

SCIENTIFIC NOTATION

Scientific notation isn't nearly as complicated as it sounds. It's just a short way to write very large or very small numbers using powers of 10—in other words, 10 with an exponent. When scientists and engineers work with very large or very small numbers, they use scientific notation, rather than writing out a number with, say, 27 zeros after it! Instead, they will write it as a number from 1 to 10 multiplied by 10 with an exponent. (You should remember factors and exponents from Chapter 5.)

So instead of always having to write 1,000,000,000,000,000,000,000,000,000 they can write 1×10^{27}. That saves a lot of space!

Let's go over some really simple rules for how to convert to scientific notation and back.

- If the power of 10 (the exponent) is *positive*, then the number is very *big*.
- If the power of 10 is *negative*, then the number is very *small*.

To rewrite a very large number into scientific notation, all you have to do is move the decimal point <u>left</u> until only one digit remains to the left of the decimal. The number of times the decimal point moves is the number of the exponent:

$$5{,}000{,}000{,}000 = 5 \times 10^9$$

For very small numbers, move the decimal point to the <u>right</u> until only one digit remains to the right of the decimal point. The number of moves to the right gives you a *negative* exponent:

$$0.000000052 = 5.2 \times 10^{-8}$$

Converting from scientific notation to standard notation is just as easy! All you do is reverse what you just did.

To convert a very large number from scientific notation to standard, move the decimal point to the <u>right</u> the same number of moves as the exponent:

$$5 \times 10^9 = 5{,}000{,}000{,}000$$

To convert a very small number from scientific notation to standard, move the decimal point to the <u>left</u> the same number of moves as the exponent:

$$5.2 \times 10^{-8} = 0.000000052$$

Let's try a sample problem:

─────────────────○─────────────────

$3.8 \times 10^4 =$

A   380
B   3,800
C   38,000
D   380,000

Here's How to Crack It

Just follow the rules to convert the number given in the question from scientific notation to standard form. Since this exponent is positive, we're going to move the decimal point to the right:

$$3.8 \times 10^4 = 3.8000 = 38{,}000$$

Now check the answer choices. Choice **C** is correct.

─────────────────○─────────────────

Once you realize it's all about counting, scientific notation is actually pretty easy, isn't it? Now try a couple on your own. The answers are located at the end of this chapter, after the final quiz.

1. $2.9 \times 10^{-3} =$
   A   0.0029
   B   0.029
   C   0.29
   D   2,900

2. Express 64,000 in scientific notation.
   A 64×10^3
   B 64×10^4
   C 6.4×10^3
   D 6.4×10^4

Standard MG 1.1

"Compare weights, capacities, geometric measures, times, and temperatures within and between measurement systems (e.g., miles per hour and feet per second, cubic inches to cubic centimeters)."

UNITS OF MEASURE

The CAHSEE will ask you to convert measurements from one kind of unit to another. You might have to convert within the same measurement system (for instance, from centimeters to millimeters—both are metric system units) or between different measurement systems (from centimeters to inches—centimeters are metric system units, inches are from the U.S. or Imperial system). It will help if you know how to set up proportions, because proportions are useful when you're comparing things that are similar sizes but are measured in different ways.

Let's go over a problem in which we set up a **proportion** in order to convert measurements.

One cubic meter is equal to about 264 gallons. About how many gallons are there in 5 cubic meters?

A   52.8 gallons

B   259 gallons

C   269 gallons

D   1,320 gallons

Here's How to Crack It

Read the question carefully. First, make sure you understand the information given in the question. We're given a conversion rule to use right off: 1 cubic meter = 264 gallons (we can ignore the "about" for these kinds of conversions).

$$1 \text{ m}^3 = 264 \text{ gal}$$

When setting up a proportion, we can write it like a fraction:

$$\frac{1 \text{ m}^3}{264 \text{ gal}}$$

We want to find out how many gallons are in 5 cubic meters. Since we don't know the number of gallons, let's call that n.

$$5 \text{ m}^3 = n \text{ gal}$$

To solve proportion problems, just set up two equal fractions. One will have all the information you know, and the other will have the missing piece that you're trying to figure out:

$$\frac{1 \text{ m}^3}{264 \text{ gal}} = \frac{5 \text{ m}^3}{n \text{ gal}}$$

Whenever you have a proportion set up like this, you can cross multiply and solve for n very easily. Cross multiplying means you can multiply the numerator of the left-hand fraction by the denominator of the right, and multiply the denominator of the right-hand fraction by the numerator of the left:

$$\frac{1 \text{ m}^3}{264 \text{ gal}} \diagup\!\!\!\!\!\diagdown \frac{5 \text{ m}^3}{n \text{ gal}}$$

Once you've done that, you can rewrite the equation, and solve for n.

$$(1)(n) = (5)(264)$$

$$n = 1{,}320 \text{ gal}$$

Check the answer choices. Choice **D** is correct.

Setting Up Proportions

Whenever you set up a proportion, make sure you set up your fractions the same way on both sides of the equal sign. Compare these examples.

$$\frac{1 \text{ m}^3}{264 \text{ gal}} = \frac{5 \text{ m}^3}{n \text{ gal}}$$

m^3 is to gal as m^3 is to gal will get you the correct answer. But...

$$\frac{1 \text{ m}^3}{264 \text{ gal}} = \frac{n \text{ gal}}{5 \text{ m}^3}$$

m^3 is to gal as gal is to m^3 is inconsistent and will lead to a wrong answer.

Rule of Thumbs

Imperial units of measure, like the inch and the foot, were based on the human body: The inch was supposedly the width of a man's thumb, and the foot is (obviously!) the length of a man's foot. You can see how that could get kind of confusing though: Whose foot? Whose thumb? That's why the metric system, which is based on scientific constants, was invented.

Now try some on your own. The answers are located at the end of this chapter, after the final quiz.

1. **One kilogram is equal to approximately 2.2 pounds. About how-many pounds are there in 40 kilograms?**

   A   18.2 pounds

   B   37.8 pounds

   C   42.2 pounds

   D   88 pounds

Name	Height
Felipe	1,632 mm
Leanna	1.62 m
Stanley	159 cm

2. **If you arranged the students named in the table above from shortest to tallest, in what order would they appear?**

   A   Leanna, Stanley, Felipe

   B   Stanley, Leanna, Felipe

   C   Leanna, Felipe, Stanley

   D   Felipe, Leanna, Stanley

3. **A speed of 3.6 kilometers per hour is equivalent to a speed of 1 meter per second. If a car were moving at a speed of 20 meters per second, what would its speed be in kilometers per hour?**

   A   5.5 kilometers per hour

   B   16.4 kilometers per hour

   C   23.6 kilometers per hour

   D   72 kilometers per hour

4. The unit for weight in the metric system is the newton. One pound equals about 4.45 newtons. If Jordan weighs 89 pounds, what is his approximate weight in newtons?

A 20 newtons

B 85 newtons

C 396 newtons

D 404 newtons

5. Arrange the following speeds in order from fastest to slowest:

$950 \dfrac{m}{min}$; $60 \dfrac{km}{hr}$; $15 \dfrac{m}{sec}$

A $60 \dfrac{km}{hr}$; $950 \dfrac{m}{min}$; $15 \dfrac{m}{sec}$

B $15 \dfrac{m}{sec}$; $950 \dfrac{m}{min}$; $60 \dfrac{km}{hr}$

C $60 \dfrac{km}{hr}$; $15 \dfrac{m}{sec}$; $950 \dfrac{m}{min}$

D $950 \dfrac{m}{min}$; $60 \dfrac{km}{hr}$; $15 \dfrac{m}{sec}$

SCALE

You can see **scale** in action in real life all over Las Vegas. For example, on top of the hotel Paris, there is a one-half scale version of the Eiffel Tower. You will see problems about scale on the test—these problems give you a scale drawing or model of an object, tell you what scale was used, and then ask you to calculate the real-life dimensions. Knowing how to set up a proportion is key here.

Standard MG 1.2

"Construct and read drawings and models made to scale."

The diagram below shows a scale drawing of the floorplan of a house. The scale used is: 1 inch (in) = 12 feet (ft).

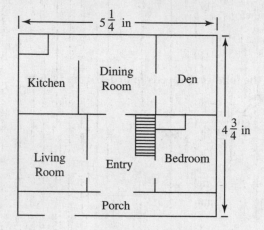

What is the length (left to right) of the house in feet?

A 51 feet

B 54 feet

C 63 feet

D 69 feet

It's Not About Weight

Other places scale is used: Maps, model skeletons of dinosaurs, and models of things like cars and planes.

Here's How to Crack It

Read the question and study the diagram carefully. Scale is the **ratio** of a given length on a drawing or model to its corresponding length in reality. In this question the scale tells you that 1 inch on the drawing corresponds to 12 feet on the real house.

Next, set up a proportion with the scale on one side and the unknown on the other side—just like in the problem we did earlier.

$$\frac{1 \text{ in}}{12 \text{ ft}} = \frac{5\frac{1}{4} \text{ in}}{x \text{ ft}}$$

Cross multiply and solve for the unknown variable. You might want to change $5\frac{1}{4}$ to 5.25 to make the calculation easier.

$(1)(x) = (5.25)(12)$ means that $x = 63$ ft.

Now check the answer choices. Choice **C** is correct.

Now try one on your own. The answer is located at the end of this chapter, after the final quiz.

Now try one on your own. The answer is located at the end of this chapter, after the final quiz.

1. **The diagram below is a scale drawing of the space shuttle. The scale used is 1 inch (in) = 14 feet (ft).**

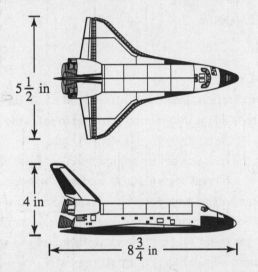

   What is the real length, in feet, from nose to tail, of the space shuttle?

   A   108.5 ft

   B   115.5 ft

   C   119 ft

   D   122.5 ft

MEASUREMENT PROBLEMS

Measurement problems will ask you to solve problems involving rates (for example, speed in miles per hour) or products (for example, work, expressed in Newton-meters). You will have to make sure the answer is labeled with the correct units. Make sure that the answer makes sense—you don't want to try to fit a 12-foot car into a 12-inch box! Look at the units in the question and think about what units the answer should be.

Standard MG 1.3

"Use measures expressed as rates (e.g., speed, density) and measures expressed as products (e.g., person-days) to solve problems; check the units of the solutions; and use dimensional analysis to check the reasonableness of the answer."

The amount of work done in moving an object is equal to the force applied to the object multiplied by the distance the object moves ($W = F \times d$). Force is measured in newtons (N), distance is measured in meters (m), and work is measured in newton-meters (N-m).

A   450 N

B   450 N-m

C   1,800 N

D   1,800 N-m

Here's How to Crack It

Read the question carefully. Don't get discouraged by all the technical terms and the formula! You have all the information you need to solve the problem right here.

First, let's look at the question again and figure out what we need to do—and what we don't. The question itself says: *If 900 N-m of work was done lifting the front end of a car 0.5 m off the ground, what force was applied?* So we need to figure out how much **force** was used. Remember that the passage tells us that force is expressed in **newtons**. Knowing that, let's look at the answer choices and see if we can use Process of Elimination to eliminate any right off the bat. Since we know that force is expressed in newtons (N), we can cross out choices B and D immediately, because they're expressed in newton-meters (N-m). We've already knocked our choices down to two, and we haven't even done any math yet!

Next, let's write down the formula given in the problem.

$$W = F \times d$$

We know from the passage that 900 N-m of *work* was done, and the car was raised a *distance* of 0.5 meters from the ground.

Now we can substitute the numbers and units given in the problem into the formula:

$$W = F \times d$$

$$900 \text{ N-m} = F \times 0.5 \text{ m}$$

Now we can solve the equation for F, the force:

$$\frac{900 \text{ N·m}}{0.5 \text{ m}} = F$$

$$1{,}800 = F$$

Since we know that force is expressed in newtons, we can see that choice C, 1,800 N, is correct.

We can also look at the units to confirm our answer. Notice that meters (m) cancels out on both sides of the equation, leaving newtons (N) as the units in which the answer is expressed.

$$\frac{900 \text{ N·m̶}}{0.5 \text{ m̶}} = \frac{F \times 0.5 \text{ m̶}}{0.5 \text{ m̶}}$$

$$1{,}800 \text{ N} = F$$

Now check the answer choices. Choice C is correct again (phew!).

——————————◯——————————

Now try some on your own. The answers are located at the end of this chapter, after the final quiz.

1. **The speed of light is 186,000 miles per second. The average distance of the Sun from Earth is 93,000,000 miles. How long does it take light from the Sun to reach Earth?**

    A   500 seconds

    B   500 miles per second

    C   17,298 seconds

    D   17,298 miles per second

Fraction Fact

Remember that when you divide by a fraction, you need to invert the fraction and then multiply. You must invert the units as well.

2. Over the 82-game regular season, the San Jose Sharks lost 328 person-games due to injury. On average, how many players missed each game due to injury?

A 3 person games

B 3 players

C 4 person games

D 4 players

3. Acceleration is the rate of change of velocity. Scientists who study motion use the following formula to find acceleration: *Acceleration =*

$$\frac{Final\ Velocity - Original\ Velocity}{Time}$$

As a jet fighter is launched from the deck of an aircraft carrier, it goes from a velocity of zero to 70 meters per second (m/sec) in 2 seconds. What is the acceleration?

A 35 m/sec

B 35 m/sec/sec

C 140 m/sec

D 140 m/sec/sec

4. Last month the Merced County School District lost 380 person days of work due to illness. If last month had 20 working days, what was the average number of persons who missed work each day due to illness?

A 19 persons

B 19 person-days

C 76 persons

D 76 person-days

CHANGES IN MEASUREMENT

Changing in measurement, converting something from units to square units or cubic units, requires a little extra thought. Be careful—converting cubic feet to cubic inches is not the same as converting feet to inches.

Let's review the relationships between inches and feet, square inches and feet, and cubic inches and cubic feet.

When we talk about inches and feet, we are talking about *length*. When we talk about square inches and square feet, we are talking about *area*. When we talk about cubic inches and cubic feet, we are talking about *volume*.

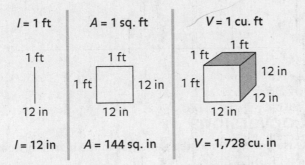

How many cubic inches are in 8 cubic feet?

A   96

B   1,152

C   1,728

D   13,824

Standard MG 2.4

"Relate the changes in measurement with a change of scale to the units used (e.g., square inches, cubic feet) and to conversions between units (1 square foot = 144 square inches or [1 ft²] = [144 in²], 1 cubic inch is approximately 16.38 cubic centimeters or [1 in³]=[16.38 cm³])."

Memorize These!

To find the area of something, we multiply the length times the width: $A = lw$.

To find the volume of something, we multiply the length times the width times the height: $V = lwh$.

Here's How to Crack It

Read the question carefully. We are converting cubic feet to cubic inches. Our diagram above tells us that 1 cubic foot is equal to 1,728 cubic inches. Let's set up a proportion to help us find out how many inches are equal to 8 cubic feet:

$$\frac{x \text{ cu. in}}{8 \text{ cu. ft}} \times \frac{1{,}728 \text{ cu. in.}}{1 \text{ cu. ft.}}$$

Now cross multiply:

$$8(1{,}728) = x = 13{,}824 \text{ cu. in.}$$

Check the answer choices. Choice **D** is correct.

Metric Conversions

Converting measurements works the same way in the metric system—but it's even easier to do the math, because it's all working with powers of ten. One cubic meter is equal to <u>one million</u> cubic centimeters.

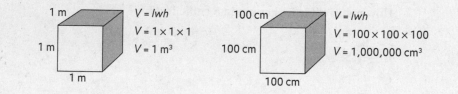

Now try some on your own. The answers are located at the end of this chapter, after the final quiz.

1. Ms. Harrington wants to have wall-to-wall carpeting installed in her living room, which measures 12 feet by 15 feet. How many square yards (yd²) of carpeting will she need?

    A 9

    B 20

    C 60

    D 180

2. The volume of a box is 8,640 cubic inches. How many cubic feet (ft³) does this equal?

A   5

B   60

C   720

D   2,880

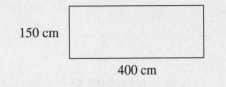

150 cm

400 cm

3. What is the area, in square meters (m²), of the rectangle above?

A   5.5

B   6

C   600

D   60,000

4. Each of the end zones on a football field measures 50 yards by 10 yards. What is the area, in square feet (ft²), of each end zone?

A   450

B   500

C   1,500

D   4,500

5. A cube has a volume of 27 cubic feet. What is the length, in inches (in), of one of the sides of the cube?

A   3

B   36

C   243

D   46,656

CHAPTER 7: MEASUREMENT AND SCIENTIFIC MATH FINAL QUIZ

Answers to this quiz can be found on page 274–276.

1. $4.7 \times 10^2 =$

   A   4.700

   B   47

   C   470

   D   4,700

5. $3.2 \times 10^{-2} =$

   A   0.0032

   B   0.032

   C   0.32

   D   320

2. Express 0.000075 in scientific notation.

   A 0.75×10^{-4}

   B 7.5×10^{-5}

   C 7.5×10^{-6}

   D 75×10^{-6}

6. Express 0.00083 in scientific notation.

   A 0.83×10^{-3}

   B 8.3×10^{-3}

   C 8.3×10^{-4}

   D 83×10^{-5}

3. $1.6 \times 10^3 =$

   A   1.6000

   B   16

   C   160

   D   1,600

7. $9.1 \times 10^5 =$

   A   9,100

   B   91,000

   C   910,000

   D   9,100,000

4. Write 5,280 in scientific notation.

   A 528×10^1

   B 52.8×10^2

   C 5.28×10^3

   D 0.528×10^4

8. The standard form of a number is 2,500,000. How would this number be-written in scientific notation?

   A 25×10^5

   B 2.5×10^6

   C 2.5×10^7

   D 0.25×10^7

9. One meter equals about 3.28 feet. In the Summer Olympics one of the events is the 400-meter run. About how many feet does that distance equal?

A   122 feet

B   1,220 feet

C   1,312 feet

D   1,320 feet

10. An automobile engine's torque (pulling power) is measured in pound-feet (lb-ft). One lb-ft is equivalent to approximately 1.4 newton-meters (N-m). If an engine's torque were 196 lb-ft, what would that be in N-m?

A   78.4 N-m

B   140 N-m

C   242.4 N-m

D   274.4 N-m

11. Arrange the following areas in order from largest to smallest:

12 sq. yd; 109 sq. ft; 15,840 sq. in

A   12 sq. yd; 109 sq. ft; 15,840 sq. in

B   109 sq. ft; 15,840 sq. in; 12 sq. yd

C   15,840 sq. in; 109 sq. ft; 12 sq. yd

D   109 sq. ft; 12 sq. yd; 15,840 sq. in

12. One kilometer equals approximately 0.62 miles. About how many miles would be the equivalent of a 10-kilometer race?

A   3.8 miles

B   6.2 miles

C   10.62 miles

D   16.2 miles

13. In Europe gasoline is sold by the liter. One gallon is equal to about 3.79 liters. If a car's gas tank had a capacity of 12 gallons, what would be its approximate capacity in liters?

A   3.2 liters

B   8.2 liters

C   15.8 liters

D   45.5 liters

14. The diagram below shows a scale drawing of a 2002 model automobile. The scale used is:
1 centimeter (cm) = 0.3 meters (m).

4.7 cm

12.1 cm

What is the length, in meters, of the actual 2002 automobile?

A   3.63 m

B   4.03 m

C   36.3 m

D   121 m

15. The diagram below is a scale drawing of a commercial fishing boat. The scale used is 1 inch (in) = 16 feet (ft).

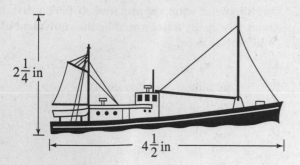

$2\frac{1}{4}$ in

$4\frac{1}{2}$ in

What is the actual length, in feet, of the fishing boat?

A   64.5 ft

B   72 ft

C   76 ft

D   88 ft

16. The scale model of the lighthouse shown in the picture below was made using a scale of 1 inch (in) = 20 feet (ft).

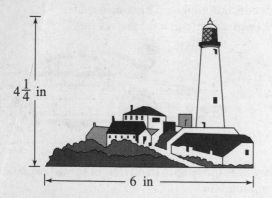

$4\frac{1}{4}$ in

6 in

What is the height, in feet, of the actual lighthouse?

A   65 ft

B   75 ft

C   85 ft

D   95 ft

17. Density equals mass per unit volume $\left(D = \dfrac{M}{V}\right)$.

The density of pure silver is 10.5 grams per cubic centimeter $\left(\dfrac{g}{cm^3}\right)$. What is the approximate mass of a pure silver bracelet that has a volume of 4 cm³?

A   2.6 g

B   2.6 g/cm³

C   42 g

D   42 g/cm³

18. The total amount of electric energy a household appliance uses depends on the power (measured in kilowatts) used by the appliance and the total time (measured in hours) it is used. The formula for electric energy is: $E = P \times t$ *Energy = Power × time*

If an average month has 30 days, and a microwave oven, rated at 1.5 kilowatts of power, is used an average of one hour a day, how much electric energy does the microwave oven use in a month?

A   20 kilowatts

B   20 kilowatt-hours

C   45 kilowatts

D   45 kilowatt-hours

19. An exhaust fan is rated at 360 cubic feet per minute (ft³/m). This means it can remove 360 cubic feet of air from a room every minute. If the fan runs for 20 minutes, how much air will be removed?

A   18 cubic feet

B   18 cubic feet per minute

C   7,200 cubic feet

D   7,200 cubic feet per minute

20. The sticker on a new car lists the average mileage as 24 miles per gallon. How far should a person be able to drive on 8 gallons of gas?

   A 3 miles per gallon

   B 3 miles

   C 192 miles per gallon

   D 192 miles

21. One inch is approximately equal to 2.54 centimeters. About how many square centimeters (cm^2) equal one square inch?

   A   2.54

   B   5.08

   C   6.45

   D   16.38

22. One acre equals 43,560 square feet. How many square yards (yd^2) does that equal?

   A   1,613

   B   3,630

   C   4,840

   D   14,520

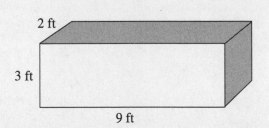

24. How many square inches are in 4 square feet?

   A   48

   B   108

   C   576

   D   6,912

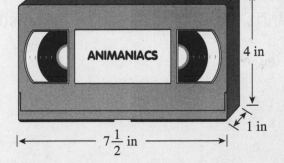

25. One cubic inch (in^3) is approximately equal to 16.38 cubic centimeters (cm^3). What is the volume, in cubic centimeters (cm^3), of the videocassette shown above?

   A   122.85

   B   204.75

   C   466.83

   D   491.40

23. What is the volume, in cubic yards (yd^3), of the box shown in the diagram above?

   A   2

   B   3

   C   18

   D   54

SWERS TO PRACTICE PROBLEMS

entific Notation
A
2. D

Scale
1. D
2. A

Changes in Measurement
1. B
2. A
3. B
4. D
5. B

Units of Measure
1. D
2. B. None
3. D
4. C
5. A

Measurement Problems
1. A
2. D
3. B
4. A

Chapter 8
Algebra

The CAHSEE features many different types of algebra problems, including translating words into math, setting up and solving equations, and manipulating algebraic expressions in a variety of ways.

Standard AF 1.1

"Use variables and appropriate operations to write an expression, an equation, an inequality, or a system of equations or inequalities that represents a verbal description (e.g., three less than a number, half as large as area A)."

WORDS INTO NUMBERS

Did you know that math is actually a kind of language? For example, when you see $3 + 4 = 7$, you automatically translate the symbols on the page into English: "three plus four equals seven" (or maybe Spanish: "tres mas quatro iguales siete"). The CAHSEE will ask you to do the opposite—to take sentences describing a situation and turn them into a mathematical equation or expression. Use variables (x or y or whatever letter you like) to represent anything you don't know. Work slowly, bit by bit, writing down each piece of the sentence as you read it, rather than trying to do the whole sentence at once.

Add 5 to a number and then divide the result by 2. The answer is 7. Which of these equations matches this scenario?

A $\quad 7 = 5 + \dfrac{n}{2}$

B $\quad \dfrac{n}{5} + 2 = 7$

C $\quad 7 = \dfrac{2}{n} + 5$

D $\quad \dfrac{n+5}{2} = 7$

Math/English Dictionary

"is" means "="
"of" means "×"
"more than" means "+"
"less than" means "−"

Here's How to Crack It

Read the question carefully. Think of an equation as a mathematical sentence that contains an equal sign (=) or a less than or greater than sign (<, >). The sentence can contain numbers and variables (a, b, x, y, n) that act like nouns, and operational signs (+, −, ×, ÷) that act like verbs or adjectives that describe what to do to the numbers or variables.

Next, find the words and phrases in the question that indicate verbs or mathematical operations. Let's start with the first sentence:

"Add 5 to a number." Since the first word is "add," we know we're going to have a $+$ sign in the equation. We're adding 5 to a number. Since we don't know what number, we'll use a variable to represent it. Let's use n for our number:

$$n + 5$$

The next sentence says:

"Divide the result by 2." The second sentence tells us we're going to divide the result of $n + 5$ by 2. We could use the $\div$ in our equation, but let's represent division like this instead so we don't have to deal with parentheses:

$$\frac{n + 5}{2}$$

"The answer is 7." This sentence is pretty easy. "The answer is" is just another way of saying "equals," which means we need an equal sign:

$$= 7$$

Next, put them all together to form an equation.

$$\frac{n + 5}{2} = 7$$

Now check the answer choices. Choice **D** is correct.

———————————◯———————————

Some questions will give you the variables directly, although they may give you more than one variable. You will have to decide what to do with the variables in these questions.

———————————◯———————————

For last week's field trip, the number of students, s, was equal to 7 times the number of adult supervisors, a. Which equation contains the same information?

A $s \cdot a = 7$

B $7 \cdot a = s$

C $7 \cdot s = a$

D $7 \cdot s = 7 \cdot a$

Here's How to Crack It

First, let's identify the variables in this problem. In the question, *s* represents the number of students, and *a* represents the number of adult supervisors.

Next, we need to find the verbs—in other words, the phrases that tell us what we're going to do with these variables.

"The number of students, *s, was equal to* 7 *times* the number of adult supervisors, *a.*"

The first verb we have in this question is "*s* was equal to." We can write that like this:

$$s =$$

The next mathematical operation in our question is "7 times the number of adult supervisors", which we can write as

$$7 \times a \text{ or } 7a \text{ or } 7 \cdot a$$

Now we can put the whole thing together:

$$s = 7 \cdot a$$

Now check the answer choices. Choice **B** is correct.

Multiple Multiples

There are a few different multiplication symbols: ×, <, (), •, and sometimes... nothing!

If there is no operation sign between a number and a variable (4*x*) you need to multiply.

Now try a couple on your own. The answers are located at the end of this chapter, after the final quiz.

1. Multiply a number by 3 and add 2 to the result. The answer is 17. Which of the following equations matches these statements?

    A $2 = 17 + 3n$

    B $3n + 2 = 17$

    C $3n = 17 + 2$

    D $3(n + 2) = 17$

2. **In a certain classroom, the number of desks, *d*, is equal to 6 times the number of rows, *r*. Which equation matches the information?**

    A $6 \cdot r = d$

    B $6 \cdot d = r$

    C $6 \cdot r = 6 \cdot d$

    D $d \cdot r = 6$

ORDER OF OPERATIONS

The CAHSEE will ask you to simplify long algebraic expressions. You don't even have to solve these problems, you just have to make them shorter! When you're simplifying expressions, it's important to do things in the right order, called the Order of Operations. But don't worry! We've got an easy way to remember this order.

PEMDAS is an acronym to help you remember the order of operations.

P	Parentheses
E	Exponents
M	Multiply (from left to right)
D	Divide (from left to right)
A	Add (from left to right)
S	Subtract (from left to right)

In other words:

1. Do all work in **parentheses** first (and remember to use PEMDAS inside the parentheses!).
2. Simplify all expressions with **exponents**.
3. **Multiply** and **divide** in order from left to right.
4. **Add** and **subtract** in order from left to right.

Another way to remember PEMDAS is to memorize the phrase, "Please Excuse My Dear Aunt Sally!"

Standard AF 1.2

"Use the correct order of operations to evaluate algebraic expressions such as $3(2x + 5)^2$."

Let's try an example.

Evaluate the following expression: $4x - 6 + 3(5 - 1) \cdot 2^2$

A $4x - 3$

B $4x + 42$

C $4x + 186$

D $4x + 570$

Here's How to Crack It

First of all, the phrase "evaluate the following expression" is just another way of saying "simplify the expression." So when you see the word "evaluate," think "simplify."

We need to simplify that long algebraic expression using the order of operations. Remember PEMDAS, and this should be a piece of cake.

Parentheses: The only operation with parentheses in this expression is $3(5 - 1)$, which we can simplify to $3(4)$:

$$4x - 6 + 3(4) \cdot 2^2$$

Exponents: 2^2 becomes 4:

$$4x - 6 + 3(4) \cdot 4$$

Multiply and **Divide**: We need to multiply and divide in order from left to right. Since we don't know what x is, we can leave $4x$ alone—it's as simple as we can make it. (There is no division to be done in this expression, so don't worry about dividing anything.) Multiplying from left to right gives us

$$4x - 6 + 12 \cdot 4$$

and then

$$4x - 6 + 48$$

Add and **Subtract**: The last step in the Order of Operations is to add and subtract in order from left to right.

$4x - 6 + 48$ can be rewritten as $4x + 48 - 6$, which gives us

$$4x + 42$$

Now check the answer choices. Choice **B** is correct.

CAHSEE can make things a bit more difficult with exponents and parentheses. You might have a problem with two sets of parentheses, or an expression with a set of parentheses and an exponent. You will have to know how to use the **distributive property** for these kinds of expressions.

The distributive property tells us how to simplify expressions that require you to multiply numbers inside parentheses by something else. The simplest way to write the distributive law is like this:

$$a(b + c) = ab + ac$$

This just means that you can multiply everything *inside* the parentheses by everything *outside* of it, working from left to right. For example:

$$5(6 + 3) = 5(6) + 5(3) =$$
$$30 + 15 = 45$$

You can test this by doing the operation another way (remember PEMDAS):

$$5(6 + 3) = 5(9) = 45$$

It looks a little trickier when you throw a variable into the mix, but you actually have to do *less* work:

$$5(x + 3) = 5x + 15$$

You don't know what x is, and you don't have any way of finding it, so don't worry about solving for it!

You will also have to solve expressions with parentheses raised to a power, like $(x + y)^2$, or two sets of parentheses multiplied by each other. You're probably not surprised to hear we've got a trick to simplifying these problems, too!

ELL TIP

The distributive property just means you are *distributing* (spreading out) the numbers inside the parentheses.

When multiplying sets of parentheses, for example $(x + 3)(x + 4)$, we can use the following acronym to help us remember the order of operations:

FOIL = First Outer Inner Last

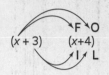

Start with the **first** figure in each set of parentheses: $x \times x = x^2$

Then do the two **outside** figures: $x \times 4 = 4x$

Then the two **inside** figures: $3 \times x = 3x$

Finally, do the last **figure** in each set of parentheses: $3 \times 4 = 12$

When you put them all together, you get

$$x^2 + 4x + 3x + 12$$
$$\text{or}$$
$$x^2 + 7x + 12$$

When you have a parentheses followed by an exponent, you can just expand the expression and use FOIL to simplify:

$$(x + y)^2 = (x + y)(x + y) = x^2 + xy + xy + y^2 = x^2 + 2xy + y^2$$

Let's try an example using FOIL:

Evaluate the following expression: $3(2x - 5)^2$

A $6x - 15$

B $6x + 25$

C $12x^2 + 75$

D $12x^2 - 60x + 75$

Here's How to Crack It

Read the question carefully. Keep in mind both PEMDAS and FOIL.

First of all, let's expand the exponent:

$$3(2x - 5)(2x - 5)$$

Now, following PEMDAS, we do the expressions in parentheses first. In order to simplify the parentheses, we'll use FOIL:

First: $2x \times 2x = 4x^2$

Outer: $2x \times -5 = -10x$

Inner: $-5 \times 2x = -10x$

Last: $-5 \times -5 = 25$

Putting it all together, we get:

$$3(4x^2 - 10x - 10x + 25)$$

Combine like terms:

$$3(4x^2 - 20x + 25)$$

Finally, use the distributive property to multiply the expression in parentheses by 3:

$$12x^2 - 60x + 75$$

Now check the answer choices. Choice **D** is correct.

Now try a couple on your own. The answers are located at the end of this chapter, after the final quiz.

1. **Evaluate the following expression: $5(2x + 3)^2$**

    A $10x + 15$

    B $10x + 9$

    C $20x^2 + 60x + 45$

    D $100x^2 + 300x + 225$

2. **The expression $4(x - 3) - 2(x - 3)$ is equivalent to**

    A 2

    B $2x$

    C $2x - 6$

    D $2x - 18$

ALGEBRAIC OPERATIONS

You're going to have to find the roots of an algebraic equation; it will also ask you to find the **multiplicative inverse** (also known as the **reciprocal**), and the **additive inverse**. Let's break this down into manageable pieces.

Algebraic Roots

When you find the roots of an algebraic equation, this means you will have to solve for all the possible answers to a variable in an equation where the variable is raised to a power—basically, you will have to find the square root of a variable. Let's look at an example.

Solve for x if $4x^2 - 8 = 92$.

A $\{-2, 2\}$

B $\{-2, 5\}$

C $\{-5, 5\}$

D $\{-10, 10\}$

"Students understand and use such operations as taking the opposite, finding the reciprocal, and taking a root. They understand and use the rules of exponents."

Here's How to Crack It

Read the question carefully. We have to solve for x, so first let's think about what we know about x. In this equation, x is the square root of x^2. Now, what do we know about square roots? A square root of a particular number is a number that, *when multiplied by itself (squared),* equals the first number. Six is the square root of 36 because 6 times 6 is 36.

In this problem, we can use Process of Elimination and eliminate choice **B** right away, because a number cannot have two square roots unless they are they positive and negative versions of the same number. Negative two and 5 are not versions of the same number, so they are out. Whenever you have to solve for the square root of a variable, always check the answer choices first and see if you can eliminate one or more of them for this reason.

Now that we've eliminated one of the answer choices, we still have three to choose from. Now we have to do some math.

First, let's get x on one side of the equation and the rest of the numbers on the other side. You can do this by adding the opposite of −8 to both sides.

$$4x^2 - 8 = 92$$
$$4x^2 - 8 + 8 = 92 + 8$$
$$4x^2 - 100$$

Now, to isolate x^2, divide each side of the equation by 4:

$$\frac{4x^2}{4} = \frac{100}{4}$$

$$x^2 = 25$$

Finally, take the square root of both sides of the equation. (Remember that the square root of a positive number has both a positive and a negative value.)

$$x^2 = 25, \text{ meaning that } x = -5 \text{ and } +5$$

The solution set is {−5, 5}. Now check the answer choices. Choice **C** is correct.

Finding Your Roots

A square root can be either positive or negative, because two negatives multiplied together result in a positive.

Inverses

In algebra, the **additive inverse** of a number is just another way of saying "opposite". The sum of any number and its inverse is always zero. For example, the opposite of 3 is 3 because their sum is zero. The opposite of $-\frac{3}{4}$ is $\frac{3}{4}$.

The **multiplicative inverse** of a number is also called its **reciprocal**. The product of any number and its reciprocal is 1. For example, the reciprocal of 3 is $\frac{1}{3}$ because their product is 1. The reciprocal of $-\frac{3}{4}$ is $-\frac{4}{3}$ because $(-\frac{3}{4})(-\frac{4}{3}) = 1$. In other words, the reciprocal of a fraction is just that fraction flipped upside down. If you're finding the reciprocal, remember to make a mixed number (such as $3\frac{1}{2}$) into an improper fraction (such as $\frac{7}{2}$).

Now try some on your own. The answers are located at the end of this chapter, after the final quiz.

1. **What is the reciprocal (multiplicative inverse) of $-3\frac{1}{2}$?**

    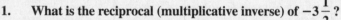

    A $-\frac{2}{7}$

    B $\frac{2}{7}$

    C $\frac{5}{7}$

    D $3\frac{1}{2}$

    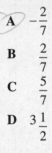

2. **Solve for x, if $8x^2 + 5 = 293$.**

    A $\{-12, 6\}$

    B $\{-6, 6\}$

    C $\{-6, 12\}$

    D $\{-12, 12\}$

3. **Solve for x, if $\frac{x}{4} = -16$.**

    A -64

    B -4

    C 4

    D 64

4. **Simplify the expression $(x^2y^3)^3$.**

   A x^5y^3

   B x^5y^6

   C x^6y^3

   D x^6y^9

5. **Solve for x, if $9x^2 - 4 = 77$.**

   A $\{-9, 9\}$

   B $\{-9, 3\}$

   C $\{-3, 3\}$

   D $\{3, 9\}$

6. **Solve for x, if $\dfrac{x}{7} - 5 = -4$.**

   A -63

   B -7

   C 7

   D 63

LINEAR EQUATIONS AND INEQUALITIES

A **linear equation** or **linear inequality** is one where none of the variables has an exponent and the variables are being added or subtracted, instead of multiplied or divided. $2x + 4 = 10$ is a linear equation. So is $x - y = 15$.

$x^2 + y = 6$ is *not* a linear equation, because x is squared.

$\dfrac{x}{y} = 4$ is *not* a linear equation because the variables are being divided.

Standard AF 4.1

"Solve two-step linear equations and inequalities in one variable over the rational numbers, interpret the solution or solutions in the context from which they arose, and verify the reasonableness of the results."

Inequalities

An inequality is an expression that uses one of the following signs instead of an equal sign:

<	(less than)
>	(greater than)
≤	(less than or equal to)
≥	(greater than or equal to)

You can solve inequalities the same way you solve equations—with one important exception. Whenever you multiply or divide an inequality by a *negative* number, the solution will have the *opposite* inequality sign: < becomes >, and ≤ becomes ≥ .

You can check whether or not your answer is right by plugging it back into the original inequality. If you didn't reverse the inequality sign after dividing both sides by a negative number, your answer will not work.

Let's start with a simple inequality.

Solve for x when $4x + 5 < 29$.

A $x < 5$

B $x < 6$

C $x < 7$

D $x < 8$

Here's How to Crack It

Remember that solving inequalities is like solving equations. If this expression had an equal sign, we would want to get the part of the expression that has the variable on one side of the equal sign all by itself. We want to do the same thing here. To do this, we'll subtract 5 from both sides.

$$4x + 5 < 29$$
$$\underline{-5 \quad -5}$$
$$4x < 24$$

Next, divide both sides by 4:

$$\frac{4x}{4} < \frac{24}{4}$$

becomes

$$x < 6$$

Now check the answer choices. Choice **B** is correct.

───────────○───────────

Now let's try a slightly more complicated problem:

───────────○───────────

Solve for x when $-4x + 5 > 15$

A $x < -3$

B $x > -3$

C $x < -5$

D $x > 5$

Here's How to Crack It

Read the question carefully. What's different about this inequality than the first one we did? If you said the coefficient of the variable is negative, you're on the right track! Remember that because we're going to be dividing by a negative number we have to flip the inequality sign.

Now that you know that, look at the answer choices again: Can we cross out any of the answer choices right now, using POE? Yes! We can cross out choices **B** and **D** because they both have the *same* inequality sign (>) as the expression in the question.

Now that we've narrowed our answers down to two, we can solve for x:

Subtract 3 from each side:

$$\begin{array}{r} -4x + 3 > 15 \\ -3 \quad -3 \\ \hline \end{array}$$

Math Term

A *coefficient* is the number that a variable is multiplied by.

Divide each side by −4 (remember to flip the inequality sign!):

$$
\begin{array}{r}
-4x \;\; > \; 12 \\
\div -4 \qquad \div -4 \\
\hline
x \qquad < -3
\end{array}
$$

$$x < -3$$

Now check the answer choices. Choice **A** is correct.

––––––––––––––––––––○––––––––––––––––––––

Now try a couple on your own. The answers are located at the end of this chapter, after the final quiz.

1. **Solve the following equation for a.**

   $3a - 9 = 15$

   A $a = 2$

   B $a = 4$

   C $a = 6$

   D $a = 8$

2. **If $p = 5$ and $q = 2$, then**

   $$\dfrac{pq + 6}{2} - 4 =$$

   A 2

   B 4

   C 6

   D 7

3. **Solve the following inequality for** x.

   $2x - 5 < 11$

   A $x < 3$

   B $x < 4$

   C $x < 6$

   D $x < 8$

4. **If** $y = 3$ **and** $z = 9$**, then** $\dfrac{yz - 6}{3} + 9 =$

   A 10

   B 12

   C 16

   D 20

5. **Solve the following inequality for** c.

   $7c + 14 > 49$

   A $c > 4$

   B $c > 5$

   C $c > 7$

   D $c > 9$

SIMPLIFYING ALGEBRAIC EXPRESSIONS

The CAHSEE will give you an equation or inequality that needs to be simplified before you can be solve it. Read the questions carefully so you know what they are asking for and so you don't do more math than you have to! Remember dear Aunt Sally—PEMDAS is crucial here.

Standard Al1 4.0

"Students simplify expressions before solving linear equations and inequalities in one variable, such as $3(2x - 5) + 4(x - 2) = 12$."

Which of the following equations is equivalent to
$$\frac{8}{x} = \frac{20}{x+3} \text{ ?}$$

A $x(x + 3) = 160$

B $8(x + 3) = 20x$

C $8x = 20(x + 3)$

D $28 = 20x + (x + 3)$

Here's How to Crack It

The equation here is set up like a proportion. (You might want to review the section on proportions in Chapter 7.) Remember that the cross-products of a proportion are equal. This means that the numerator in the fraction on the left × the denominator on the right = the denominator on the left × the numerator on the right. So for $\frac{a}{b} = \frac{c}{d}$, $ad = bc$. Cross multiply to rewrite the equation in a form that can be solved:

$$8(x + 3) = 20x$$

Look at the answer choices. Choice **B** is correct.

When simplifying inequalities, remember to combine like terms and follow PEM-DAS. In addition, remember to flip the sign when multiplying or dividing by a negative number.

Which of the following inequalities is equivalent to
$5x - 2(4 - x) > 3x + 2$?

A $5x - 8 - 2x > 3x + 2$

B $7x + 8 > 3x + 2$

C $7x - 8 > 3x + 2$

D $10x + 2x > 3x + 2$

Here's How to Crack It

Recall the order of operations. In this problem, the first step is to use the distributive property to multiply the terms inside the parentheses by −2.

So $5x - 2(4 - x) > 3x + 2$ becomes

$$5x - 8 + 2x > 3x + 2$$

(Remember, −2 multiplied by 4 equals -8, but −2 times -x equals +2x, because a negative times a negative always equals a positive.)

Next, combine like terms:

So $5x - 8 + 2x > 3x + 2$ becomes

$$7x - 8 > 3x + 2$$

Now check the answer choices. Choice **C** is correct.

Now try a few on your own. The answers are located at the end of this chapter, after the final quiz.

1. **Which equation is equivalent to $\dfrac{15}{n} = \dfrac{10}{n-1}$?**

    A $15(n-1) = 10n$

    B $25 = n + (n-1)$

    C $15n = 10(n-1)$

    D $n(n-1) = 150$

2. **Which of the following inequalities is equivalent to $3 + 2x < 5(x - 2)$?**

    A $3 + 2x < 5x - 2$

    B $3 + 2x < 5x - 7$

    C $3 + 2x < 5x - 8$

    D $3 + 2x < 5x - 10$

3. **Which equation is equivalent to $\dfrac{6}{y} = \dfrac{9}{y+2}$?**

    A $y(y + 2) = 54$

    B $15 = y + (y + 2)$

    C $9y = 6(y + 2)$

    D $6y = 9(y + 2)$

4. **Which of the following inequalities is equivalent to $4a - (3 - a) < 2a + 1$?**

    A $4a - 3 - a < 2a + 1$

    B $5a - 3 < 2a + 1$

    C $5a + 3 < 2a + 1$

    D $12a + a < 2a + 1$

5. $\dfrac{16}{x-3} = \dfrac{40}{x}$

Which of the following equations is equivalent to the one shown above?

A $x(x-3) = 640$

B $x + (x-3) = 56$

C $40x = 16(x-3)$

D $40(x-3) = 16x$

ALGEBRA AND ABSOLUTE VALUE

Equations and inequalities that contain absolute values may have more than one solution. Remember, absolute value is the number of units a number is from zero on the number line. It does not matter if the number is positive or negative. Therefore, $|3| = 3$, and $|-3| = 3$, because both 3 and -3 are 3 units away from 0. If you see a question on the CAHSEE like this the correct answer will be the set containing *all* the possible solutions to the equation.

Standard AI1 3.0

Students solve equations and inequalities involving absolute values.

Given that n is an integer, what is the solution set of $7 - 3|n| > 1$?

A $\{-2, -1, 0, 1, 2\}$

B $\{-2, -1, 0, 1\}$

C $\{-1, 0, 1, 2\}$

D $\{-1, 0, 1\}$

Here's How to Crack It

First, notice that the integer, n, is expressed in terms of absolute value. Remember that this means n can be either positive *or* negative. Next, isolate the terms that contain the variable on one side of the inequality—just like we did in the exercises on inequalities earlier. You can do this by subtracting 7 from both sides.

$$7 - 3|n| > 1$$
$$7 - 7 - 3|n| > 1 - 7$$
$$-3|n| > -6$$

Now divide both sides by –3.

$$\frac{-3|n|}{-3} > \frac{-6}{-3}$$

$$|n| < 2$$

Remember: Dividing by a negative number changes the direction of the inequality symbol. Now, substitute the values given in the answer choices for |n| to see which work, and which don't. Let's start with A, because it encompasses all the other sets given in the answer choices.

$$|n| < 2$$

$|-2| < 2$: If $n = -2$, the statement is false, because the absolute value of -2 is equal to 2, not less than 2. This means we can cross out choices **A** and **B**, because they both have -2 in their sets. Let's move on to the values in choice **C**:

$|-1| < 2$: If $n = -1$, the statement is true, so keep choices **C** and **D**, because they both have -1 in their sets.

$|0| < 2$: If $n = 0$, the statement is true. We can still keep choices **C** and **D**, because they both also contain 0. Both **C** and **D** also have 1 in their sets, so let's skip that and move on to 2, to see if we can eliminate **C**.

$|2| < 2$: If $n = 2$, the statement is false, because the absolute value of two is equal to 2, not less than 2. That means we can cross out choice C, which leaves us with choice D.

We can check our work by substituting one of the false values into the statement:

$$7 - 3|n| > 1$$

can be rewritten as:

$$7 - 3(2) > 1$$

Now we can solve this easily by simplifying it:

$$7 - 6 > 1$$
$$1 > 1$$

That doesn't make any sense, does it? But if we substitute one of the values in the set in choice **D**, we can see that

$$7 - 3(-1) > 1$$

becomes

$$7 + 3 > 1$$
$$10 > 1$$

This is obviously true. Therefore, the solution set has {–1, 0, 1}. Choice **D** is correct.

———————————○———————————

Now try a few on your own. The answers are located at the end of this chapter, after the final quiz.

1. **Given that x is an integer, find the solution set of the inequality $12 - 5\,|x| > -3$**

   A {–3, –2, –1, 0, 1, 2, 3}

   B {–3, –2, –1, 0, 1, 2}

   C {–2, –1, 0, 1, 2}

   D {–2, –1, 0, 1, 2, 3}

2. **Solve for y, if you know that y is an integer:**
   $$|y + 5| = 8$$

   A {–13, 3}

   B {–3, 3}

   C {–3, 13}

   D {–13, 13}

3. **Solve for a (assuming that a is an integer): $3\,|a| = 15$**

   A {–5, 0}

   B {–5, 0, 5}

   C {–5, 5}

   D {0, 5}

4. **Assuming that x is an integer, what is the solution set of the following inequality?**

$$|x - 3| < 2$$

A {−1, 0, 1}

B {4, 3, 2}

C {5, 1}

D {5, 4, 3, 2, 1}

Standard AF 2.1

"Interpret positive whole-number powers as repeated multiplication and negative whole-number powers as repeated division or multiplication by the multiplicative inverse. Simplify and evaluate expressions that include exponents."

POWERS

Some questions on the CAHSEE will ask you to simplify expressions that have variables with exponents. Treat variables with exponents just as you would normal number bases with exponents. (Review exponents in Chapter 5 if you need to.) Here are some more tips for working with exponents:

- A positive exponent means you multiply the base number by itself over and over: $2^3 = 2 \cdot 2 \cdot 2 = 8$

- A negative exponent means you divide the base number by itself over and over: $2^{-3} = \dfrac{1}{2^3} = \dfrac{1}{2} \cdot \dfrac{1}{2} \cdot \dfrac{1}{2} = \dfrac{1}{8}$

- It might help to recall what you learned earlier about scientific notation: Consider the example 2.7×10^{-3}. Moving the decimal 3 places to the left, which we do when we translate scientific notation into standard notation, gives us 0.0027. Using the rules of negative exponents, $2.7 \times 10^{-3} = \dfrac{2.7}{10^3} = \dfrac{2.7}{10 \times 10 \times 10} = \dfrac{2.7}{1{,}000} = 0.0027$. It's the same thing.

- You can rewrite negative exponents as positive exponents by taking the reciprocal of the base. For example, $x^{-4} = \dfrac{1}{x^4}$, or $\dfrac{1}{y^{-3}} = y^3$.

- Use the reciprocal to get rid of negative exponents and combine exponents of the same base.

Simplify the following expression: $\dfrac{a^2 b^{-2} c^{-1}}{2^{-2} c^2}$

A $\quad \dfrac{a^2 b^{-1} c^{-1}}{2^{-1} 2^{-1} c^2}$

B $\quad \dfrac{a^2 c}{2^{-2} c^2}$

C $\quad \dfrac{4a^2}{b^2 c^3}$

D $\quad \dfrac{a^2}{b^2 c^3}$

Here's How to Crack It

First, notice there are three negative exponents in the expression: b^{-2}, c^{-1}, and $\dfrac{1}{2^2}$.

We want to get rid of the negative exponents by multiplying by the reciprocals, which are $\dfrac{1}{b^2}$, $\dfrac{1}{c^2}$, and 2^2, respectively. Now we can rewrite the expression using only positive exponents.

$$\frac{a^2 b^{-2} c^{-1}}{2^{-2} c^2} = \frac{2^2 a^2}{b^2 c^2 c^1}$$

Next clear the exponent from the 2 and combine any exponents of the same base. Remember that when combining exponents with the same base, you *add* the exponents together.

$$\frac{2^2 a^2}{b^2 c^2 c^1} = \frac{4a^2}{b^2 c^3}$$

Now check the answer choices. Choice **C** is correct.

In this next example, don't let negative exponents fool you—just use the same techniques we've been doing!

Simplify the expression $5x^{-2}$

A $\dfrac{25}{x^2}$

B $\dfrac{1}{(5x)^2}$

C $(5x)^{-1}(5x)^{-1}$

D $\dfrac{5}{x^2}$

Here's How to Crack It

Read the question carefully. First, remind yourself what a negative exponent means. A negative exponent means repeated division by the base number. This means that x^{-2} can be written as $\dfrac{1}{x^2}$. Be careful! The negative exponent applies only to the x and not to the 5.

Next, rewrite the expression by changing the negative exponent to a positive exponent.

Step 1: $5x^{-2} = \dfrac{5}{x^2}$

Now look at the answer choices. Choice **D** is correct.

Now try a few on your own. The answers are located at the end of this chapter, after the final quiz.

1. Simplify the following algebraic expression: $\dfrac{3x^{-2}}{x^2 y^3}$

A $\dfrac{3}{x^4 y^3}$

B $\dfrac{1}{9x^4 y^3}$

C $\dfrac{1}{9y^3}$

D $\dfrac{3}{y^3}$

2. Simplify the expression below.

$(4x)^{-2}$

A $16x^2$

B $\dfrac{4}{x^2}$

C $\dfrac{1}{4x^2}$

D $\dfrac{1}{16x^2}$

MULTIPLYING AND DIVIDING MONOMIALS

A **monomial** is an expression consisting of a number multiplied by one or more variables, such as $5a^5b^3$. (A *polynomial* is one or more monomials that are added or subtracted, such as $7a^4 + 9c^3$. We'll talk about polynomials later.) If you are asked to simplify a monomial expression just combine like terms—just like we were doing in the previous section. Let's take a look.

Simplify the expression below:

$(3xy^3z^2)(8x^2yz^2)$

A $11x^2y^3z^2$

B $11x^3y^4z^4$

C $24x^2y^3z^2$

D $24x^3y^4z^4$

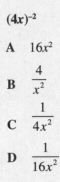

Standard AF 2.2

"Multiply and divide monomials; extend the process of taking powers and extracting roots to monomials when the latter results in a monomial with an integer exponent."

Here's How to Crack It

Remind yourself of the rules that govern the multiplication of variables with exponents. To multiply, you add the exponents. For example, $2^2 \times 2^3 = 2^{2+3} = 2^5$.

Next, multiply the numbers and variables in one monomial by those in the other monomial, using the distributive property:

$$(3xy^3z^2)(8x^2yz^2) = (3 \times 8) \times (x \times x^2) \times (y^3 \times y) \times (z^2 \times z^2)$$

Next, simplify the expression using the rules of exponents.

$$24 \times (x^{1+2}) \times (y^{3+1}) \times (z^{2+2})$$

This can be simplified even further to:

$$24x^3y^4z^4$$

Now check the answer choices. Choice **D** is correct.

Now let's try an expression involving division.

Simplify the expression $\dfrac{12a^2b^4c^3}{-4a^2bc^2}$

A $-3a^4b^5c^5$

B $-3b^3c$

C $8a^4b^5c^5$

D $8b^3c$

When multiplying, exponents are added but coefficients are multiplied.

$x = x^1$

Don't forget that a variable with no exponent really has an exponent of 1!

Here's How to Crack It

Read the question carefully. Remember the rules that govern the division of variables with exponents. To divide, you are going to subtract the bottom exponent from the top exponent. For example, $\frac{2^5}{2^3} = 2^{5-3} = 2^2$.

To simplify the expression, we need to divide the numbers and variables in the monomial in the numerator by those of the monomial in the denominator. First, let's expand the expression so we can see what we're dealing with:

$$\frac{12a^2b^4c^3}{-4a^2bc^2} = \frac{12}{-4} \times \frac{a^2}{a^2} \times \frac{b^4}{b} \times \frac{c^3}{c^2}$$

Next, simplify the expression using the rules of exponents. Remember to subtract the exponents:

$$-3 \times a^{2-2} \times b^{4-1} \times c^{3-2}$$

Remember that a^{2-2} becomes a^0, which equals 1, and c^{3-2} becomes c^1, which is usually written as c.

$$-3b^3c$$

Look at the answer choices. Choice **B** is correct.

──────────○──────────

Now try a couple on your own. The answers are located at the end of this chapter, after the final quiz.

1. Simplify $\dfrac{8x^3y^6}{2xy^2}$

   A $4x^2y^4$

   B $4x^4y^8$

   C $16x^2y^4$

   D $16x^4y^8$

The Zero Effect

Any number raised to the zero power (x^0) *always* equals 1.

2. Simplify the following expression: $(5ab^3c^2)(-2ab^2c)$

  A $-2.5bc$

  B $3bc$

  C $3a^2b^5c^3$

  D $-10a^2b^5c^3$

Standard AI1 5.0

"Students solve multistep problems, including word problems, involving linear equations and linear inequalities in one variable and provide justification for each step."

SOLVING MULTISTEP ALGEBRAIC PROBLEMS

These problems can be equations, inequalities, or word problems that require you to set up an equation or an inequality. Read these carefully. Sometimes you will be asked to solve the equation or inequality. Other times you will merely be asked for the first step in solving it, or to name a property illustrated by that equation or inequality. Don't lose out on points by reading too quickly or carelessly, and don't do a lot work you don't have to! Take your time and be sure you understand what they are asking.

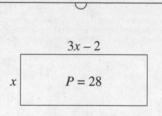

The length of a rectangle is 2 less than 3 times its width. The perimeter is 28. What are the dimensions of the rectangle?

  A 7×4

  B 8×6

  C 10×4

  D 12×2

Here's How to Crack It

First, remind yourself of the formula for the perimeter of a rectangle. Perimeter equals two times the length plus two times the width ($P = 2l = 2w$). Plug the information given in the question into the formula for the perimeter.

$P = 28$

$l = 3x - 2$

$w = x$

$P = 2l + 2w$

$$28 = 2(3x - 2) + 2x$$

Next, simplify the equation—remember PEMDAS! Do the work in parentheses first—use the distributive property to get rid of them:

$$28 = 2(3x - 2) + 2x \text{ becomes } 28 = 6x - 4 + 2x$$

Now, combine like terms.

$$28 = 6x - 4 + 2x \text{ becomes } 28 = 8x - 4$$

Next, isolate the variable (x) by adding 4 to both sides.

$$28 + 4 = 8x - 4 + 4 \text{ becomes } 32 = 8x$$

Finally, solve for x by dividing both sides by 8.

$$\frac{32}{8} = \frac{8x}{8}$$

$$4 = x$$

But wait! There's more! Just because we've solved for x doesn't mean we're done. In the final step you need to substitute the value of x in the expressions given for length and width. First, look at the answer choices again. Now that we know that $x = 4$, and x is the width of the rectangle, are there any choices we can eliminate? Yes, there are! Only choices **A** and **C** contain 4, so our answer has to be either **A** or **C**—we can eliminate **B** and **D**.

Now we need to find the length of the rectangle. We know that $w = x$, and $x = 4$. Since the length of the rectangle equals $3x - 2$, we can substitute 4 for x and get the length:

$l = 3x - 2$
$l = 3(4) - 2$
$l = 12 - 2$
$l = 10$

The dimensions of the rectangle are 10×4. Choice **C** is correct.

You can check your work by substituting the values you got for the length and the width of the rectangle back into the formula for perimeter. $P = 2l + 2w$ becomes $28 = 2(10) + 2(4)$, which simplifies to $28 = 20 + 8$ or $28 = 28$. It works!

Now try a couple on your own. The answers are located at the end of this chapter, after the final quiz. Remember to read each question carefully! If it doesn't ask you to solve for *x*, don't waste your time!

1. **Which property is illustrated by $3(2x - 5) = 6x - 15$?**

   A   associative property

   B   commutative property

   C   distributive property

   D   transitive property

2. **To solve for *x* in $\dfrac{x}{8} + 3 = 7$, what should be your first step?**

   A   Apply the distributive property.

   B   Add −3 to each side.

   C   Divide each side by 7.

   D   Multiply each side by 8.

3. **Which property is illustrated by $3x + 5 = 5 + 3x$?**

   A   associative property

   B   commutative property

   C   distributive property

   D   transitive property

4. **Edgar rented a car while on vacation. The rental agency charges \$45 for the first day, and \$30 for each additional day. If Edgar's car rental bill was \$165, for how many days did he rent the car?**

   A   4

   B   5

   C   6

   D   7

5. Given that n is a positive integer, what is the solution set of the following inequality?

$2n - 5 < 3$

A   {0, 1, 2, 3}

B   {0, 1, 2, 3, 4}

C   {1, 2, 3}

D   {1, 2, 3, 4}

MULTISTEP PROBLEMS WITH MONOMIALS AND POLYNOMIALS

You will be given combinations of monomials and polynomials and be asked to add, subtract, multiply or divide them. **Polynomials** are just groups of monomials separated by + or –. The CAHSEE will probably not ask you to solve for a variable, just to find an expression that answers the question. All you have to do with these is remember and apply the techniques we've already discussed, like PEMDAS, FOIL, and how to deal with exponents. Let's try some.

Standard Al1 10.0

"Students add, subtract, multiply, and divide monomials and polynomials. Students solve multistep problems, including word problems, by using these techniques."

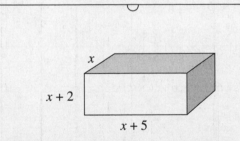

The height of a rectangular box is 2 units longer than the width, and the length is 5 units longer than the width. Which expression could represent the box's volume?

A $3x + 7$

B $x^2 + 7x + 10$

C $x^3 + 10x$

D $x^3 + 7x^2 + 10x$

Here's How to Crack It

Read the question and study the diagram carefully. Remember the formula for the volume of a rectangular solid is $V = lwh$ (Volume = length × width × height). Substitute the values given in the question into the formula.

$$l = x + 5$$
$$w = x$$
$$h = x + 2$$
$$V = lwh$$
$$V = (x + 5)(x)(x + 2)$$

Next, multiply the three sets of parentheses. It's probably easier if you multiply the two **binomials**—$(x + 5)$ and $(x + 2)$—first. Use the FOIL method (First, Outside, Inside, Last).

$$(x + 5)(x + 2)$$

First: $x \cdot x = x^2$

Outside: $x \cdot +2 = +2x$

Inside: $+5 \cdot x = +5x$

Last: $+5 \cdot +2 = +10$

Now combine like terms: $x^2 + 7x + 10$

Next, multiply this answer (which is $l \times h$, don't forget) by x (the width). Use the distributive property.

$$x(x^2 + 7x + 10) = x^3 + 7x^2 + 10x$$

Now check the answer choices. Choice **D** is correct.

As you can see, sometimes you have to recall a few formulas to answer these questions. What formula do you need for the next one?

———————————○———————————

The lengths of the sides of a triangle are represented by $x^2 - 16$, $x^2 + 5x + 6$, and $x^2 - 4x + 3$. Which of the following expressions could represent the perimeter of the triangle?

A $x^2 + x + 7$

B $3x^2 + x - 7$

C $3x^2 - x + 9$

D $3x^3 + 9x^2 + 25$

Here's How to Crack It

Remind yourself how to find the perimeter of a triangle. The perimeter of any polygon (*polygon* is another word for "shape") is the sum of the lengths of all the sides. So to find the perimeter of this triangle, you need to add the three sides together.

$$\text{side } 1 = x^2 - 16$$
$$\text{side } 2 = x^2 + 5x + 6$$
$$\text{side } 3 = x^2 - 4x + 3$$

We can write our formula like this: $x^2 - 16 + x^2 + 5x + 6 + x^2 - 4x + 3$, but that looks pretty unwieldy, doesn't it? An easier way to add the sides together is to stack the expressions, like this:

$$\begin{array}{r} x^2 - 16 \\ x^2 + 5x + 6 \\ \underline{x^2 - 4x + 3} \\ 3x^2 + x - 7 \end{array}$$

Now check the answer choices. Choice **B** is correct.

———————————○———————————

Sometimes you'll need to work backwards to find the piece of the puzzle that the question is asking for. Remember, if you know the formula, you can solve for any part of it. Just plug in what you do know to find out what you don't know.

The area of a rectangle is represented by the expression $12a^4 + 20a^3 - 4a^2$. If the width is represented by the expression $4a^2$, which of the following expressions could represent the length?

A $3a^2 + 5a$

B $3a^2 + 5a - 1$

C $4a^2$

D $12a^4 + 20a^3$

Don't Forget!

Subtract exponents when you divide.

Here's How to Crack It

Remind yourself how to find the area of a rectangle. The formula for the area of a rectangle is $A = lw$. If you know the area and you know the width, then $l = \dfrac{A}{w}$

Divide the polynomial that represents the area by the monomial that represents the width.

$$\frac{12a^4 + 20a^3 - 4a^2}{4a^2}$$

Remember that dividing by $4a^2$ is the same as multiplying by $\dfrac{1}{4a^2}$. Now just apply the distributive property: Divide each figure in the numerator by $4a^2$ and remember how to word with exponents. (Psst! That means subtract the exponents when you divide.)

$$\frac{12a^4}{4a^2} + \frac{20a^3}{4a^2} - \frac{4a^2}{4a^2}$$

$$3a^2 + 5a - 1$$

Now check the answer choices. Choice **B** is correct.

Now try a couple on your own. The answers are located at the end of this chapter, after the final quiz.

1. In the trapezoid shown above, two sections of the longer base are represented by x and $x + 6$, the shorter base by $x + 3$, and the height by $x + 4$. Which of the following expressions could represent the area of the trapezoid? [Area of a trapezoid $= \dfrac{1}{2}(b_1 + b_2)h$]

   A $\dfrac{3x + 9}{2}$

   B $\dfrac{4x + 13}{2}$

   C $\dfrac{3x^2 + 36}{2}$

   D $\dfrac{3x^2 + 21x + 36}{2}$

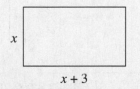

x

$x + 3$

2. In the rectangle shown above, the length is 3 units longer than the width. Which of the following could represent the area of the rectangle?

   A $x^2 + 3x$

   B $x^2 - 9$

   C $x^2 + 3x + 3$

   D $x^2 + 6x + 9$

CHAPTER 8: ALGEBRA FINAL QUIZ

Answers can be found on pages 276–279.

1. Ramon is thinking of a number. He says that if you divide the number by 4, and then add 3 to the result, the answer is 8. Which equation could be used to find the number Ramon is thinking of?

   A $\dfrac{n+3}{4} = 8$

   B $3 = 8 + \dfrac{n}{4}$

   C $\dfrac{n}{4} + 3 = 8$

   D $\dfrac{4}{n} = 8$

2. For a certain chemical compound, the number of hydrogen atoms, H, is equal to 2 more than twice the number of carbon atoms, C. Which of the following equations agrees with the information?

   A $2 \cdot C + 2 = H$

   B $2 \cdot H = 2 \cdot C + 2$

   C $2 \cdot C = H + 2$

   D $\dfrac{H}{C} = 2$

3. If you multiply a number by 5 and then subtract 7, the result is 23. Which of these equations can be used to find the unknown number?

   A $7 = 23 - 5n$

   B $5(n - 7) = 23$

   C $5n = 7$

   D $5n - 7 = 23$

4. In an ecosystem, the number of deer, d, is equal to 8 times the number of wolves, w. Which of the following equations contains the same information?

   A $w \cdot d = 8$

   B $8 \cdot w = 8 \cdot d$

   C $8 \cdot w = d$

   D $8 \cdot d = w$

5. When 1 is added to 2 times a number, the result is 15. Which of these equations matches this statement?

   A $1 = 15 + 2n$

   B $2(n + 1) = 15$

   C $\dfrac{n}{2} + 1 = 15$

   D $2n + 1 = 15$

6. Evaluate the following algebraic expression:

   $2(5x - 3)^2$

   A $10x - 6$

   B $10x + 9$

   C $50x^2 + 18$

   D $50x^2 - 60x + 18$

7. Evaluate the expression below.

   $4(2x + 1) - 22 - 3(x - 5)$

   A $5x - 3$

   B $5x + 3$

   C $5x - 33$

   D $11x - 33$

8. Evaluate the following expression:

   $4(y - 3)^2 + 5(2y - 6)$

   A $14y - 42$

   B $4y^2 + 34y + 66$

   C $4y^2 - 14y + 6$

   D $4y^2 - 14y + 66$

9. Evaluate the expression below.

$3a^2 - 5 - (a^2 + a - 3)$

A $2a^2 + a - 2$

B $2a^2 + a - 8$

C $2a^2 - a - 2$

D $4a^2 - a - 8$

10. Evaluate the following expression:

$9x^2 - 8x + 4 - 2(x - 2)^2$

A $7x^2 - 4$

B $7x^2 - 8x - 4$

C $7x^2 - 16x - 4$

D $9x^2 - 10x + 8$

11. Evaluate the expression below.

$5x^2 - 16x + 12 - (2x^2 - 8x + 8)$

A $3x^2 + 8x - 4$

B $3x^2 - 8x + 4$

C $3x^2 - 8x + 20$

D $3x^2 - 24x + 20$

12. What is the opposite (additive inverse) of $5\frac{1}{4}$?

A $-5\frac{1}{4}$

B $-\frac{4}{21}$

C $\frac{4}{21}$

D $\frac{17}{21}$

13. Find the positive value of $\sqrt{6.25}$.

A 2.05

B 2.5

C 3.05

D 3.5

14. Solve for x, if $4x^2 + 6 = 150$.

A $\{-12, 12\}$

B $\{-6, 6\}$

C $\{6, -12\}$

D $\{12, -6\}$

15. Simplify the expression $\dfrac{(a^4 b^{-3})^2}{a^2 b}$.

A $\dfrac{a^6}{b^7}$

B $\dfrac{a^4}{b^6}$

C $a^4 b^4$

D $a^6 b^5$

16. What is the reciprocal (multiplicative inverse) of $1\frac{1}{4}$?

A $-1\frac{1}{4}$

B $-\frac{4}{5}$

C $\frac{1}{5}$

D $\frac{4}{5}$

17. Solve for x, if $1 - \dfrac{x}{5} = 3$.

   A   -15

   B   -10

   C   10

   D   20

18. Solve the following equation for n.

$3 - 2n = 7$

   A $n = -5$

   B $n = -2$

   C $n = 2$

   D $n = 5$

19. Solve the following inequality for d.

$20 - 8d < 4$

   A $d < -3$

   B $d > -3$

   C $d < 2$

   D $d > 2$

20. Which of the following inequalities is equivalent to $7y - 11 > 2y - 3(5 - y)$?

   A $7y - 11 > 2y - 15 - 3y$

   B $7y - 11 > 5y - 15$

   C $7y - 11 > 5y + 15$

   D $7y - 11 > 6y + 3y$

21. Which of the following equations is equivalent to $4(2b + 1) = 17 - 3(2b - 5)$?

   A $8b + 1 = 17 + 6b - 5$

   B $8b + 1 = 17 - 6b - 5$

   C $8b + 4 = 17 + 6b - 15$

   D $8b + 4 = 17 - 6b + 15$

22. Which of the following inequalities is equivalent to $2n - 3 < 5(n - 1)$?

   A $2n - 3 < 5n - 6$

   B $2n - 3 < 5n - 5$

   C $2n - 3 < 5n - 4$

   D $2n - 3 < 5n - 1$

23. Which equation is equivalent to $\dfrac{3}{x} = \dfrac{5}{x+4}$?

   A $5x = 3(x + 4)$

   B $5(x + 4) = 3x$

   C $15 = x(x + 4)$

   D $x + (x + 4) = 8$

24. Which of the following inequalities is equivalent to $9a - 5(2 - a) \leq 2(6a - 2)$?

   A $4a - 10 < 8a - 4$

   B $4a - 10 < 12a - 2$

   C $14a - 10 < 12a - 4$

   D $14a + 10 < 12a - 4$

25. Which equation is equivalent to $4m(2 - 1) = 5(m + 3 - 30)$?

   A $6m - m = 5m + 15 - 30$

   B $8m - m = 5m + 15m - 30$

   C $8m - 4m = 5m + 15 - 30$

   D $8m - 4m = 5m + 15m - 30$

26. Which equation is equivalent to $-h(1 - 6) = 6h - 10$?

    A $7h = 6h - 10$

    B $-h + 6 = 6h - 10$

    C $h - 6 = 6h - 10$

    D $5h = 6h - 10$

27. Solve for b, assuming that b is an integer:

    $|2b - 6| = 8$

    A $\{-7, 1\}$

    B $\{-1, 7\}$

    C $\{-1, 1\}$

    D $\{7, -1\}$

28. Given that n is an integer, what is the solution set of the inequality $15 - 4|n| > 3$?

    A $\{-3, 3\}$

    B $\{-3, -2, -1, 0, 1, 2, 3\}$

    C $\{-2, -1, 0, 1, 2\}$

    D $\{-1, 0, 1\}$

29. Solve for h:

    $|h - 9| = 5$

    A $\{14, 4\}$

    B $\{14, -4\}$

    C $\{4, -14\}$

    D $\{4, -4\}$

30. Given that x is an integer, what is the solution set of the inequality $|x - 1| \leq 3$?

    A $\{-2, 4\}$

    B $\{-2, -1, 0, 1, 2, 3, 4\}$

    C $\{-1, 0, 1, 2, 3\}$

    D $\{0, 1, 2\}$

31. Solve for y, assuming that y is an integer:

    $2|y| - 5 = 1$

    A $\{-3, 3\}$

    B $\{-2, 3\}$

    C $\{2, -3\}$

    D $\{6, 4\}$

32. Assuming that n is an integer, find the solution set of the inequality $4 - |n| > 2$.

    A $\{-3, -2, -1, 0, 1, 2, 3\}$

    B $\{-2, 2\}$

    C $\{-2, -1, 0, 1, 2\}$

    D $\{-1, 0, 1\}$

33. Simplify the expression below.

    $\dfrac{2^{-2}}{c^2}$

    A $4c^2$

    B $\dfrac{1}{4c^2}$

    C $\dfrac{4}{c^2}$

    D $\dfrac{c^2}{4}$

34. **Simplify the following algebraic expression:** $\dfrac{a^2b^{-4}}{b^{-3}c^{-2}}$

   A a^2bc^2

   B $\dfrac{c^2}{a^2b}$

   C $\dfrac{a^2c^2}{b}$

   D $\dfrac{a^2c^2}{b^7}$

35. **Simplify the expression below.**

$$\dfrac{1}{3x^{-2}}$$

   A $\dfrac{x^2}{9}$

   B $\dfrac{x^2}{3}$

   C $3x^2$

   D $9x^2$

36. **Simplify the following expression:** $(-3x^{-3}y)^2$

   A $\dfrac{-3y^2}{x^6}$

   B $\dfrac{y^2}{9x^6}$

   C $\dfrac{-9y^2}{x^6}$

   D $\dfrac{9y^2}{x^6}$

37. **Simplify the following algebraic expression:** $(5c^{-1})2d^2$

   A $\dfrac{d^2}{25c^2}$

   B $\dfrac{5d^2}{c^2}$

   C $\dfrac{25d^2}{c^2}$

   D $\dfrac{25c^2}{d^2}$

38. **Simplify the expression below.**

$$\dfrac{xy^2}{z^4}$$

   A xy^2z^4

   B xy^2z^{-4}

   C $\dfrac{x}{y^2-z^{-4}}$

   D $\dfrac{z^4}{xy^{-2}}$

39. **Simplify** $(-3xy2z^3)^2$

   A $3x^2y^4z^6$

   B $-3x^2y^4z^6$

   C $9x^2y^4z^6$

   D $-9x^2y^4z^6$

40. **Simplify the expression below.**

$$\dfrac{-15x^3y^5}{-3xy^2}$$

   A $-5x^2y^3$

   B $5x^2y^3$

   C $-5x^4y^7$

   D $5x^4y^7$

41. **Simplify the expression** $(9a^2b^2)(2ab^3)$

   A $18a^2b^6$

   B $18a^3b^5$

   C $18a^3b^6$

   D $18a^5b^5$

42. Write the following expression in its simplest form.

$$\frac{10x^2yz^2}{15xy^2}$$

A $\dfrac{2x}{3z}$

B $\dfrac{2xz}{3}$

C $\dfrac{10x^2}{5yz}$

D $\dfrac{10xy}{15z}$

43. Simplify $(4a^2b^4c^3)^2$

A $4a^4b^6c^5$

B $4a^4b^8c^6$

C $16a^4b^6c^5$

D $16a^4b^8c^6$

44. Simplify the following expression:

$$\frac{42a^5b^4c^2}{6a^4bc}$$

A $7a^9b5c^3$

B $7ab^3c$

C $36a^9b^5c^3$

D $36ab^3c$

$5x - 7 = 13$

45. To solve for x in the equation above, which of the following should be your first step?

A Apply the distributive property.

B Add -7 to each side.

C Add $+7$ to each side.

D Divide each side by 5.

46. The cost of a long-distance telephone call is $0.80 for the first three minutes and $0.20 for each additional minute. What is the greatest number of whole minutes for a telephone call if the cost cannot exceed $3.00?

A 11

B 12

C 13

D 14

47. Solve for x if $2(3x + 11) + 5 = 3(4x - 7)$.

A $x = 6$

B $x = 7$

C $x = 8$

D $x = 9$

48. Which property is illustrated by the following equation?

$$5x + (2x + 5) = (5x + 2x) + 5$$

A associative property

B commutative property

C distributive property

D transitive property

$$3 - 2(y - 4) < 1$$

49. To solve for y in the inequality above, which of the following should be your first step?

   A   Apply the distributive property.

   B   Add -3 to each side.

   C   Add $+3$ to each side.

   D   Divide each side by -2.

50. The sum of $5x^2 + 3x + 15$ and $x^2 - 16$ is

   A $4x^2 - 3x - 1$

   B $6x^2 - 1$

   C $6x^2 + 3x - 1$

   D $5x^4 + 3x^3 + 15x^2$

51. If the expression $12x^4y^3$ represents the area of a rectangle and $4x^2y$ represents the width, which of the following could represent the length?

   A $3x^2y^2$

   B $3x^6y^4$

   C $8x^2y^2$

   D $48x^6y^4$

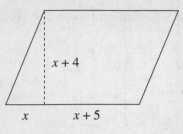

52. In the parallelogram shown above, two sections of the base are represented by x and $x + 5$, and the height by $x + 4$. Which of the following expressions could represent the area of the parallelogram? (Area of a parallelogram $= bh$)

   A $3x + 9$

   B $2x^2 + 20$

   C $2x^2 + 9x + 20$

   D $2x^2 + 13x + 20$

ANSWERS TO PRACTICE PROBLEMS

Words Into Math
1. B
2. A

Order of Operations
1. C
2. C

Algebraic Operations
1. A
2. B
3. A
4. D
5. C
6. C

Algebra and Absolute Value
1. C
2. A
3. C
4. B

Powers
1. A
2. D

Multiplying and Dividing Monomials
1. A
2. D

Linear Equations and Inequalities
1. D
2. B
3. D
4. C
5. B

Simplifying Algebraic Expressions
1. A
2. D
3. C
4. B
5. D

Solving Multistep Algebraic Problems
1. C
2. B
3. B
4. B
5. C

Multistep Problems with Monomials and Polynomials
1. D
2. A

Chapter 9
Geometric Shapes

Be Prepared

Prepare your diagrams and equations before you start any geometry problem!

Standard MG 2.1

"Use formulas routinely for finding the perimeter and area of basic two-dimensional figures and the surface area and volume of basic three-dimensional figures, including rectangles, parallelograms, trapezoids, squares, triangles, circles, prisms, and cylinders."

You will see a bunch of questions on the CAHSEE about geometric shapes. Before you dive into these problems, do a few things to avoid careless mistakes:

- Label everything you know on the diagram.
- Draw diagrams if they are not provided.
- Write formulas before you start using them.

Take a little bit of time at the beginning to save yourself a lot more time at the end!

PERIMETER, AREA, SURFACE AREA AND VOLUME

You will have to find the **perimeter** or **area** of a two-dimensional figure, or the **surface area** or **volume** of a three-dimensional figure. You'll be given all but the most common formulas, so make sure you know how to find things like the area of a rectangle ($A = lw$) and the volume of a cube ($V = lwh$).

6. The diagram below shows a trapezoid drawn inside a rectangle. To find the perimeter of the rectangle, simply add the lengths of the sides: $8 + 12 + 8 + 3 + 6 + 3 = 40$ cm. Or, create the equation: $2(12) + 2(8) = 40$ cm.

    [Perimeter of a rectangle $= 2l + 2w$

    Area of a triangle $= \dfrac{1}{2} bh$

    Area of a trapezoid $= \dfrac{1}{2} (b_1 + b_2)h$]

    What is the area of the shaded portion of the rectangle?

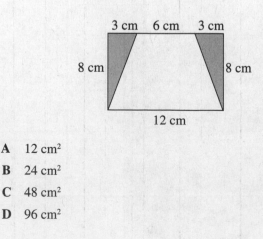

A   12 cm²

B   24 cm²

C   48 cm²

D   96 cm²

Here's How to Crack It

First, make sure you know what the question is asking you to find. The question gives you the formula for the area of a trapezoid—but if you read the question carefully, you should realize that you only need to know how to find the area of a triangle. Why is that? Look at the diagram carefully. The shaded portion of the rectangle is actually *two congruent triangles*. In this case, the test takers actually gave you too much information to try to trip you up. Luckily, they also gave you the formula for the area of a triangle. All you have to do is plug in the measurements from the diagram.

$$A = \frac{1}{2}bh$$

$$\frac{1}{2} \times 3 \times 8 = 12 \text{ cm}^2$$

The two shaded triangles are congruent (the same shape), so all you have to do is multiply the area of one triangle by two to get the area of the shaded portion of the rectangle.

$$\text{Shaded Area} = 2 \times 12 \text{ cm}^2 = 24 \text{ cm}^2$$

Now check the answer choices. Choice **B** is correct.

To check your work, you can find the area of the trapezoid and subtract it from the area of the surrounding rectangle (the two triangles). The area of the trapezoid is $A = \frac{1}{2}(b_1 + b_2)h$, or $A = \frac{1}{2} \times 18 \times 8$, which equals 72 cm². The area of the rectangle is $A = lw = 12 \times 8$, or 96 cm².

$$96 - 72 = 24 \text{ cm}^2$$

24 cm² is the area of the two triangles. You can be sure that answer is most likely correct because you got the same answer using both methods.

Now try a couple on your own. The answers are located at the end of this chapter, after the final quiz.

Cube *a*   **Cube *b***

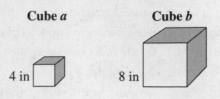

4 in   8 in

1. In the diagram above, the two cubes have sides of 4 in and 8 in.

    What is $\dfrac{volume\ of\ Cube\ a}{volume\ of\ Cube\ b}$?

    A $\dfrac{1}{8}$

    B $\dfrac{1}{6}$

    C $\dfrac{1}{4}$

    D $\dfrac{1}{2}$

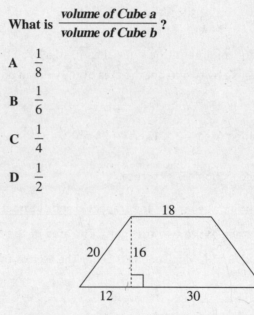

2. In the diagram above, what is the area of the trapezoid?

    $$A = \frac{1}{2}(b_1 + b_2)h$$

    A   336 square units

    B   384 square units

    C   480 square units

    D   600 square units

CONGRUENCE

Two figures are **congruent** if all corresponding sides and angles are equal. You'll be given a diagram of two figures and some information about them, and you'll have to determine if the figures are congruent. Sometimes you will be given two congruent figures and asked to identify the congruent parts of the figures.

Let's review some tips on how to identify congruent figures.

When comparing figures to determine whether or not they are congruent, it's very important to compare *corresponding* parts. Corresponding parts are matching parts of two congruent figures.

You can use these handy abbreviations to help you remember how to determine if two triangles are congruent:

SSS **(side-side-side)**	3 sides of one triangle are congruent to their corresponding sides in the other triangle.
SAS **(side-angle-side)**	2 sides and the included angle of one triangle are congruent to their corresponding sides and angles in the other triangle.
ASA **(angle-side-angle)**	2 angles and the included side of one triangle are congruent to their corresponding angles and side in the other triangle.
AAS **(angle-angle-side)**	2 angles and a non-included side of one triangle are congruent to their corresponding angles and side in the other triangle.

The $\cong$ sign means "is congruent to."

Standard MG 3.4

"Demonstrate an understanding of conditions that indicate two geometrical figures are congruent and what congruence means about the relationships between the sides and angles of the two figures."

Now let's try an example:

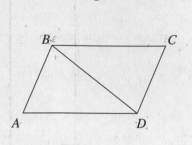

In the diagram above, $\overline{BD}$ is a diagonal of parallelogram ABCD. $\angle ABD \cong \angle CDB$. Which of the following statements must be true to prove that $\triangle ABD \cong \triangle CDB$?

A $\overline{AB} \cong \overline{CD}$

B $\angle ABC \cong \angle BDC$

C $\overline{AB} \cong \overline{BC}$

D $\angle CBD \cong \angle BDC$

Here's How to Crack It

Read the question and study the diagram carefully. Remember that congruent means "of equal measure." Next, look at the two triangles you are trying to prove congruent. Ask yourself, "What corresponding parts do I already *know* are congruent?"

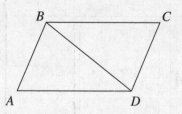

The question tells us that angle ADB is congruent to angle CBD. We can write this like this:

$$\angle ADB \cong \angle CBD$$

We also know that line BD is shared by both triangles. We can write it like this:

$$\overline{BD} \cong \overline{BD}$$

Now ask yourself, "What *other* corresponding parts need to be congruent to prove the two triangles congruent?"

If $\overline{AB} \cong \overline{CD}$ **SAS**

If $\angle ADB \cong \angle CBD$ **ASA**

If $\angle BAD \cong \angle DCB$ **AAS**

Look at the answer choices. Do any of them match those conditions?

A: Yes—**SAS**

B: No

C: No

D: No

Choice **A** is correct.

───────────────○───────────────

Now try one on your own. The answers are located at the end of this chapter, after the final quiz.

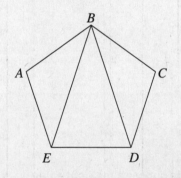

1.   **Figure *ABCDE* is a pentagon where $\angle BAE \cong \angle BCD$ and $\angle AEB \cong \angle CDB$. Which of the following bits of information is needed to prove that $\triangle ABE \cong \triangle CBD$?**

    A $\angle BAE \cong \angle ABD$

    B $\overline{AB} \cong \overline{CD}$

    C $\angle BED \cong \angle BCD$

    D $\overline{AE} \cong \overline{CD}$

THE PYTHAGOREAN THEOREM

The CAHSEE tests the **Pythagorean theorem** by giving you a diagram of a **right triangle**—or some other figure containing a right triangle—and providing you with the length of two of the sides. You will have to find the length of the third side. So let's review Pythagoras's Big Idea:

> In a right triangle, the square of the hypotenuse is equal to the sum of the squares of the two legs.

Or, to put it another way:

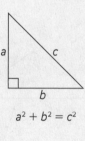

$$a^2 + b^2 = c^2$$

$$a^2 + b^2 = c^2$$

The *hypotenuse* is the side opposite the right angle.

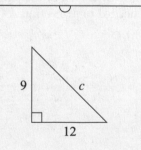

In the diagram above, what is the value of *c*?

A   8

B   15

C   21

D   225

Standard MG 3.3

"Know and understand the Pythagorean theorem and its converse, and use it to find the length of the missing side of a right triangle and the lengths of other line segments and, in some situations, empirically verify the Pythagorean theorem by direct measurement."

Here's How to Crack It

Read the question and study the diagram carefully. Remember, a triangle with a square in the corner means it's a right triangle. We already know the formula for finding the hypotenuse ($a^2 + b^2 = c^2$). Now, we have to plug in the values we've been given for the legs and do the math:

$$a^2 + b^2 = c^2$$
$$9^2 + 12^2 = c^2$$
$$9(9) + 12(12) = c^2$$
$$81 + 144 = c^2$$
$$225 = c^2$$

We're not done yet! It's very easy to forget that you need to solve for c, *not c^2*:

$$\sqrt{225} = \sqrt{c^2}$$

Don't worry if you don't know the square root of 225 off the top of your head—you don't need to. Instead, let's use POE to narrow down our answer choices. We already know that 225 is the square of c, not c itself, so we can eliminate choice **D** right off the bat. Now, let's just work from the top and see which number multiplied by itself equals 225.

If you remember your multiplication tables, you should be able to eliminate choice **A** right away: $8 \times 8 = 64$. Let's move on to B:

$15 \times 15 = 225$

Look at that! $15^2 = 225$. Choice **B** is correct.

Not all Pythagorean theorem problems are so simple, though. Sometimes you'll need to use the Pythagorean theorem to solve one step of a more complex problem.

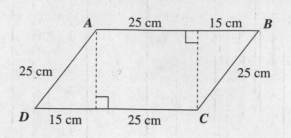

In the diagram above, figure *ABCD* is a parallelogram.
What is its area in square centimeters (cm²)?
(Area of a parallelogram = *bh*)

A   300 cm²

B   375 cm²

C   500 cm²

D   800 cm²

Here's How to Crack It

Read the question carefully to figure out what you need in order to find the area. The formula $A = bh$ tells you that you need to know how long the base and the height are. The base is line CD $\overline{CD}$, and the height is the dashed line. When you look at the dashed line in the parallelogram, what do you see? A right triangle. That means you should use the Pythagorean theorem to find the height, h.

Let's look at the triangle on the left. We know the length of one side of the triangle is 15 cm. We also know the length of the hypotenuse (the side opposite the right angle) is 25 cm. We can plug these values into our formula to find the length of the third side of the triangle (which is the height of the parallelogram, remember):

$a^2 + b^2 = c^2$
$15^2 + h^2 = 25^2$
$225 + h^2 = 625$ (subtract 225 from both sides)
$h^2 = 400$

Now we have to find the square root of 400. We know that it must be between 15 and 25, right? Let's try to narrow that range down by picking a number right in between those and finding its square. We'll start with 20.

$$20 \times 20 = 400$$

That was easy! 20 is the square root of 400, which means that $h = 20$ cm.

Now we can find the area of the parallelogram, using the formula the question gives us.

$$A = bh$$
$$b = 15 + 25 = 40$$
$$h = 20$$
$$A = 40 \times 20$$
$$A = 800 \text{ cm}^2$$

Now check the answer choices. Choice **D** is correct.

———————○———————

Now try a few on your own. The answers are located at the end of this chapter, after the final quiz.

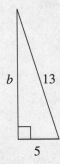

1. **The diagram shown above is a right triangle. What is the value of *b*?**

    A   8

    B   12

    C   14

    D   194

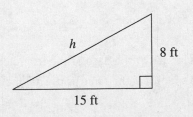

2. **The figure shown above is a right triangle. What is the length, in feet (ft), of *h*?**

    A   10 ft

    B   12 ft

    C   17 ft

    D   23 ft

AREA OF COMPLEX FIGURES

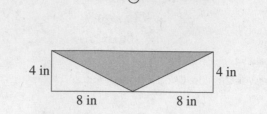

The CAHSEE will give you a diagram that combines two or more basic figures: a square inside a circle, a triangle in a rectangle, and so forth. You will have to find the area that results from adding or subtracting the two areas of those figures.

Standard MG 2.2

"Estimate and compute the area of more complex or irregular two- and three-dimensional figures by breaking the figures down into more basic geometric objects."

Candice is cutting two wedges from a 4-inch by 16-inch piece of paper, as shown in the figure above. What is the area of the piece that remains (the shaded area)?

(Area of a triangle = $\frac{1}{2}bh$)

A 16 in²

B 32 in²

C 64 in²

D 96 in²

Here's How to Crack It

Read carefully to be sure you know what the question is asking you to find. Then decide which formulas you need. Look at the shaded section of the diagram. You are being asked to find the area of that section—what do you notice about that shaded section? That's right! It's a triangle. All you have to do is find the area of a triangle. If you look at the diagram carefully, you'll see that you already have all the information you need—no fancy footwork required.

We already know the area of a triangle equals $\frac{1}{2}bh$.

The diagram gives us the length of the base of the triangle: 8 inches + 8 inches = 16 inches. The height of the triangle is the same as the height of the rectangle: 4 inches.

Now all you have to do is Plug In the numbers:

$A = \frac{1}{2}bh$

$A = \frac{1}{2} \times 16 \times 4$

$A = 32$ in²

Check the answer choices. Choice **B** is correct.

———————————○———————————

Now try some on your own. The answers are located at the end of this chapter, after the final quiz.

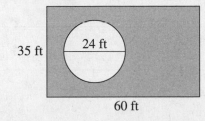

1. **Ms. Conner installed a round above ground pool in her backyard as shown in the diagram above. The grass-covered backyard measures 60 feet by 35 feet, and the pool is 24 feet in diameter. What is the approximate area, in square feet, of the remaining grass (the shaded area)?**

   (Area of a circle = πr^2; $\pi = 3.14$)

   A 1,200

   B 1,650

   C 2,550

   D 3,000

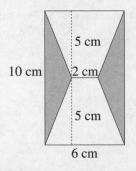

2. **Carrie is cutting an hourglass shape (that is actually two identical trapezoids placed end-to-end) from a rectangular piece of cloth as shown in the diagram above. What is the area of the shaded portion of the cloth?**

   (Area of a trapezoid = $\dfrac{1}{2}(b_1 + b_2)h$)

   A 20 cm²

   B 40 cm²

   C 60 cm²

   D 80 cm²

RECTANGULAR SOLIDS

You will be given a labeled diagram of a three-dimensional object made from one or more rectangular solids, like a cube, box, or cylinder. You will then be asked to find the perimeter, surface area, or volume. You may also be asked to compare the surface areas or volumes of two objects of different sizes. Make sure you know some of the most common formulas, like the volume of a rectangular solid ($V = lwh$), and the area of a circle ($A = \pi r^2$).

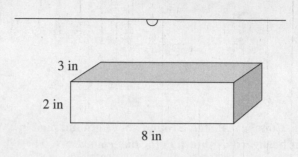

A brick measures 8 inches long, 3 inches wide, and 2 inches high. What is the volume, in cubic inches (in³), of the brick?

A 13

B 24

C 40

D 48

Here's How to Crack It

Read the question and study the diagram carefully. Remember that the formula for the volume of a rectangular solid is *Volume = length × width × height*. Plug In the measurements given by the diagram.

$$V = lwh$$
$$V = 8\text{ in} \times 3\text{ in} \times 2\text{ in}$$
$$V = 48\text{ in}^3$$

Now check the answer choices. Choice **D** is correct.

Standard MG 2.3

"Compute the length of the perimeter, the surface area of the faces, and the volume of a three-dimensional object built from rectangular solids. Understand that when the lengths of all dimensions are multiplied by a scale factor, the surface area is multiplied by the square of the scale factor and volume is multiplied by the cube of the scale factor."

Surface Area vs. Volume

The **surface area** of a rectangular solid is *not* the same as its volume. The surface area is the sum of all the areas of each side of the solid. All rectangular solids have six faces (like the faces of a numbered die in a board game).

You can find the surface area of the brick from the sample problem above in four easy steps.

Step 1: Find the surface area of the largest side and multiply it by 2:

$$A = lw = 8 \text{ in} \times 3 \text{ in} = 24 \text{ in}^2$$
$$24 \times 2 = 48 \text{ in}^2$$

Step 2: Find the surface area of the mid-sized side and multiply it by 2:

$$A = lh = 8 \text{ in} \times 2 \text{ in} = 16 \text{ in}^2$$
$$16 \times 2 = 32 \text{ in}^2$$

Step 3: Find the surface area of the smallest side and multiply it by 2:

$$A = wh = 3 \text{ in} \times 2 \text{ in} = 6 \text{ in}^2$$
$$6 \times 2 = 12 \text{ in}^2$$

Step 4: Total Surface Area:

$$48 \text{ in}^2 + 32 \text{ in}^2 + 12 \text{ in}^2 = 92 \text{ in}^2$$

Area Is Area Is Area

The surface area is still area: It's measured in units squared (cm^2, in^2).

Now try some on your own. The answers are located at the end of this chapter, after the final quiz.

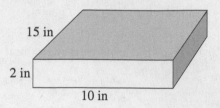

1. **Anita is wrapping a birthday present. The box measures 15 inches by 10 inches by 2 inches. What is the minimum number of square inches of wrapping paper needed to cover all the surfaces of the box?**

   A   150

   B   300

   C   360

   D   400

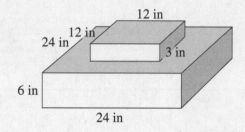

2. **Mr. Anderson, the football coach, built the pedestal shown above for an awards dinner.**

   What is $\dfrac{\textit{Volume of the Top Step}}{\textit{Volume of the Bottom Step}}$

   A $\dfrac{1}{16}$

   B $\dfrac{1}{8}$

   C $\dfrac{1}{4}$

   D $\dfrac{1}{2}$

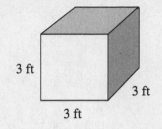

3 ft

3 ft

3 ft

3. Kadeesha's computer arrived in a cube-shaped box. What is the volume of the box in cubic feet (ft³)?

A   9

B   18

C   27

D   36

CHAPTER 9: GEOMETRIC SHAPES FINAL QUIZ

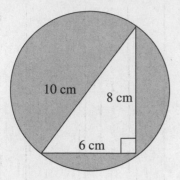

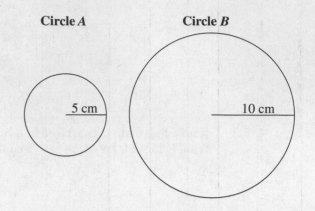

Circle *A*   Circle *B*

1. In the diagram above, the hypotenuse of the right triangle is a diameter of the circle. What is the area of the shaded portion of the circle?

    (Area of a triangle = $\frac{1}{2}bh$;

    Area of a circle = πr^2; $\pi = 3.14$)

    A   30.5 cm²

    B   54.5 cm²

    C   78.5 cm²

    D   290 cm²

3. Circle *A* has a radius of 5 cm, and Circle *B* has a radius of 10 cm.

    What is $\dfrac{Area\ of\ Circle\ A}{Area\ of\ Circle\ B}$?

    ($A = \pi r^2$; $\pi = 3.14$)

    A $\dfrac{1}{4}$

    B $\dfrac{1}{2}$

    C $\dfrac{\pi}{4}$

    D $\dfrac{\pi}{2}$

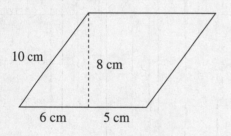

2. In the figure above, what is the area of the parallelogram? (Area of a parallelogram = *bh*)

    A   48 cm²

    B   80 cm²

    C   88 cm²

    D   110 cm²

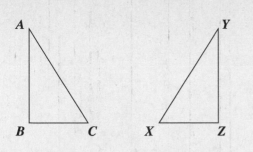

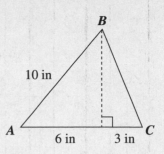

4. In the diagram above, $\triangle ABC \cong \triangle YZX$. $\overline{AB} \cong \overline{YZ}$, $\overline{AC} \cong \overline{YX}$ and $\overline{BC} \cong \overline{ZX}$. Which of the following angles in $\triangle YZX$ is congruent to $\angle ABC$?

A $\angle YXZ$

B $\angle XYZ$

C $\angle YZX$

D $\angle ZYX$

6. What is the area, in square inches (in²), of triangle ABC?

(Area of a triangle = $\dfrac{1}{2} bh$)

A 36 in²

B 45 in²

C 72 in²

D 90 in²

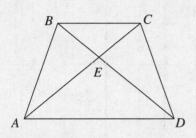

5. Figure $ABCD$ shown above is a trapezoid. Diagonals AC and BD intersect at point E. Side $\overline{AB} \cong$ side $\overline{CD}$, and $\angle AEB \cong \angle DEC$. Which of the following statements could be used, if it were true, to prove that $\triangle ABE \cong \triangle DCE$?

A $\overline{AB} \cong \overline{BD}$

B $\angle ABE \cong \angle DCE$

C $\overline{AE} \cong \overline{DE}$

D $\angle CBD \cong \angle BCA$

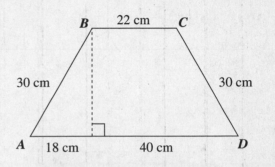

7. In the diagram above, Figure $ABCD$ is a trapezoid. What is its area in square centimeters (cm²)?

(Area of a trapezoid = $\dfrac{1}{2}(b_1 + b_2)h$)

A 648 cm²

B 744 cm²

C 960 cm²

D 1,920 cm²

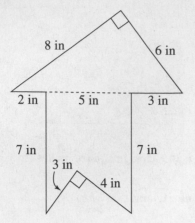

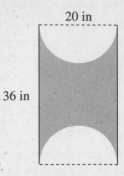

8. The figure shown above can be viewed as a rectangle with one right triangle on top and another right triangle removed from the bottom. What is the area of the figure?

   (Area of a triangle = $\frac{1}{2}bh$)

   A   42 in²

   B   47 in²

   C   53 in²

   D   59 in²

10. The above figure is made by removing a semicircle from each end of a rectangle measuring 36 in by 20 in. What is the area of the shaded region?
    (Area of a circle = πr^2; $\pi = 3.14$)

    A   157 in²

    B   314 in²

    C   406 in²

    D   563 in²

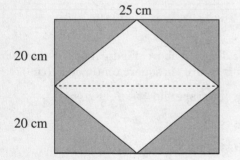

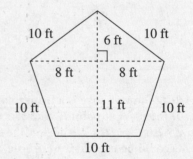

9. Jeff's assignment is to cut the largest possible diamond from a piece of cardboard that measures 40 cm by 25 cm. About how many square centimeters will the area of the remaining cardboard (shaded area) be?

   A   250

   B   500

   C   750

   D   1,000

11. For her technology project, Autumn drew up plans for a pentagonal deck. She noticed that it is actually a combination of a triangle and a trapezoid. What is the area, in square feet, of the proposed deck?

   [Area of a triangle = $\frac{1}{2}bh$; Area of a trapezoid = $\frac{1}{2}(b_1 + b_2)h$]

   A   48

   B   69

   C   143

   D   191

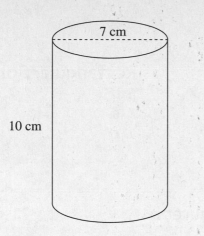

12. Tom wants to cover up the label wrapped around the can of dog food shown above. What is the approximate surface area of the label? (Circumference of a circle = πd)

A 70 cm²

B 220 cm²

C 385 cm²

D 1,540 cm²

14. Each small cube in this puzzle measures 2 centimeters on all sides. What is the volume, in cubic centimeters (cm³), of the entire puzzle?

A 8

B 27

C 108

D 216

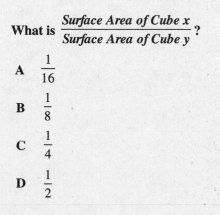

13. The two cubes shown above have sides of 4 inches and 8 inches, respectively.

What is $\dfrac{Surface\ Area\ of\ Cube\ x}{Surface\ Area\ of\ Cube\ y}$?

A $\dfrac{1}{16}$

B $\dfrac{1}{8}$

C $\dfrac{1}{4}$

D $\dfrac{1}{2}$

ANSWERS TO PRACTICE PROBLEMS

Perimeter, Area, Surface Area and Volume
1. A
2. C

The Pythagorean Theorem
1. B
2. C

Rectangular Solids
1. D
2. B
3. C

Congruence
1. D

Area of Complex Figures
1. B
2. A

Chapter 10
Geometric Graphs

When you think of geometry you probably think about shapes like the triangles and parallelograms and cubes we discussed in the previous chapter. But geometry is also about space and the position of things in space. **Graphing** is a way of representing things in two dimensions—on what we call a Cartesian grid, or **coordinate plane**. Graphs and charts are also used to represent how things change over time (such as how much gas prices have risen this year!). The CAHSEE will test you on your understanding of graphing by asking you to read and interpret graphs and charts, how to graph equations, and how to represent slope.

GRAPHS

You may be shown a graph representing an equation and then be asked to identify the equation represented by the graph.

Standard AF 1.5

"Represent quantitative relationships graphically and interpret the meaning of a specific part of a graph in the situation represented by the graph."

The line on the graph below represents which of the following equations?

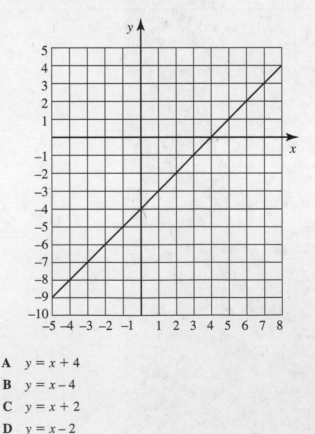

A $y = x + 4$

B $y = x - 4$

C $y = x + 2$

D $y = x - 2$

Here's How to Crack It

Study the graph carefully and try to find the relationship between x and y. An easy way to do this is to make a table of some of the x-values (that is, where the line falls on the x-axis of the graph, let's say from –2 to +2) and their corresponding y-values—where the line falls on the y-axis.

x	–2	–1	0	1	2
y	–6	–5	–4	–3	–2

Next, look for a pattern in the way the value of y changes in response to changes in the value of x.

It appears that the value of y is always 4 less than the value of x, doesn't it?

We can write an equation that says "the value of y is 4 less than the value of x" like this:

$$y = x - 4$$

Now check the answer choices. Choice **B** is correct.

You could also have plugged values from the graph into the answer choices to see which fit. For example, you know the line touches the point (0, –4). Plugging $x = 0$ and $y = -4$ into the answer choices, only **B** works.

Reading Graphs

When you look at a graph for the first time, pay attention to the shape of the line. If the line is *rising* from *left to right*, it means that as x is increasing, y is also increasing. If the line is *falling* from *left to right*, it means that as x is increasing, y is decreasing. Finally, if the line is *flat*, it means that y *always remains the same*.

Sometimes the CAHSEE will give you a graph representing a real-world situation and ask you to interpret what the graph means about the situation. What numbers are being tracked by this graph? Is it dollars on one axis and time on the other axis? Are profits increasing or decreasing? Lots of different kinds of information can be shown using a graph, so be sure to read carefully.

The graph below shows the monthly cost charged by two companies for using a cell phone. MobilTel has an initial fee of $15 and charges $0.10 per minute of call time. TeleCom has an initial fee of $30 and charges $0.08 per minute of call time after 200 minutes.

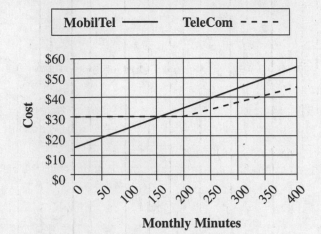

MobilTel costs less than TeleCom

A   if there are less than 150 minutes of call time.

B   if there are less than 200 minutes of call time.

C   if there are more than 200 minutes of call time.

D   no matter how many minutes of call time there are.

Here's How to Crack It

Study the graph carefully. Is one line is higher than the other?

At the left side of the graph, the line for TeleCom is higher than the line for MobilTel, indicating that MobilTel costs less in the beginning. After a certain number of minutes, the line for MobilTel is higher than the line for TeleCom, indicating that now TeleCom costs less.

Now, locate the exact point at which the two lines cross. They cross at $30 and 150 minutes, right?

It seems that up to 150 minutes, MobilTel costs less. *After* 150 minutes, TeleCom costs less.

Now look at the answer choices. Choice **A** is correct.

———————⎯◯⎯———————

Now try one on your own. The answers are located at the end of this chapter, after the final quiz.

1. **The graph below represents which of the following equations?**

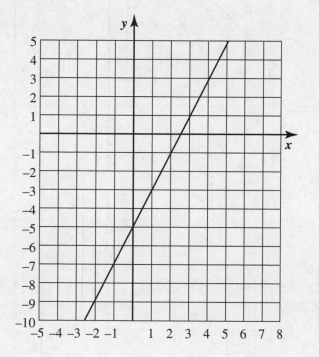

    A $y = x - 2$

    B $y = x + 2$

    C $y = 2x - 5$

    D $y = 2x + 5$

GRAPHING FUNCTIONS

These questions are concerned with how to graph functions such as $y = x^2$ or $y = x^3$. You should be familiar not only with the basic coordinate system but also with the basic shapes of those graphs.

Which of these could be the graph of the equation: $y = -(x^3)$?

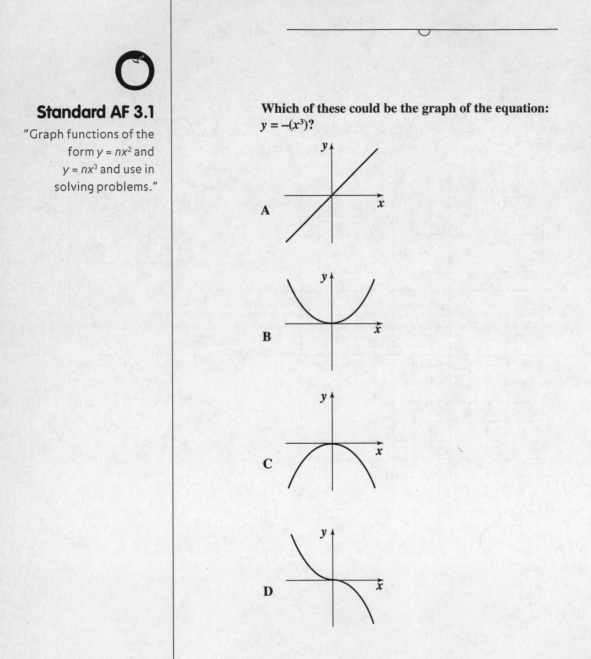

Here's How to Crack It

In this problem, instead of using a graph to write an equation, we have to use an equation to draw a graph. We can still use a table of x- and y-values to help us do this. This time around, we'll choose a range of numbers that could represent x and then solve for y, in order to fill out the table.

$$y = -(x^3)$$

Let's use the same numbers we used in the first sample problem for x: –2, –1, 1, and 2.

x	–2	–1	1	2
y				

Now we can plug in the x-values and solve for y. We'll do one for you here, and let you do the rest:

$$y = -(2)^3 = -(2 \times 2 \times 2) = -8$$

x	–2	–1	1	2
y	8	1	–1	–8

Try to recognize a pattern in the data and how this pattern might affect the graph. It appears that when x is negative, y is positive and when x is positive, y is negative. In addition, as x moves away from zero, y changes rapidly—from 1 to 8.

Next, make a small sketch of a graph with the points in the table plotted on it.

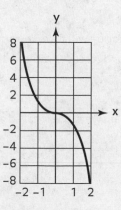

Slippery Slope
When y changes very quickly, the line will always be very steep.

Now check the answer choices. You can use POE to eliminate the graphs in **A**, **B**, and **C** because they clearly don't match up with the x- and y-values you found for the equation. Choice **D** is correct.

Exponential Functions

The graph functions of the form $y = nx^2$ and $y = nx^3$ are *exponential* functions. That means they show unusually rapid increases or decreases—also called rapid growth or rapid decay.

For example, look at the graph below that shows the projected world population for the year 2050.

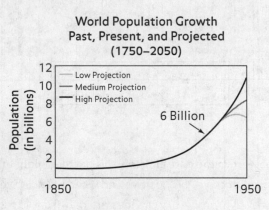

The earth had less than 1 billion people on it in 1750, and 6 billion by the year 2000. If the earth's population continues to grow like this, it may reach 10 billion by 2050! This is an example of exponential growth.

The graph of an exponential function will never be a straight line. It will always be a smooth curve that increases or decreases rapidly. Keep this in mind when using POE to rule out answer choices.

Now try one on your own. The answers are located at the end of this chapter, after the final quiz.

1. **Which of the following equations could the graph below represent?**

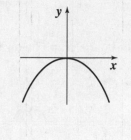

A $y = x - 3$

B $y = x^3$

C $y = -(2x^2)$

D $y = 2x^2$

LINEAR FUNCTIONS AND SLOPE

You will be shown a graph with two points on a line labeled as ordered pairs (x, y). The first number in an ordered pair is the x-coordinate, and the second is the y-coordinate. You will have to compute the **slope** of the line. Let's review what slope is and how to find it.

Slope just means the steepness of the line: the bigger the number, the steeper the slope. So a line with a slope of 5 has a steeper incline than a line with a slope of 2. The sign of the slope, positive or negative, tells you which way the line goes: up or down. Positive is up, negative is down. The formula for finding slope is

$$\text{Slope} = \frac{change\ in\ y}{change\ in\ x}$$

The *change in y* is also called **rise**, and *change in x* is also called **run**. We can also write the formula for slope this way:

$$\frac{rise}{run} = \frac{y_1 - y_2}{x_1 - x_2}$$

What if the line falls instead of rising? Well, that just means it rose a negative amount. If it went down two units, the rise would be –2.

When you compute the slope of a line, all you have to do is Plug In the x- and y-values of two points on the line.

Let's try an example.

Standard AF 3.3

"Graph linear functions, noting that the vertical change (change in y-value) per unit of horizontal change (change in x-value) is always the same and know that the ratio ('rise over run') is called the slope of a graph."

The slope of the line on the graph below is

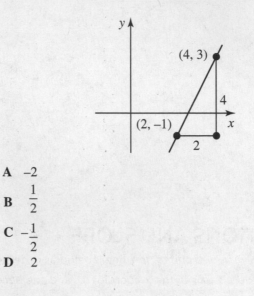

A –2

B $\dfrac{1}{2}$

C $-\dfrac{1}{2}$

D 2

Here's How to Crack It

Read the question and study the diagram carefully. First, recall the formula for the slope of a line on a graph. This one is easy because the change in y (4) and the change in x (2) are given to you right there on the graph. You can find the slope easily by dividing the rise by the run: $\dfrac{4}{2} = 2$.

Now check the answer choices. Choice **D** is correct.

Watch Your Step

When determining slope, it doesn't matter which two points on the line you choose. The important thing is to take both the *x*-value and the *y*-value from the *same point* on a line.

If you only had the *x*- and *y*-coordinates, you could have substituted them into the formula and computed the slope that way.

$$(x_1, y_1) = (4, 3)$$

$$(x_2, y_2) = (2, -1)$$

$$\text{Slope} = \frac{change\ in\ y\ value}{change\ in\ x\ value} = \frac{y_2 - y_1}{x_2 - x_1} = \frac{3 - (-1)}{4 - 2} = \frac{4}{2} = 2$$

You could also have noticed that the line was going up as it moved to the right. That means the slope must be positive, eliminating **A** and **C**.

Now try some on your own. The answers are located at the end of this chapter, after the final quiz.

1. **The slope of the line on the graph below is**

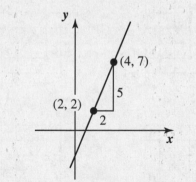

A $-\dfrac{3}{2}$

B $-\dfrac{2}{3}$

C $\dfrac{2}{3}$

D $\dfrac{3}{2}$

2. **What is the slope of the line below?**

A $-\dfrac{5}{2}$

B $-\dfrac{2}{5}$

C $\dfrac{2}{5}$

D $\dfrac{5}{2}$

Standard MG 3.2

"Understand and use coordinate graphs to plot simple figures, determine lengths and areas related to them, and determine their image under translations and reflections."

COORDINATE GRAPHS

These questions look at simple figures plotted on a graph. You will be given the vertices—the *x*- and *y*-coordinates—of the points of the figure. You may be asked to identify the figure. They might give you three vertices and ask you where the fourth one is. You also may be asked to identify a given figure after it has been reflected across an axis. You may be asked to identify a figure after it's been translated or reflected elsewhere on the graph. Understanding the basic shapes and an ability to move around the coordinate grid are both key skills for these questions.

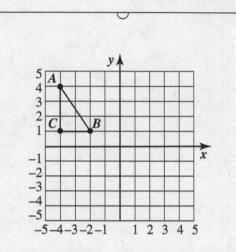

Triangle *ABC* is reflected across the *y*-axis. Which of the following shows the result of this reflection?

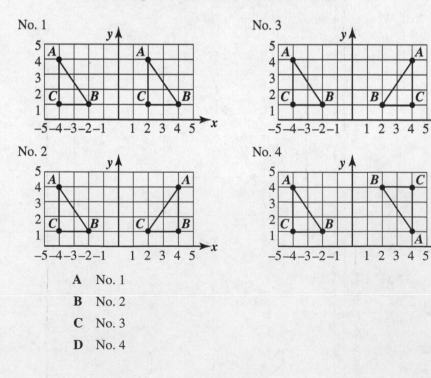

A   No. 1

B   No. 2

C   No. 3

D   No. 4

Here's How to Crack It

Read the question and study the diagram carefully—pay close attention to where vertices A, B, and C are located on the graph. Recall that a reflection is just what it sounds like: a mirror image of the original figure. So a reflection across the y-axis means that the y-axis is acting like a mirror. You can use POE to rule out the wrong answers.

In No. 1, the orientation of the triangle has not changed at all; the whole triangle has just slid to the right, instead. You know that when you look in a mirror, your left arm looks as if it's your right arm and vice versa. You can rule out answer choice **A**.

In No. 2, the triangle *looks* like it is a mirror image. However, the right angle that was at C in the original triangle is now at B. This would not occur as a result of a simple reflection. You can cross out choice **B**.

In No. 3, the triangle appears to be a mirror image, and the vertices correspond to the original triangle. It seems like No. 3 could be the correct answer. Keep it.

In No. 4, not only have left and right been reversed, but so have up and down. When you look in a mirror, is the image upside down? Of course not! Eliminate **D**. Choice **C** is correct.

○

You may also be given the (x, y) coordinates of the vertices of a figure and asked what kind of figure it is. You can draw the figure on the axes to see what it is.

○

The vertices of a quadrilateral are the points (2, 2), (2, 6), (6, 2), and (6, 6). What kind of quadrilateral is it?

A   Cube

B   Pentagon

C   Square

D   Trapezoid

Here's How to Crack It

Plot the 4 points given in the question on a piece of graph paper. Then connect the points with straight lines to form a quadrilateral (4-sided figure).

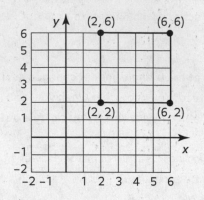

You can see that the sides of the quadrilateral are all 4 units long, which makes it a square. Now look at the answer choices. Choice **C** is correct.

Now try one on your own. The answers are located at the end of this chapter, after the final quiz.

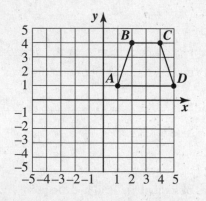

1. **Trapezoid *ABCD* is reflected across the *y*-axis. What are the coordinates of the image points of vertices A, B, C, and D?**

    A   *A* (–5, 1), *B* (–4, 4), *C* (–2, 4), *D* (–1, 1)

    B   *A* (1, –1), *B* (2, –4), *C* (4, –4), *D* (5, –1)

    C   *A* (–1, –1), *B* (–2, –4), *C* (–4, –4), *D* (–5, –1)

    D   *A* (–1, 1), *B* (–2, 4), *C* (–4, 4), *D* (–5, 1)

EQUATIONS OF LINES

The CAHSEE will ask you to prove that a given point lies on the graph of a particular linear equation. In some cases you will be given one coordinate of a point and an equation and asked to solve for the other coordinate. Let's look at one of those now.

Point $(n, -1)$ lies on the line whose equation is $x - 2y = 3$. What is n's value?

A -2

B 1

C 3

D 5

Standard AI1 7.0

"Students verify that a point lies on a line, given an equation of the line. Students are able to derive linear equations."

Here's How to Crack It

Read the question carefully. First, make sure you understand what the question is asking. If a point lies on the line for an equation, then the x- and y-values of the point make the equation true. For example, point $(2, 3)$ lies on the line $x + y = 5$ because $2 + 3 = 5$.

The question is asking you to determine what the x-value of point $(n, -1)$ has to be to make the equation $x - 2y = 3$ true. Substitute n for x and -1 for y in the equation, then solve for n.

$$x - 2y = 3$$
$$n - 2(-1) = 3 \text{ becomes } n + 2 = 3$$
$$n + 2 - 2 = 3 - 2 \text{ becomes } n = 1$$

Now look at the answer choices. Choice **B** is correct.

Let's look at another one.

Which point lies on the line that represents the equation $2x - y = 7$?

A (0, 6)

B (1, 9)

C (2, 3)

D (5, 3)

PITA Tip

If the values in the answer choices make the equation true, that's it! You've found the right choice!

Here's How to Crack It

Because only one of the four choices will satisfy the equation, you can use POE here to eliminate the incorrect choices. Start with answer choice A, and substitute the *x*- and *y*-values into the equation, and then check to see if they make it true.

A: $2x - y = 7$ becomes $2(0) - 6 = 7$, or $0 - 6 = 7$.
  Because $- 6 = 7$ is false, you can get rid of **A**.

B: $2x - y = 7$ becomes $2(1) - 9 = 7$, or $2 - 9 = 7$.
  - 7 does not equal 7, so you can rule out **B**.

C: $2x - y = 7$ becomes $2(2) - 3 = 7$, or $4 - 3 = 7$.
  $1 = 7$ is false, so you can eliminate **C**.

Now, by Process of Elimination, we've determined that **D** is almost certainly the correct answer. But let's make sure by solving the equation:

D: $2x - y = 7$ becomes $2(5) - 3 = 7$, or $10 - 3 = 7$.
  $7 = 7$ is true.
  Choice **D** is correct.

Interception!

The *y*-intercept is the place where a line crosses the *y*-axis.

Other questions will give you the coordinates of two points and ask you to derive the equation of the line formed by those two points. When you write, or "derive", an equation of a line, the slope is expressed as *m*. The equation of the line needs to be in **slope-intercept** form: $y = mx + b$. You need to find the slope, *m*, and the *y*-intercept, *b*.

Remember the slope formula: $\text{Slope} = m = \dfrac{y_2 - y_1}{x_2 - x_1}$.

Write an equation of the line that contains the points (2, 7) and (5, 13).

Here's How to Crack It

First, determine the slope by using the two points given.

$$m = \frac{y_2 - y_1}{x_2 - x_1} \qquad \text{Let } (2, 7) = (x_1, y_1) \text{ and } (5, 13) = (x_2 - y_2).$$

$$m = \frac{13 - 7}{5 - 2} = \frac{6}{3} = 2 \qquad \text{The slope equals 2.}$$

Next, use the x- and y-values of either of the points to find the value of b. Let's use (2, 7). So $y = 7$, $m = 2$, and $x = 2$.

$$y = mx + b$$

$$7 = 2(2) + b$$

$$7 = 4 + b$$

$$3 = b$$

Now write the equation by replacing m and b with their numerical values.

$$y = 2x + 3$$

This is an equation of a line that contains the points (2, 7) and (5, 13).

Now try some on your own. The answers are located at the end of this chapter, after the final quiz.

1. Point $(3, b)$ lies on the line whose equation is $3x + y = 13$. What is the value of b?

    A −3

    B 1

    C 4

    D 7

2. Which of the following points lies on the line that represents the equation $7x − 4y = 2$?

    A $(−1, −2)$

    B $(1, 2)$

    C $(2, 3)$

    D $(2, 4)$

Standard Al1 6.0

"Students graph a linear equation and compute the x-and y-intercepts (e.g., graph $2x + 6y = 4$)."

GRAPHING LINEAR EQUATIONS

You will be asked to compute the x- or y-intercept of a line from its linear equation, which will usually not be in slope-intercept form ($y = mx + b$). It will help you to convert the equation into slope-intercept form. If the problem asks you to match the graph and the equation, be sure to match the y-intercept (where the line crosses the y-axis) and make sure the slope fits. Remember that with slope, the bigger the number, the steeper the slope, and that positive is up and to the right, negative is down and to the right. Keep these properties of the graphs of linear equations in mind and you'll be able to knock off incorrect answers.

Let's look at an example.

What are the coordinates of the y-intercept of the line whose equation is $2y = 4x + 6$?

A (0, 3)

B (0, 6)

C (2, 0)

D (3, 0)

Here's How to Crack It

Read the question carefully. First, remind yourself what is meant by the "y-intercept." The y-intercept is the point where the graph of a linear equation crosses the y-axis. Remember that *at* the y-axis, the x-coordinate of a point is *always* going to be zero. So you can use POE to eliminate the answer choices that do *not* show x as zero right away. Cross out **C** and **D** right off the bat.

Now we can find the coordinates of the y-intercept of the line by rewriting the equation from the question in the form: $y = mx + b$. In order to do that, we need to isolate y, so divide both sides by 2:

$$\frac{2y}{2} = \frac{4x + 6}{2}$$

That leaves us with $y = 2x + 3$.

Remember that when a linear equation is written in this form, m is the slope of the line and b is the y-coordinate of the y-intercept. Therefore, in the graph of the equation $y = 2x + 3$, $m = 2$ and the y-intercept is (0, 3).

Now look again at the answer choices. Choice **A** is correct.

You could also have solved this by drawing a graph of the equation given in the question. To do this, you need to assign some values for x and then solve for the values for y. Then plot the points on a coordinate graph and connect them with a straight line.

x	y
–3	–3
–2	–1
–1	1
0	3
1	5
2	7
3	9

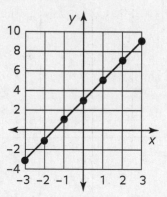

Intercepted Again

The x-coordinate of the y-intercept is always 0 because every point located on the y-axis has an x-value of 0. Likewise, the y-coordinate of the x-intercept is always 0 because every point on the x-axis has a y-value of 0.

Next, find the coordinates of the point where the graph of the equation crosses the y-axis.

The graph crosses the y-axis at the point with coordinates (0, 3).

Now try some on your own. The answers are located at the end of this chapter, after the final quiz.

1. **What are the coordinates of the *y*-intercept of the line whose equation is 2*y* = 8*x* + 4?**

    A (0, 2)

    B (0, 4)

    C (2, 0)

    D (4, 0)

2. **What is the *x*-intercept of the line 2*x* + *y* = 10?**

    A (−2, 0)

    B (0, 5)

    C (0, 10)

    D (5, 0)

PARALLEL LINES AND SLOPE

The CAHSEE will test you on the concept of the slopes of parallel lines. You will be given the equation of a line and have to choose which equation represents a line that's parallel to it. It will usually help to re-arrange some equations into slope-intercept form ($y = mx + b$). The most important thing to remember is:

> Parallel lines have the same slope.

Standard AI1 8.0

"Students understand the concept of parallel lines and how their slopes are related."

The line whose equation is $y = 4x + 3$ is parallel to the line whose equation is

A $\quad y = \dfrac{1}{4}x - 4$

B $\quad y = -4x + 3$

C $\quad y = 4x + 5$

D $\quad y = -\dfrac{1}{4}x - 3$

Here's How to Crack It

Remember that two parallel lines have the same slope. So we want to find the equation that has the same slope as the equation of the line in the question. In this question, the equation is already in slope-intercept form ($y = mx + b$), so it's easy to find the slope for this line: 4 (because 4 is in the m position).

Now, all we have to do is look at the equation in each of the answer choices, and figure out which one has a slope of 4.

Out of all of the answer choices, only the equation in C ($y = 4x + 5$) has a 4 in the slope position. Don't be fooled by the -4 in choice B! Choice C is the one you want. Easy!

As long as you remember that parallel lines have the same slope, but different y-intercepts, you should be able to handle these questions. Sometimes you'll be given equations that aren't in slope-intercept form. This is no big deal! To rewrite the equations so they *are* in slope-intercept form, just get y by itself on one side of the equal sign.

Let's try one.

     The line whose equation is $3x - y = 4$ is parallel to the line whose equation is

    A $4x = y + 3$

    B $y - 4 = 3x$

    C $y - 4 = -3x$

    D $y = 4$

Start by rearranging the equation $3x - y = 4$ to the form $y = mx + b$.

First, add y to both sides:

$$3x - y + y = 4 + y$$
$$3x = 4 + y$$

Now subtract 4 from both sides to get y all by itself:

$$3x - 4 = y$$

If it looks a little strange because y is on the right side of the equation this time, don't worry! It still means the same thing. But we can write the equation like this instead:

$$y = 3x - 4$$

Now we can see that the slope of the original equation is 3.

Next, all we have to do is put each of the answer choices in the form $y = mx + b$. Then, use POE to see which line has the same slope as the original.

    A: $4x = y + 3$

Rewrite the equation so that y is on the left side by itself.

$$y + 3 = 4x$$
$$y + 3 - 3 = 4x - 3$$
$$y = 4x - 3$$

The slope is 4, so you can rule out **A**.

Then do the same for **B**, **C**, and **D**.

B:	$y = 3x + 4$	The slope is 3, so hang on to **B**.
C:	$y = -3x + 4$	The slope is -3, so you can rule out **C**.
D:	$y = 0x + 3$	The slope is 0, so you can rule out **D**.

The correct choice is **B**.

———————————◯———————————

Now try some on your own. The answers are located at the end of this chapter, after the final quiz.

1. **Which of the following is an equation of a line that is parallel to the line whose equation is $y = 3x - 6$?**

    A $y = -3x + 2$

    B $y = -\dfrac{1}{3}x - 10$

    C $y = \dfrac{1}{3}x + 5$

    D $y = 3x + 4$

2. **Which of the following is best describes the graphs of two parallel lines?**

    A They have the same slope, but different y-intercepts.

    B They have different slopes, but the same y-intercept.

    C They have the same slope, and the same y-intercept.

    D They have different slopes, and different y-intercepts.

Standard Al1 9.0

"Students solve a system of two linear equations in two variables algebraically and are able to interpret the answer graphically. Students are able to solve a system of two linear inequalities in two variables and to sketch the solution sets."

SYSTEMS OF LINEAR EQUATIONS

You will be given two linear equations, each containing two variables. You will have to solve them either algebraically, or by graphing them to find where the lines formed by the equations intersect. The correct answer will be the ordered pair (x, y) that satisfies *both* equations. You may have to do this with some inequalities too.

Which ordered pair is the solution set for this system of equations?

$$y = 3x + 1$$

$$x = y - 3$$

A (–1, 2)

B (1, 4)

C (2, 5)

D (2, 7)

Here's How to Crack It

First, make sure you understand what you have to do. You need to determine which ordered pair (x, y) makes *both* equations true. Each of equations above has two variables, x and y, so it's going to be impossible to solve either equation by itself. However, you can use something called substitution to solve them together.

Look at the second equation. Since it says that $x = y - 3$, you can substitute $y - 3$ for the x in the first equation, and then solve for y.

Substitute $y - 3$ in place of x:

$$y = 3(y - 3) + 1$$

Distribute the 3 over the parentheses:

$$y = 3y - 9 + 1$$

Combine like terms:

$$y = 3y - 8$$

Subtract y from both sides, in order to get y on only one side of the equal sign:

$$0 = 2y - 8$$

Then add +8 to both sides, so that y is alone:

$$8 = 2y$$

Divide both sides by 2:

$$\frac{8}{2} = \frac{2y}{2}$$

$$4 = y$$

Now that we know the value of y, we can start our POE. Which answer choice has y as 4? Only B.

But, if we wanted to check our answers, we could go back and substitute 4 in place of y in the second equation.

$$x = y - 3$$
$$x = 4 - 3$$
$$x = 1$$

The ordered pair that satisfies both equations is (1, 4), confirming that the correct answer is **B**.

Don't forget PITA

You can also solve a system of equations by substituting each of the answer choices into the equations. The one choice that makes <u>both</u> equations true will be the correct answer.

You can also solve a system of equations like this graphically. Construct a graph of each equation given in the question, and then plot both lines on the same set of axes. (If you need to, go back and look at "Graphing Linear Equations".) If you work carefully, your graph should look like the figure on the next page.

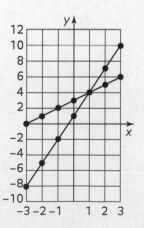

See how the lines of the two equations intersect at the point (1, 4)? This is the *solution set* for the system of equations in the question, and the same pair of coordinates you found algebraically just now.

Now try some on your own. The answers are located at the end of this chapter, after the final quiz.

1. **Which ordered pair is the solution set for this system of equations?**

   $2x - 5y = 6$

   $x + 5y = 18$

   A $(-2, -2)$
   B $(-2, 4)$
   C $(3, 3)$
   D $(8, 2)$

2. **Which ordered pair is the solution set for this system of equations?**

   $2x = 5y + 8$

   $x = y + 1$

   A $(-2, -3)$
   B $(-1, -2)$
   C $(4, 3)$
   D $(9, 2)$

CHAPTER 10: GEOMETRIC GRAPHS FINAL QUIZ

Answers can be found on page 280–282.

1. The average monthly temperatures in the cities of Los Angeles and New York are shown in the graph below.

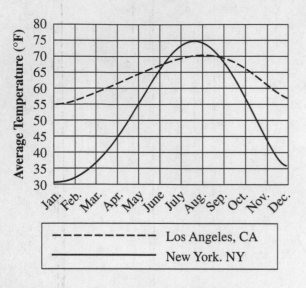

Los Angeles is warmer than New York

A the entire year except for March–May.

B the entire year except for June–September.

C the entire year except for September–November.

D the entire year without exception.

2. Which of these graphs could be the graph of the equation $y = 3x^2$?

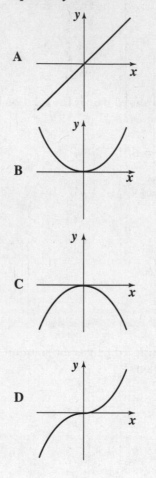

3. Which graph in the answer choices could be the graph of the equation: $y = x - 2^2$?

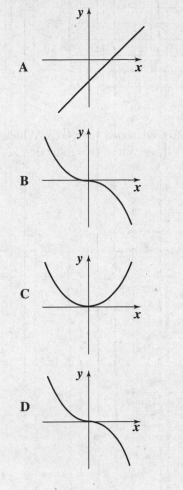

A

B

C

D

4. The slope of the line on the graph below is

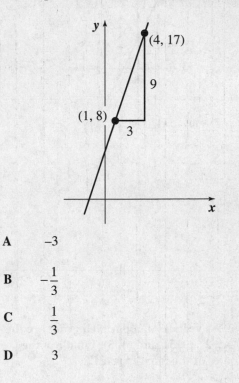

A   −3

B $-\dfrac{1}{3}$

C $\dfrac{1}{3}$

D   3

5. The slope of the line shown on the graph below is

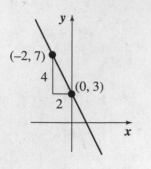

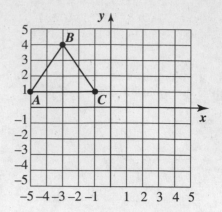

A   −2

B $-\dfrac{1}{2}$

C $\dfrac{1}{2}$

D   2

7. Triangle *ABC* is reflected across the *x*-axis. Which of the following shows the result of this reflection?

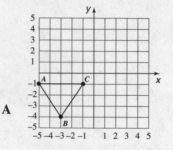

A

6. Three of the vertices of a parallelogram are the points (−2, 2), (0, 5), and (4, 5). What are the coordinates of the fourth vertex?

A   (1, 2)

B   (2, 2)

C   (3, 2)

D   (6, 2)

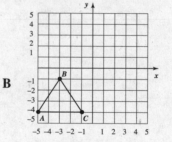

B

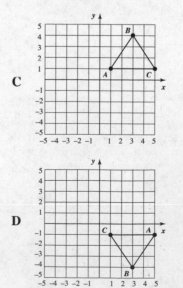

C

D

8. The graph of which of the following equations contains the points (–1, 2) and (2, 11)?

   A $y = x + 3$

   B $y = 2x + 4$

   C $y = 3x + 5$

   D $y = 4x + 3$

9. Point $(a, -2)$ lies on the line whose equation is $2x - 6y = 14$. What is the value of a?

   A   –1

   B   1

   C   4

   D   13

10. Which of the following points lies on the line that represents the equation $6x + 2y = 10$?

    A   (0, 6)

    B   (–1, 2)

    C   (2, 1)

    D   (2, –1)

11. The graph of which of the following equations contains the point (–2, 9)?

    A $x + y = 7$

    B $x - y = 11$

    C $x + 3y = 9$

    D $3x - 2y = 5$

12. Point $(3, n)$ lies on the line whose equation is $4x + 3y = 6$. What is the value of n?

    A   –6

    B   –2

    C   2

    D   6

13. Which of the following points does not lie on the graph of the equation $2x + 5y = 16$?

    A   (–2, 4)

    B   (3, 2)

    C   (8, 0)

    D   (10, –1)

14. The graph of which of the following equations contains the points (–2, 1) and (2, 9)?

    A $y = x + 3$

    B $y = x + 7$

    C $y = 2x + 5$

    D $y = 4x + 1$

15. Point $(q, -2)$ lies on the line whose equation is $9x + 3y = 21$. What is the value of q?

    A   –3

    B   –2

    C   3

    D   13

16. The line whose equation is $3x - 5y = 15$ has a y-intercept with coordinates

    A   (–3, 0).

    B   (0, –3).

    C $(\frac{3}{5}, -3)$.

    D $(\frac{3}{5}, 0)$.

17. What is the x-intercept of the line $5x + 2y = 20$?

    A   (0, 4)

    B   (0, 10)

    C   (4, 0)

    D   (4, 10)

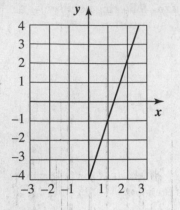

18. The graph above represents which of the following equations?

A $y = x - 4$

B $y = x + 2$

C $y = 2x + 4$

D $y = 3x - 4$

19. What are the coordinates of the y-intercept of the line whose equation is $5x - 3y = 15$?

A $(-5, 0)$

B $(-3, 0)$

C $(0, 3)$

D $(0, -5)$

20. What is the x-intercept of the line $2y - 5x = 10$?

A $(-5, 0)$

B $(-2, 0)$

C $(0, 5)$

D $(0, -2)$

21. Which of the following equations has a y-intercept and an x-intercept whose coordinates are $(0, 0)$?

A $y = 2x$

B $y = 2x + 5$

C $y = 2x - 5$

D $y = 3x - 3$

22. The line whose equation is $y = 2x + 5$ is parallel to the line whose equation is

A $y = \dfrac{1}{2}x - 3$

B $y = -2x + 9$

C $y = 2x - 1$

D $y = -\dfrac{1}{2}x + 5$

23. Which of the following lines is parallel to $2x + y = 5$?

A $y - 2x = 5$

B $y = 2x + 2$

C $2x - y = 5$

D $y = -2x - 6$

24. A line parallel to a line of the equation $3x - 4y = 16$ would have a slope equal to

A $-\dfrac{4}{3}$

B $-\dfrac{3}{4}$

C $\dfrac{3}{4}$

D $\dfrac{4}{3}$

25. Which of the following lines is not parallel to $y = 3x - 8$?

A $3x - y = 5$

B $3x + y = 8$

C $3x = y - 8$

D $6x - 2y = 15$

26. What is the slope of a line whose equation is
    $2y = x - 14$?

    A -1

    B $\dfrac{1}{2}$

    C 1

    D 2

27. Which of the following lines is parallel to
    $3x + 2y = 12$?

    A $2y = 3x - 6$

    B $2y - 3x = 12$

    C $3y = 2x + 8$

    D $3x = 4 - 2y$

28. A line parallel to the line whose equation i
    $6x + 3y = 15$ would have a slope equal to

    A -2

    B $-\dfrac{1}{2}$

    C $\dfrac{1}{2}$

    D 2

29. Which ordered pair is in the solution set for the
    following system of inequalities?

    $x - y > 1$

    $y < 2x - 1$

    A $(0, -2)$

    B $(0, -1)$

    C $(-1, -1)$

    D $(-2, -1)$

30. Which ordered pair is the solution set for this system
    of equations?

    $3x = 7y + 1$

    $x = y - 1$

    A $(-5, -2)$

    B $(-2, -1)$

    C $(2, 3)$

    D $(5, 2)$

31. Which ordered pair is the solution set for this system
    of equations?

    $3x + y = 5$

    $y = 5x - 3$

    A $(-2, 1)$

    B $(-1, 8)$

    C $(1, 2)$

    D $(2, -1)$

32. Which ordered pair is the solution set for this system
    of equations?

    $2y + x = 8$

    $x + y = 5$

    A $(-2, 7)$

    B $(2, -5)$

    C $(2, 3)$

    D $(4, 1)$

ANSWERS TO PRACTICE PROBLEMS

Graphs
1. C

Graphing Functions
1. C

Linear Functions and Slope
1. A
2. D

Coordinate Graphs
1. D

Equations of Lines
1. C
2. C

Graphing Linear Equations
1. A
2. D

Parallel Lines and Slope
1. D
2. A

Systems of Linear Equations
1. D
2. B

Chapter 11
Statistics

Statistics is the type of math used to collect, measure, and analyze data. That sounds really dry and uninteresting, but the fact is that you see statistics used every single day. Every time you read the sports page for the latest sports stats ("stats" as in "statistics," right?), or hear the results of the latest political poll on the news at night, you're seeing statistics in action. Every study that tells you what food is good for you or warns us about climate change uses statistics to analyze the information. The CAHSEE will test you on how well you understand statistical techniques, and your ability to read and interpret statistical data in real-world situations.

Standard SDAP 1.1

"Compute the mean, median, and mode of data sets."

MEAN, MEDIAN, AND MODE

The CAHSEE will ask you to find the mean, the median, and the mode of a set of numbers. Let's quickly review what mean, median, and mode are before moving on to some sample problems.

The **mean** is the same as the *average* of a set of numbers. To find the mean of a group of several different numbers, you add the numbers together, then divide the total by the actual number of items added.

The **median** is the middle number of a set of numbers. If you line up all the numbers in a set in order and point to the middle one, that's the median. It's often the same thing as the mean—but not always!

The **mode** is the number that occurs the most often in a set of numbers.

So, if your set is [2, 3, 5, 9, 9], the mean is 6.6, the median is 5, and the mode is 9.

The table below shows the daily high temperatures (in degrees Fahrenheit) for three cities over four days.

High Temperatures

	Mon.	Tues.	Wed.	Thurs.
Boston	62	59	46	49
Chicago	49	47	47	45
San Francisco	63	61	62	64

What was Boston's mean high temperature over the four days?

A 46

B 50

C 54

D 62

Here's How to Crack It

Read the question and study the table carefully. Notice that the question is asking you about Boston, but the table also gives you information about Chicago and San Francisco. Do we need to know what the temperature is in Chicago to find the mean temperature in Boston? No! They have nothing to do with each other! Go ahead and cross out the temperatures for Chicago and San Francisco; you won't need them at all.

Next, find the mean (average) of the Boston temperature readings by adding all the Boston temperatures together, and dividing by 4—the number of days of readings:

$$62 + 59 + 46 + 49 = 216$$

$$216 \div 4 = 54$$

The mean of this set of numbers is 54.

Now check the answer choices. Choice **C** is correct.

Slow Down!

The CAHSEE is untimed. Make sure you read every question and graph carefully. Don't make careless mistakes by rushing to the answer choices. If you rush through the question, you may not realize what information you need to answer it correctly.

Now try some on your own. The answers are located at the end of this chapter, after the final quiz.

1. In the first seven games of the basketball season, Cindy scored 8, 2, 12, 6, 8, 4, and 9 points. What was her mean number of points scored per game?

   A   6

   B   7

   C   8

   D   9

2. Kafir's grades on five math quizzes are 9, 7, 10, 6, and 10. What is the median of his quiz grades?

   A   8

   B   8.4

   C   9

   D   9.5

Ages of Players on the Soccer Team

Age (years)	Number of Players
11	2
12	8
13	6
14	3
15	1

3. The ages of the players on the town's traveling soccer team are listed in the table above. What is the mode of the soccer team's ages?

   A   12

   B   12.5

   C   12.65

   D   13

SORDID STATISTICS

Advertising agencies have learned how to manipulate statistics to make it *appear* that the data support their claims about a product. When you read an advertisement, or see a commercial on TV, make sure to consider all the data, especially numbers in fine print. Don't believe everything you read—make your own decision!

You don't have to have a sophisticated understanding of complex statistics to answer the questions the CAHSEE will ask you about this section. You just have to identify claims that advertisements make that are based on a set of data. In some cases you'll have to decide whether the claim the ad is making is valid, or whether it is in some way deceptive or misleading.

Standard SDAP 2.5

"Identify claims based on statistical data and, in simple cases, evaluate the validity of the claims."

Mall Name	Number of Cars Stolen	Number of Years Open
Metro	600	15
Suburban	150	3

The table shown above appears in a local newspaper ad. The ad claims, "*Suburban Mall* is safe! We have had one-fourth the number of cars stolen from our parking areas that *Metro Mall* has." Why is this claim not valid?

A The ad's claim should read, "twenty-five percent fewer cars stolen."

B The ad's claim should read, "one-third the number of cars stolen."

C On average *Metro Mall* has had more cars stolen per year.

D On average *Suburban Mall* has had more cars stolen per year.

Here's How to Crack It

Read the question and table carefully. Pay special attention to the term "not valid." In statistics "valid" means "well grounded on evidence; able to withstand criticism." So the question is telling us right off that the ad is claiming something that is *not* supported by the evidence given in the table. We have to decide *why* what the ad claims is wrong.

First, let's figure out *how* the ad is wrong. Valid means "well grounded on the evidence." Is the claim well grounded? Well, the ad says, "We have had one-fourth the number of cars stolen from our parking areas that *Metro Mall* has." 150 is one-fourth of 600, so this seems to be true.

However, valid also means "able to withstand criticism." Is the ad able to stand up to criticism? Let's look at the numbers in the last column of the table. *Metro Mall* has been open for 15 years, but *Suburban Mall* has only been open for three. Because *Metro Mall* has been in business five times longer than *Suburban Mall* you would expect the number of cars stolen to be greater for *Metro Mall*, wouldn't you? If a column labeled "Number of Cars Stolen Per Year" were added to the table, the numbers would be 40 for *Metro Mall* and 50 for *Suburban Mall*! The ad is giving you the hard facts in the table, true, but it's manipulating the way the information in the claim is presented to make *Suburban Mall* look better. The claim is deceptive and, therefore, not valid.

Finally, look at the answer choices. Answer choice **D** is correct.

───────────────○───────────────

Now try one on your own. The answers are located at the end of this chapter, after the final quiz.

Aurora Investments
The #1 *Equity Income Fund*

**The Aurora Investments Equity Income Fund was ranked #1
out of 22 equity income funds since its inception,
10/31/86, through 10/31/01 by Lipper, Inc.**

Call or e-mail to request a fund profile or prospectus.

	Total Return	Rank (Lipper)
1-year	2.62%	#18
5-year	10.87%	#21
10-year	13.54%	#5
Since inception	11.48%	#1

1. **The ad shown above appeared in a financial news magazine. Why is Aurora Investments's claim to have the #1 Equity Income Fund <u>misleading</u>?**

   A The claim should read, "ranked #18 out of 200."

   B Based on Total Return over the past 1, 5, and 10 years, Aurora Investments Equity Income-Fund was <u>not</u> ranked #1.

   C The claim should read, "ranked #5 out of 44."

   D Aurora Investments Equity Income Fund has been ranked #1 based on Total Return since 10/31/86.

PROBABILITIES

Probability is the *chance* that something will happen. Probabilities are always expressed as a fraction between 0 and 1, or as a percentage between 0 and 100. You might have to convert the probability from one form to another. If there is a 30% chance of rain, that is the same as a .03 probability of rain, or roughly $\frac{1}{3}$. On the test, you will be asked to calculate the probability that a particular event will occur, as expressed as a fraction, percentage, or ratio (1:1).

The formula for finding the probability of an event can be written as

$$P = \frac{\text{the number of ways that an event can occur}}{\text{the number of possible outcomes}}$$

Let's take a look at some examples.

Sally has the following change in her purse: three quarters, two dimes, one nickel, and two pennies. What is the probability that, if she picks a coin without looking, she will <u>not</u> pick a penny?

A $\frac{1}{8}$

B $\frac{1}{4}$

C $\frac{1}{2}$

D $\frac{3}{4}$

Here's How to Crack It

Read the question carefully. You are being asked to find the probability that an event will *not* occur. First, determine all the possible outcomes. There are eight coins in Sally's pocket, so there are eight possible outcomes—one for each coin. Next, calculate the probability—the chance—that the event described *will* occur. So we are going to figure out how likely it is that Sally *will* pick a penny, and then use that answer to figure out how likely it is that she will *not*. Sounds confusing! But it's actually pretty simple once the steps are all broken down.

Remember that to find the probability of an event you divide the number of ways an event can occur by the number of possible outcomes.

Standard SDAP 3.3

"Represent probabilities as ratios, proportions, decimals between 0 and 1, and percentages between 0 and 100 and verify that the probabilities computed are reasonable; know that if *P* is the probability of an event, 1 – *P* is the probability of an event not occurring."

How Low Can You Go?
Remember, when you're working with fractions, always reduce the fractions as much as possible.

Step 1: Since there are two pennies in Sally's pocket, there are two possible ways she could pick a penny, out of eight. $P(\text{penny}) = \frac{2}{8} = \frac{1}{4}$.

So the probability of Sally picking a penny out of her pocket is $\frac{1}{4}$.

Now we want to find the probability of Sally picking anything *but* a penny out of her pocket.

Remember that probability is always expressed as an amount between 1 and 0. So if P is the probability that an event will occur, then we can say that $1 - P$ is the probability that an event will not occur.

Step 2: Subtracting P from 1, we get $NP(\text{not penny}) = 1 - P(\text{penny}) = 1 - \frac{1}{4} = \frac{3}{4}$.

The probability that Sally will *not* pick a penny is $\frac{3}{4}$. Now check the answer choices. Choice **D** is correct.

―――――――――――○―――――――――――

Now try one a few your own. The answers are located at the end of this chapter, after the final quiz.

1. Eduardo has a set of dominoes that consists of twenty-eight tiles. Seven of the tiles have the same number of dots on both halves and are called doubles. The player to draw a double first begins the game. What is the theoretical probability that the first tile Eduardo draws will be a double?

   A $\frac{1}{28}$

   B $\frac{1}{14}$

   C $\frac{1}{7}$

   D $\frac{1}{4}$

2. For a genetics experiment related to eye color, Reba placed twenty plastic disks (ten brown and ten clear) in a small container. She shook the container and picked a disk at random five times, replacing the disk after each pick. Each time she picked a brown disk. If Reba picks a disk at random one more time, what is the theoretical probability that she will pick a clear disk?

A $\frac{1}{10}$

B $\frac{1}{5}$

C $\frac{1}{2}$

D $\frac{2}{3}$

3. A fair spinner has equal-sized sections numbered 1–7. If you spin it one time, what is the probability that the spinner will <u>not</u> stop on an even number?

A $\frac{1}{3}$

B $\frac{3}{7}$

C $\frac{1}{2}$

D $\frac{4}{7}$

Standard SDAP 3.1

"Represent all possible outcomes for compound events in an organized way (e.g., tables, grids, tree diagrams) and express the theoretical probability of each outcome."

COMPOUND EVENTS

Some probabilities are the result of two events that happen in sequence, one after the other—in other words, they're *compounded*. For example, what is the probability that it will rain AND you'll forget your umbrella? That's an example of a **compound event** (and Murphy's Law). You will need to be able to draw a diagram of the possible outcomes as well as to figure the theoretical probability of a possible outcome. **Theoretical probability is** just another term for probability: It's the *probability* of one event happening out of all the *possible* outcomes of a situation. You can find it using the same formula you used for probability in the previous section.

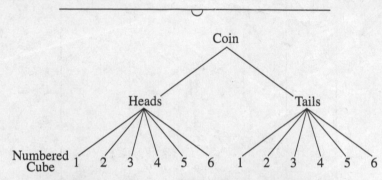

Nicole tosses a coin and rolls a numbered cube. The tree diagram above represents all the possible outcomes.

What is the theoretical probability that Nicole will toss tails and roll an even number?

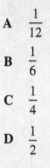

A $\frac{1}{12}$

B $\frac{1}{6}$

C $\frac{1}{4}$

D $\frac{1}{2}$

Here's How to Crack It

Read the question and examine the diagram carefully. Remember, theoretical probability just means "probability." The question is asking you to find the probability of two things happening in this situation: the probability that Nicole will come up with tails in her coin toss, and the probability that Nicole will roll an even number on the cube. First, let's figure out the probability of each one of those possible events separately.

Step 1: Because tossing a coin has only two possible outcomes, heads or tails, the probability of Nicole tossing tails is 1 out of 2, or $\frac{1}{2}$.

Step 2: Rolling a numbered cube has six possible outcomes, one for each side. Of the six possible outcomes, three are even numbers: 2, 4, and 6. Therefore, the probability of rolling an even number is 3 out of 6, or $\frac{1}{2}$.

Finally, we have to figure out the probability of both of those events occurring. We can find the combined (as in "compound," right?) probability of two independent events by multiplying the probability of the first event (A) by the probability of the second event (B):

$$P(A) \cdot P(B)$$

Step 3: The probability of both tossing tails and rolling an even number is the product of the probabilities of each independent event.

$$P(\text{tails}) \cdot P(\text{even}) = \frac{1}{2} \cdot \frac{1}{2} = \frac{1}{4}$$

The "theoretical probability" that Nicole will toss tails and roll an even number is $\frac{1}{4}$.

Now check the answer choices. Choice **C** is correct.

Now try one on your own. The answers are located at the end of this chapter, after the final quiz.

$0 > P > 1$

The probability of an event occurring is *always* a number between 0 and 1. If you get an answer that is less than 0 or greater than 1, go back and check your work for errors.

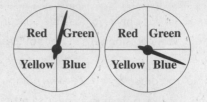

1. Both spinners in the above diagram are fair. Martin spins each spinner one time. All the possible outcomes can be displayed in a table similar to the one below.

	Second Spinner			
First Spinner	Blue	Green	Red	Yellow
blue				
green				
red				
yellow				

What is the theoretical probability that one of the two spinners will stop on red and the other spinner will stop on green?

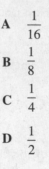

A $\frac{1}{16}$

B $\frac{1}{8}$

C $\frac{1}{4}$

D $\frac{1}{2}$

Standard SDAP 3.5

"Understand the difference between independent and dependent events."

INDEPENDENT AND DEPENDENT EVENTS

We know that compound events are made up of two or more simple events. The CAHSEE is also going to test you on how to analyze compound events, and how to determine if the events that make up a compound event are **independent events** or **dependent events**. Independent events are just that—they are independent of each other. In other words, one independent event has no influence on the outcome of another independent event. A dependent event is just the opposite—its outcome *depends* on another event. Let's take a look.

Which of the following pairs describes two <u>dependent</u> events?

A Picking an ace from a standard deck of 52 cards without replacing it; picking another ace

B Drawing a Q from a box of 26 different alphabet tiles; drawing a 7 from a jar of tiles numbered 0 to 9

C Picking a green gumdrop from a dish containing 20 each of eight assorted colors; picking a white marble from a bag containing 4 white marbles and 6 black marbles

D Flipping a coin that comes up tails; rolling a number cube and getting 6

Here's How to Crack It

Read the question carefully, and remember the meaning of dependent events. If the outcome of one event affects the outcome of another event, these events are dependent. Let's use answer choice **A** as an example of how to determine if an event is dependent (and as a bonus, see if we can eliminate it).

Imagine that two people are going to play a card game. Each picks a card from a standard deck of 52 cards to see who deals first. The probability that the first person will pick an ace is $\frac{4}{52}$, or $\frac{1}{13}$. If the first person picks an ace, what is the probability that the second person will pick an ace?

The ace picked by the first person is <u>not</u> replaced in the deck of cards. That means there are 51 cards left, three of which are aces. The probability that the second person will pick an ace is $\frac{3}{51}$, or $\frac{1}{17}$. The probability of the second person picking an ace is less than the first person. The outcome of the first event has affected the outcome of the second event. These events are dependent. Since we're looking for two dependent events, let's keep **A**, but keep looking at all the answer choices to make sure there's not a better answer.

Drawing a letter from a box of alphabet tiles does not affect whether or not you'll draw a number from a jar of number tiles, so we can get rid of **B**.

Picking a gumdrop from a dish does not affect picking a white marble from a bag, so we can eliminate **C**.

Flipping a coin does not affect rolling a number cube, so we can rule out **D**.

As we suspected, choice **A** is correct!

To find the probability of two <u>independent</u> events, use the formula
$$P(A \text{ and } B) = P(A) \cdot P(B)$$

To find the probability of two <u>dependent</u> events, use the formula
$$P(A \text{ and } B) = P(A) \cdot P(B \text{ following } A)$$

Now try a couple on your own. The answers are located at the end of this chapter, after the final quiz.

1. **Which of the following pairs describes two <u>dependent</u> events?**

   A Picking a white T-shirt from a drawer that contains 3 white T-shirts and 2 gray T-shirts; rolling a number cube and getting a 5

   B Flipping a coin that comes up tails; drawing a diamond from a standard deck of cards

   C Picking a boy from a class of 15 girls and 15 boys; picking a second boy from the remaining students

   D Drawing a black pawn from a bag that contains 8 black pawns and 8 white pawns; spinning a 1-to-8 spinner and getting an even number

2. **A bag contains 7 black checkers and 3 red checkers. Once a checker is picked, it is not replaced. What is the probability of picking 2 red checkers?**

   A $\dfrac{1}{15}$

   B $\dfrac{9}{100}$

   C $\dfrac{21}{100}$

   D $\dfrac{3}{10}$

DISPLAYING DATA

These types of questions are all about reading the information in charts and graphs. The information is always going to be right there in the chart—the CAHSEE will not ask you about any data or information that isn't given to you, so just keep your eyes open and read the charts carefully and you should have no problems.

Standard SDAP 1.1
"Know various forms of display for data sets; use the forms to display a single set of data or to compare two sets of data."

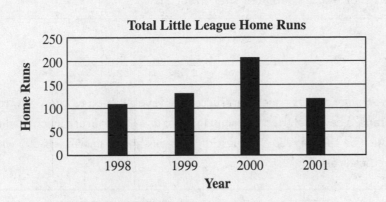

The above graph shows the total number of Little League home runs per year. Which of the following is true based on the graph?

A   The teams drank more milk in the year 2000.

B   The teams hit the most home runs in 1998.

C   The teams hit almost twice as many home runs in 2000 as they did in 1998.

D   The teams hit about twice as many home runs in 1998 as they did in 2000.

Here's How to Crack It

Study the bar graph carefully. It shows you the total number of home runs in the years 1998 through 2001. Read the question carefully and make sure you understand what information it is asking you to find.

No, go through each answer choice, and check its validity against the graph. Then use POE to cross out the answer choices that don't fit.

Answer choice **A** says that the teams drank more milk in 2000. The graph doesn't say anything about milk consumption, does it? We can eliminate choice **A**.

Answer choice **B** states that the teams hit the most home runs in 1998. On the graph, the bar for 1998 doesn't go as high as it does for all the other years. That means more home runs were hit in all the *other* years! Cross off choice **B**.

Answer choice **C** states that the teams hit almost twice as many home runs in 2000 as they did in 1998. That seems right, but compare the numbers on the graph. In 1998, around 100 home runs were hit. In 2000, about 200 home runs were hit. That's about twice as many home runs! Keep choice **C**, but check choice **D** to be sure.

Answer choice **D** states that the teams hit about twice as many home runs in 1998 as they did in 2000. We already found that the fewest home runs were hit in 1998! Cross off choice **D**. **C** is definitely the correct answer.

───────────────◯───────────────

To answer many of these questions successfully, you'll need to know how to read a circle graph, a bar graph, and a straightforward line graph. Brush up on reading all of those. Also be sure to read the question carefully and to answer exactly what they are specifically asking.

───────────────◯───────────────

The hourly temperatures in Beijing, China, over a 4-hour period on Jan. 16, 2002, are shown in the graph below.

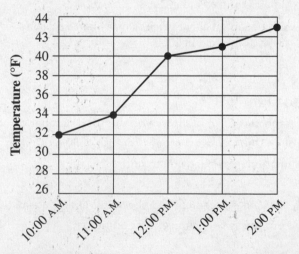

During which hour did the temperature increase the most?

A   10:00 A.M. to 11:00 A.M.

B   11:00 A.M. to 12:00 P.M.

C   12:00 P.M. to 1:00 P.M.

D   1:00 P.M. to 2:00 P.M.

Here's How to Crack It

Read the question and study the graph carefully. First, ask yourself, "How is the greatest increase indicated on a graph?" The greatest increase will be the part of the graph with the steepest slope (i.e., the part that is most uphill). Next, identify the part on the graph where the slope is the steepest. The graph is steepest between 11:00 A.M. and 12:00 P.M., right?

Now look at the answer choices. Choice **B** is correct.

———————○———————

Now try some on your own. The answers are located at the end of this chapter, after the final quiz.

**Votes Received by Candidates
A, B, C, D, and E**

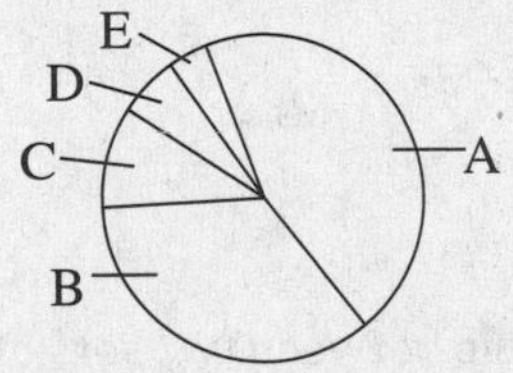

1. The above pie graph shows votes divided among 5 candidates running for student government positions. Approximately what fraction of the vote did candidate C receive?

    A $\dfrac{1}{2}$

    B $\dfrac{1}{4}$

    C $\dfrac{1}{10}$

    D $\dfrac{1}{25}$

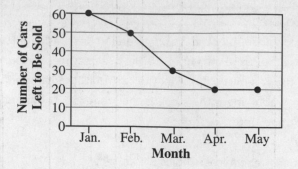

Standard SDAP 1.2

"Represent two numerical variables on a scatter plot and informally describe how the data points are distributed and any apparent relationship that exists between the two variables (e.g., between time spent on homework and grade level)."

2. The above graph shows the number of cars left at a dealership at the beginning of each month. The dealership buys its inventory of cars only once a year, at the beginning of January. During which month were the greatest number of cars sold?

A January

B February

C March

D April

SCATTER PLOTS

Scatter plots show the relationship between two sets of data by *scattering* individual dots across a graph. You will be asked whether there is a pattern in the distribution of the dots (also known as data points). You'll need to determine if there is a pattern (i.e., if the points have a particular shape, and also whether that pattern shows a relationship between the two variables).

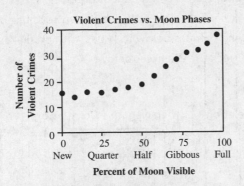

Violent Crimes vs. Moon Phases

Law officials in a city did a study to see if the number of violent crimes committed was related to the "fullness" of the moon. The results of the study are shown in the scatter plot pictured above. Based on the data, what conclusion can be drawn?

A The number of violent crimes increases as the fullness of the moon increases.

B The number of violent crimes decreases as the fullness of the moon increases.

C The number of violent crimes remains the same as the fullness of the moon increases.

D The number of violent crimes is not at all related to the fullness of the moon.

Here's How to Crack It

Study the scatter plot. You can see that the values for the two variables (number of crimes and phases of the moon) are plotted as ordered pairs (*x*, *y*) on a coordinate graph. Look at the pattern the dots make. If the pattern of plotted points slopes upward, the relationship is positive, meaning that the values of the two variables both increase in relation to each other. If it slopes downward, the relationship is negative, meaning that as one variable increases, the other decreases. If there is no apparent pattern, the two sets of data are most likely unrelated. What does the pattern in this scatter plot tell us?

Although the left side of the graph is rather flat, the right side shows a definite upward slope. It appears that the number of violent crimes committed increases as the "fullness" of the moon (percent of the moon visible) increases from 50% to 100%. Now check the answer choices. Choice **A** is correct.

Drawing the Line

When you're looking for trends among the data points in a scatter plot, it can help to draw a "best-fit" line. This type of line is drawn so that about half of the data points are above it and half are below it. A best-fit line makes it easier to see the slope of the graph. Check the examples below.

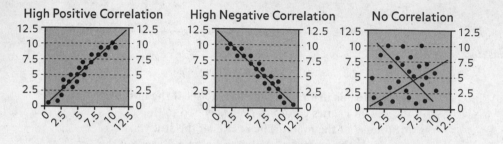

High Positive Correlation   High Negative Correlation   No Correlation

Now try one on your own. The answer is located at the end of this chapter, after the final quiz.

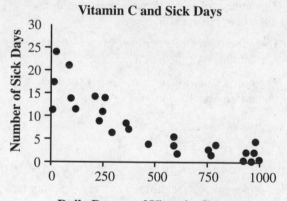

Vitamin C and Sick Days

Number of Sick Days

Daily Dosage of Vitamin C (mg)

1.   **For her end-of-year biology project, Cindy took a random survey of 30 students in her school. She asked each student how much vitamin C they took each day, and how many days they were out sick this year. The results of her survey are shown above. What conclusion can Cindy draw that is supported by her data?**

   A   The number of sick days increases as the dosage of vitamin C increases.

   B   The number of sick days decreases as the dosage of vitamin C increases.

   C   The number of sick days is not affected by the dosage of vitamin C.

   D   There is no relationship between the number of sick days and the dosage of vitamin C.

CHAPTER 11: STATISTICS FINAL QUIZ

Answers can be found on page 282–283.

1. The table below shows the number of hours three students spent watching TV over a four-week period.

    Number of Hours Spent Watching TV

	Week 1	Week 2	Week 3	Week 4
Tricia	15	18	13	20
Jose	9	12	11	14
Rosa	11	13	8	12

    What is Rosa's mean number of hours per week watching TV?

    A   10

    B   11

    C   12

    D   13

2. Ms. Walcott's science class did an experiment to determine the boiling point of tap water. The thirteen lab groups got the following results (in degrees Celsius):

    98, 100, 99, 97, 101, 100, 99, 102, 98, 101, 100, 99, 100

    What is the median temperature of the class results for the boiling point of tap water?

    A   99

    B   99.5

    C   100

    D   100.5

Average Number of Rainy Days

Month	Rainy Days	Month	Rainy Days
Jan.	13	July	11
Feb.	11	Aug.	9
Mar.	14	Sept.	8
Apr.	13	Oct.	9
May	13	Nov.	12
June	11	Dec.	13

3. The table above shows the average number of rainy days in each month for a city. What is the mode of the monthly numbers?

    A   11

    B   11.4

    C   11.5

    D   13

Company Name	Number of Autos Recalled by Factory	Number of Autos Manufactured
American Motors	4,500	750,000
Pacific-Rim Auto	3,000	300,000

4. Using the data in the table shown above, *Pacific-Rim Auto* advertised, "We had 33 percent fewer autos recalled by the factory than *American Motors* had." What is <u>deceptive</u> about this advertisement?

    A   On average *Pacific-Rim Auto* had more factory recalls per 1,000 autos manufactured.

    B   The advertisement should read, "50-percent fewer autos recalled."

    C   On average *American Motors* had more factory recalls per 1,000 autos manufactured.

    D   The advertisement should read, "three-fourths fewer autos recalled."

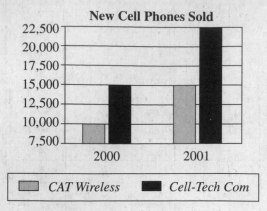

New Cell Phones Sold

Legend: ☐ CAT Wireless ■ Cell-Tech Com

5. In its TV commercials *CAT Wireless* used the graph shown above, claiming, *"CAT Wireless* sales have increased twice as fast as our nearest competitor's, *Cell-Tech Com."* What is <u>misleading</u> about this claim?

   A Both companies increased sales by 50 percent, but the bottom of the graph has been cut off to make it appear that *Cell-Tech Com* sales have increased twice as fast.

   B The claim should read, "two-thirds faster than our nearest competitor."

   C The claim should read, "50 percent faster than our nearest competitor."

   D Both companies increased sales by 50 percent, but the bottom of the graph has been cut off to make it appear that *CAT Wireless* sales have increased twice as fast.

6. A deck of cards used to play a card game has 25 red cards, 25 green cards, 25 blue cards, 25 yellow cards, and 8 wild cards. Approximately what is the theoretical probability that the first card dealt will be a wild card?

   A 7%

   B 25%

   C 75%

   D 93%

7. A vending machine contains an equal number of mini-helmets representing each of the 32 pro-football teams. What is the probability that the first mini-helmet to come out will <u>not</u> be that of the San Diego Chargers?

   A $\dfrac{1}{32}$

   B $\dfrac{1}{3}$

   C $\dfrac{1}{2}$

   D $\dfrac{31}{32}$

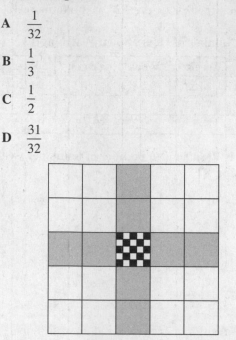

8. At the local bazaar, contestants are invited to toss quarters at a large square made up of smaller squares as shown above. If a quarter lands inside a gray square, the contestant wins a small prize. If a quarter lands inside the center checkerboard square, the contestant wins a large prize. What is the probability that a tossed quarter will land inside either a gray square or the center checkerboard square?

   A 0.04

   B 0.32

   C 0.36

   D 0.64

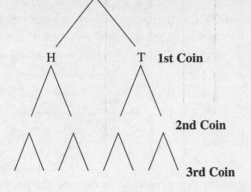

H   T   1st Coin

2nd Coin

3rd Coin

9. Valerie tosses three coins. A tree diagram similar to the one shown above can be used to represent all the possible outcomes. (It has been partially filled in.)

What is the theoretical probability that two of Valerie's coins will turn up heads, and one will come up tails?

A $\dfrac{3}{8}$

B $\dfrac{1}{4}$

C $\dfrac{1}{8}$

D $\dfrac{1}{16}$

10. Which of the following is an example of <u>dependent</u> events?

A   Flipping two coins

B   Rolling two number cubes

C   Selecting two books from a shelf that contains twenty books

D   Spinning a 1–4 spinner twice

11. Cynthia's collection of DVD movies includes four action movies, three comedies, three mysteries, two science fiction, and three horror. If she picks two movies at random without replacing them, what is the probability that she will pick two comedies?

A $\dfrac{1}{35}$

B $\dfrac{1}{25}$

C $\dfrac{1}{5}$

D $\dfrac{3}{70}$

12. Which of the following pairs describes two <u>dependent</u> events?

A   Flipping a coin that comes up heads; picking a strawberry cream candy from a box that contains 40 candies, two of which are strawberry creams

B   Drawing a queen from a standard deck of 52 cards without replacing; drawing an ace from the remaining cards

C   Spinning a 1–12 spinner and landing on a number that is a multiple of 3; picking a jelly doughnut from a box that contains twelve different doughnuts

D   Picking a grape ice pop from a box that contains three each of orange, strawberry, raspberry, and grape; rolling a number cube and getting a 1

13. Eduardo rolls two 1–6 number cubes. What is the probability that their sum will equal 12?

A $\dfrac{1}{36}$

B $\dfrac{1}{30}$

C $\dfrac{1}{18}$

D $\dfrac{1}{6}$

14. The following graph shows the world population from 1750 to 2000.

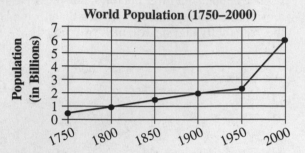

During which period did the world population have its greatest increase?

A 1800–1850

B 1850–1900

C 1900–1950

D 1950–2000

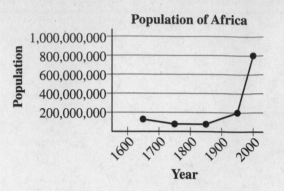

15. The above line graph shows data on the population of Africa. Which of the following statements is **not** true?

A Between 1650 and 1750, the population slightly declined.

B Between 1750 and 1850, there was little change in the population.

C Africa's population increased dramatically after 1950.

D The population in 2000 was about 800,000.

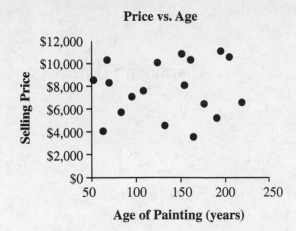

Price vs. Age

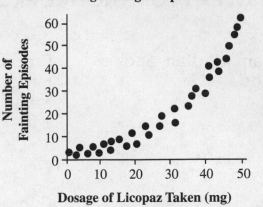

Fainting Among Licopaz Users

16. An art dealer wondered whether there was a relationship between the age of a painting and its value at auction. He gathered some data on the subject, and plotted the data on the scatter plot shown above. What can he conclude based on these data?

   A   As a painting gets older, its selling price increases.

   B   As a painting gets older, its selling price decreases.

   C   As a painting gets older, its selling price remains the same.

   D   The age of a painting and its selling price are not related.

17. A pharmaceutical company was forced to withdraw its new drug, Licopaz, from the market because some people taking it reported fainting episodes. The company did a study comparing the number of fainting episodes to the dosage of the drug taken. The results of the study are shown in the diagram above. Based on the data, what conclusions can be drawn?

   A   The dosage of Licopaz has no effect on the number of fainting episodes.

   B   As the dosage of Licopaz increases, the number of fainting episodes decreases.

   C   As the dosage of Licopaz increases, the number of fainting episodes increases.

   D   The dosage of Licopaz and the number of fainting episodes are not related.

ANSWERS TO PRACTICE PROBLEMS

Mean, Median, and Mode
1. B
2. C
3. A

Statistics
1. B

Probabilities
1. D
2. C
3. D

Compound Events
1. B

Independent and Dependent Events
1. C
2. A

Displaying Data
1. C
2. B

Scatter Plots
1. B

Chapter 12
Graphing
Statistics

This chapter combines the graphs we looked at in Chapter 10 and the statistics we looked at in Chapter 11, to let us graph statistical results.

Standard AF 3.4

"Plot the values of quantities whose ratios are always the same (e.g., cost to the number of an item, feet to inches, circumference to diameter of a circle). Fit a line to the plot and understand that the slope of a line equals the quantities."

RATIOS AND GRAPHS

You've probably already figured out that a set of points on a graph can be connected to form a line. In these questions you will be asked to calculate the slope of that line. Remember the formula for slope:

$$\frac{rise}{run} = \frac{y_2 - y_1}{x_2 - x_1}.$$

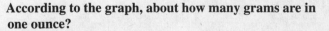

Trey found some food packages around the house. He noticed that the weight was given in both ounces and grams. A graph of his observations is shown to the left.

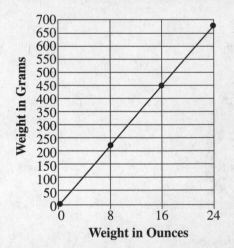

According to the graph, about how many grams are in one ounce?

A 24

B 28

C 32

D 36

Here's How to Crack It

Study the graph carefully and recall the formula for the slope of a line.

$$\text{Slope} = \frac{change\ in\ y\ value}{change\ in\ x\ value} = \frac{y_2 - y_1}{x_2 - x_1}$$

The line of this graph originates at (0, 0), which means that x_1 and y_1 are both 0. So for any other point on the line, the y-value divided by the x-value equals the slope.

$$\frac{y_2 - y_1}{x_2 - x_1} = \frac{y_2 - 0}{x_2 - 0} = \frac{y_2}{x_2}$$

Now choose any point on the line and divide the y-value by the x-value. Let's pick the point with coordinates (16, 450), because that point doesn't require us to estimate either the x- or y-values.

$$\frac{y_2}{x_2} = \frac{450}{16} = 28.125$$

Look at the answer choices. Remember, the question says "about," so the answer choice you pick just has to be the closest to the answer you got. Choice **B** is correct.

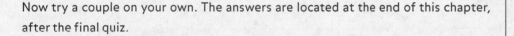

Now try a couple on your own. The answers are located at the end of this chapter, after the final quiz.

Make It Easy for Yourself

Whenever you can, choose a point on the line with an x-value that is a number that is easy to divide by.

1. **Jerome wants to purchase a large number of tickets so his family can see him play in Friday night's basketball game. The graph below shows how the total cost depends on the number of tickets purchased.**

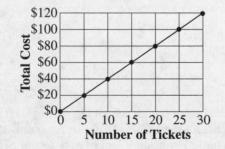

According to the graph, how much does a single ticket cost?

A $2

B $4

C $6

D $8

2. Marissa is thinking about participating in a 10 km run. However, she is having difficulty understanding how long a kilometer is. She did some research about miles and kilometers. The data she gathered are shown in the graph below.

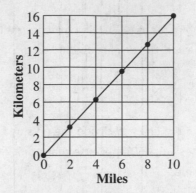

According to the data, how many kilometers are there in one mile?

A   0.5

B   1.2

C   1.6

D   3.2

CONJECTURES

These kinds of questions are about figuring out what you know based on the information you've been given. You'll be given a description of a real-life situation. Based on that information you'll need to make a hypothesis or a deduction (in other words, you have to make an educated guess). So, if they provide you with this piece of information and with that piece of information, what conclusion does that lead you to? In some cases you'll need to justify your hypothesis.

The senior class at a high school has 96 boys. Of that, 25 are on the football team, 18 are in the band, and 5 belong to both. How many senior boys do not belong to either group?

A   48

B   53

C   55

D   58

Here's How to Crack It

Read the question carefully. First, try to picture the situation described in the question. It will probably help to make a diagram that represents the situation.

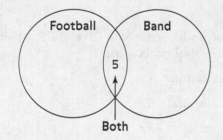

This diagram represents how many boys are involved in football and band. We need to find how many out of 96 in the entire class are *not* involved in either. But to do that, we have to figure out how many boys this diagram represents.

First, let's figure out how many boys are only on the football team. Then we'll do the same for the band.

Football (25) − Both (5) = Football only (20)
Band (18) − Both (5) = Band only (13)

Now go back to your diagram and fill in the new information.

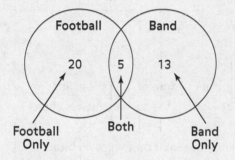

Add all the numbers up.

Football only (20) + Band only (13) + Both (5) = 38 boys

Then subtract that amount from the total number of senior boys.

96 − 38 = 58 senior boys who do not belong to either group.

Now check the answer choices. Choice **D** is correct.

You might see some questions like this on the CAHSEE that use geometry.

If $\overline{AB}$ is perpendicular to both $\overline{CD}$ and $\overline{EF}$, which of the following statements is true?

A $\overline{CD}$ intersects $\overline{EF}$

B $\overline{CD}$ is congruent to $\overline{EF}$

C $\overline{CD}$ is parallel to $\overline{EF}$

D $\overline{CD}$ is perpendicular to $\overline{EF}$

Here's How to Crack It

Read the question carefully. First, try to picture the scenario described in the question. Make a drawing of what you think it should look like.

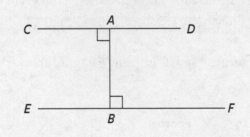

Now that you've got a clear picture of how these lines are arranged, all you have to do is use POE to decide which is the correct answer choice.

A: No, it does not appear as if they will ever intersect.

B: No, this is not necessarily true.

C: Yes, they certainly appear to be parallel.

D: No, they could not possibly be perpendicular.

Choice **C** is correct.

Now try some on your own. The answers are located at the end of this chapter, after the final quiz.

1. **If a parallelogram is not a rectangle, which statement is not true?**

   A   The opposite sides are equal in length.

   B   The opposite angles are equal in measure.

   C   The opposite sides are parallel.

   D   The diagonals are equal in length.

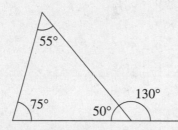

2. **Rachel noticed a pattern about the base of a triangle. She formulated a conjecture that the exterior angle formed is always equal to the sum of the two opposite angles. Which statement best justifies Rachel's conjecture?**

   A   An acute angle is always less than 90°.

   B   An obtuse angle is always greater than 90°.

   C   A right angle is always 90°.

   D   The sum of the angles of a triangle is 180°.

VERIFYING RESULTS WITH ESTIMATION

These questions ask you to solve problems by estimating rather than by precisely working them out. Round numbers to a value that is easy to work with and remember to keep your common sense with you at all times! It's important that the answer make sense, given the dimensions provided in the problem. You might want to review the sections on scale and units of measurement in Chapter 7. Remember not to put a 12-foot car in a 12-inch garage!

Standard MR 2.1

"Use estimation to verify the reasonableness of calculated results."

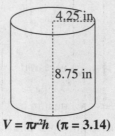

4.25 in

8.75 in

$$V = \pi r^2 h \quad (\pi = 3.14)$$

Donna used the formula $V = \pi r^2 h$ to find the volume of the cylinder above. The answer she got was 321.4 in³. She suspected that she had made an error because she had estimated the volume to be about

A $3 \times 3 \times 4 \times 9 = 324$

B $3 \times 4 \times 4 \times 9 = 432$

C $4 \times 4 \times 4 \times 9 = 576$

D $314 \times 4 \times 2 = 2{,}512$

Rounding

When you round decimals, round UP to the nearest whole number if the decimal ends in a 5 or higher; round DOWN if the decimal ends in 4 or lower.

Here's How to Crack It

Remember that estimating is all about making it easy on yourself, because you don't need an exact answer. Round off the dimensions of the cylinder to the nearest whole number, and do the same for π. Then solve for an approximation of the answer that Donna thinks she should have gotten.

Round 4.25 to 4 in
Round 8.75 to 9 in
Round 3.14 to 3

Next, plug the rounded numbers into the formula.

$V = \pi r^2 h$
$V = 3 \times 4^2 \times 9$
$V = 3 \times 16 \times 9$

Check the answer choices. Choice **B** is correct.

Using estimation, which value below is closest to the value of 2,744.8 ÷ 7.15?

A   40

B   400

C   4,000

D   40,000

Here's How to Crack It

It will help to use the best method for rounding the numbers in the question. If you round to the nearest whole number, you will get $\frac{2,745}{7} = 392.14$.

If you round 2,744.8 to the nearest ten, you will get $\frac{2,740}{7} = 391.43$.

If you round 2,744.8 to the nearest hundred, you will get $\frac{2,700}{7} = 385.71$.

Notice that the math when you round like this is not any easier than the original problem? That's because 7 doesn't go into those numbers evenly.

Instead, let's try rounding to the nearest *compatible* number—that is, the nearest numbers that divide evenly. Since we know we need to divide by 7, let's round 2,744.8 to the nearest number that is compatible with 7. 2,744.8 is close to 2,700, but 7 won't divide easily into that, will it? How about if you round in the other direction? Dividing 2,800 by 7 is easier—we can tell because 7 divides easily into 28, which is a factor of 2,800.

$$\frac{2,800}{7} = 400$$

Now check the answer choices. Choice **B** is correct.

Keep It Simple

When you're rounding, be sure to pick numbers that make the math easy for you. That's the whole point!

Now try some on your own. The answers are located at the end of this chapter, after the final quiz.

1. **By rounding, which of the following is the best estimate of 225 × 387?**

    A   80

    B   800

    C   8,000

    D   80,000

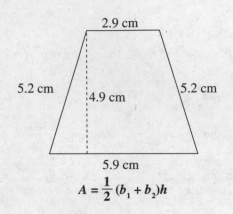

$$A = \frac{1}{2}(b_1 + b_2)h$$

2. **Using her calculator, Gail found the area of the trapezoid shown above to be 27.19 cm². She decided to double-check her figures because she had estimated the area to be approximately**

    A $\frac{1}{2} \times 9 \times 5 = 22.5$

    B $\frac{1}{2} \times 11 \times 5 = 27.5$

    C $1 \times 9 \times 5 = 45$

    D $1 \times 11 \times 5 = 55$

ESTIMATING WITH GRAPHS

The CAHSEE will also test you on how well you can read graphs and estimate projected results—results that fall outside the range of graph. You'll need to be able to draw a line based on given points and see where it would extend past the end of the graph. You'll also need to estimate the value of an unknown point on that line. Let's look at an example.

The California Department of Energy published statistics regarding statewide energy consumption. The graph below shows these data for 1997–2001.

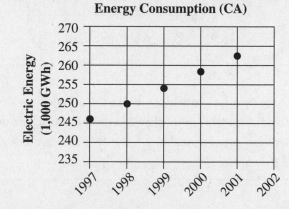

Based on these statistics, about how many thousands of gigawatt-hours of electric energy will probably be consumed in 2002?

A   259

B   266

C   270

D   275

Standard MR 2.3

"Estimate unknown quantities graphically and solve for them by using logical reasoning and arithmetic and algebraic techniques."

Here's How to Crack It

First, look to see if there is a trend in the data. You can do this by drawing a "best-fit" line on the graph (see the paragraph on "Drawing the Line" in Chapter 11 for a refresher if you need to). Extend this line until it reaches the vertical line labeled "2002."

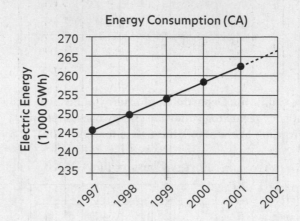

Energy Consumption (CA)

"Best Fit" Fits Everywhere

You can draw a "best-fit" line on a bar graph as well. Simply place a point at the top and center of each bar, and then connect the points.

Now look at where the best-fit line (which we also call a trend line) hits the 2002 line. It hits that line at a point a little higher than 265 on the *y*-axis, and definitely lower than 270. Now check the answer choices. B is the only choice that's in between 265 and 270, so choice **B** is correct.

Now try some on your own. The answers are located at the end of this chapter, after the final quiz.

1. The graph below shows the number of spectators at a local sports team's home games from 1993 through 1998.

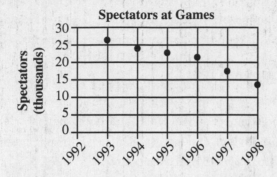

Spectators at Games

Based on these data, what was the most likely number of spectators at home games reported in 1992?

A 23,000

B 25,000

C 27,000

D 30,000

2. The U.S. Environmental Protection Agency (EPA) released statistics concerning carbon dioxide (CO_2) emissions into the air. The statistics for 1990–1999 are shown on the graph-below.

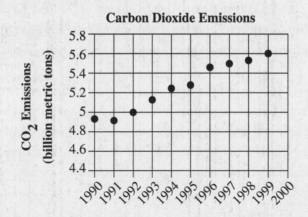

Carbon Dioxide Emissions

If the trend continues, what would the **probable** amount of CO_2 emissions have been for the year 2000?

A 5.5 billion metric tons

B 5.6 billion metric tons

C 5.7 billion metric tons

D 5.8 billion metric tons

Standard MR 2.4

"Make and test conjectures by using both inductive and deductive reasoning."

REASONING

You will be required to look at a set of statements and then use inductive and deductive reasoning to determine what conclusion could be drawn from them. Let's not dwell on those terms, but you can read about them if you want. Really, what the CAHSEE wants is to make sure you can draw proper conclusions.

That doesn't sound like math, you say! Well, no, it doesn't. You won't have to use arithmetic or algebra or geometry to answer these types of questions. But math is about more than numbers and variables and mathematical operations. When it comes down to it, math is all about reasoning from known facts—like observations and general rules—to reach a logical conclusion.

> ## What Kind of Reasoning?
> - When you use **inductive reasoning,** you observe many *specific* examples and then make a rule based on what you observed.
> - When you use **deductive reasoning** you already have a *general* rule and you use it to make a *specific* prediction.

Here's an example of reasoning.

Samantha states: I have observed that every time I throw a ball up in the air, it falls back down. Based on my observations, I predict that whenever I throw a ball up in the air, it will fall back down.

Martin states: The law of gravity states that what goes up must come down. Therefore, I predict that if I throw a ball up in the air, it will come back down.

Samantha's argument is based on her own observations; she's using inductive reasoning. Martin's argument is based on the law of gravity, a general rule he already knows, so he's using deductive reasoning. Inductive reasoning goes from the specific to the general, while deductive reasoning goes from the general to the specific.

The CAHSEE tests your reasoning skills, but you won't see a question asking you the difference between inductive and deductive reasoning. Instead, you'll see a set of statements and you'll have to choose which conclusion best fits the statements. This is kind of like the best fit lines from the previous problems, but in this case, you have to connect words instead of points to project the answer.

Let's try an example:

While getting ready to play a hockey game, Jason stated the following:

If I do not tape my stick blade, I will not be able to control the puck.

If I am not able to control the puck, I will play poorly.

If I play poorly, my team will not win the game.

Which of the following conclusions can be drawn from Jason's statements?

A If his team did not win the game, Jason was not able to control the puck.

B If he tapes his stick blade, Jason's team will win the game.

C If he is not able to control the puck, Jason did not tape his stick blade.

D If his team wins the game, Jason taped his stick blade.

Here's How to Crack It

Read the question and the statements carefully, and keep in mind the two ways of coming to a conclusion we just talked about.

None of the statements say anything about making many observations, do they? They're more like general rules that Jason believes. Therefore, we can conclude that this question is about deductive reasoning. That means we're going to use Jason's rules to come to the conclusion that makes the most logical sense. Let's work through each answer choice, using POE as we go to find the best answer.

A: If his team did not win the game, Jason was not able to control the puck.

Can you think of a reason why this statement might not be true? Perhaps Jason *was* able to control the puck, but his team *still* did not win the game because their goal-keepers played poorly. That means you can eliminate A.

Nothing But the Truth

Don't think *too* hard about reasoning questions! Stick to what you know *must* be true from the statements.

B: If he tapes his stick blade, Jason's team will win the game.

Can you think of a reason the team could have lost, even though Jason taped his stick blade? Again, maybe their goalkeeper played poorly. Therefore, you can eliminate **B**.

C: If he is not able to control the puck, Jason did not tape his stick blade.

Perhaps Jason *did* tape his stick blade, but he *still* was not able to control the puck. Maybe the ice was poor and the puck kept bouncing. Thus, you can eliminate **C**.

D: If his team wins the game, Jason taped his stick blade.

For this statement, it helps to work backward through the rules that Jason gave us. If Jason's team won the game, according to Jason's statements, what had to happen? Jason had to play well, because if he played poorly, his team wouldn't win, right? If he played well, then he was able to control the puck, according to his second statement. And if he was able to control the puck, then he taped his stick blade. So if he taped his stick blade, then he controlled the puck, he played well, and his team won. **D** is the correct choice.

———————————○———————————

Now try some on your own. The answers are located at the end of this chapter, after the final quiz.

1. **Before leaving for work one morning, Mr. Grant stated the following to himself:**

    If I do not take the roast beef out of the freezer, it will not thaw in time.

    If the roast beef does not thaw, I will not be able to cook it.

    If I am not able to cook it, we will not have roast beef for dinner.

    Which of the following conclusions can be drawn from Mr. Grant's statements?

    A   If they do not have roast beef for dinner, it did not thaw in time.

    B   If Mr. Grant takes it out of the freezer, they will have roast beef for dinner.

    C   If they have roast beef for dinner, Mr. Grant took it out of the freezer.

    D   If it does not thaw in time, Mr. Grant did not take the roast beef out of the freezer.

2. **Tyeisha's first two quiz grades in Sociology were C and C−. Which of the following conjectures is the result of inductive reasoning?**

    A   The final exam counts for 25% of this course's grade.

    B   Late papers will be reduced one letter grade per day late.

    C   *The Grapes of Wrath* is required reading for this course.

    D   I will most likely get no higher than a C in this course.

GENERALIZING RESULTS

These questions require you to apply a demonstrated principle to a new problem. You will be shown a problem that has already been solved, as well as the strategy that was used to solve it. You will then apply that strategy to a new problem. That's what we mean by "applying a demonstrated principle." Let's take a look at an example.

Standard MR 3.3

"Develop generalizations of the results obtained and the strategies used and apply them to new problem situations."

Hector solved a problem like the one shown below using the formula *distance* = *speed* × *time* ($d = st$). He reasoned that the time (t) would be the same for two trains. He let d represent the distance one train covered, and ($n - d$) represent the distance the other train covered (n = total distance for both trains). Use the same strategy to solve the problem below.

Train A leaves Los Angeles heading north to San Francisco at a speed of 80 miles per hour. At the same time, Train B leaves San Francisco heading south to Los Angeles at a speed of 50 miles per hour. If the total distance between the two cities is 390 miles, when will the two trains pass each other?

A 1 hour after leaving their respective cities

B 2 hours after leaving their respective cities

C 3 hours after leaving their respective cities

D 4 hours after leaving their respective cities

Here's How to Crack It

First, read the entire question carefully. Then, go back and read the first paragraph again. Make sure you understand how Hector solved his problem. Now, let's list the information that we have about the problem we have to solve.

Train A: speed = 80 mph
Train B: speed = 50 mph
Total distance = 390 mile

Next, we'll use the formula that Hector used, $d = st$, to write an equation for each train. Let d represent the distance Train A will be from L.A. when it meets Train B, and let ($390 - d$) represent the distance from San Francisco for Train B.

Train A: $d = 80t$

Train B: $390 - d = 50t$

Next, add the two equations, and then solve for t. We can do this by stacking the equations on top of each other so the equal signs are aligned, and adding the like terms together:

$$d = 80t$$

$$390 - d = 50t$$

$$390 = 80t + 50t$$

Now solve for t:

$$390 = 130t$$

$$3 = t$$

Go a Little Farther

Once you know the time, you can find the distance each train traveled by using same formula: $d = st$. In this problem Train A is $d = st$, or $d = 80 \times 3$, which is 240 miles. Train B is $d = st$, or $d = 50 \times 3$, which is 150 miles. The two trains will pass each other 3 hours after leaving their respective cities at a point that is 240 miles north of L.A. and 150 miles south of San Francisco.

The two trains will pass each other 3 hours after leaving their respective cities. Now check the answer choices. Choice **C** is correct.

Now try some on your own. The answers are located at the end of this chapter, after the final quiz.

1. **Nancy solved a problem similar to the one shown below. She let A represent the adult's age and C represent the child's age. She set up two equations, one for now, and one for n years from now. She then solved the system of equations. Use the same strategy to solve the problem below.**

   Michele's grandmother is now eleven times older than Michele. In five years her grandmother will be six times older than Michele will be. How old is Michele now?

   A 4 years old

   B 5 years old

   C 6 years old

   D 7 years old

2. Adam solved a problem like the one that follows. He let x represent the number of one type of coin, and used nx and $(n \pm x)$ to represent the others. He then multiplied each expression by the value of the coin it represented. Finally he wrote an equation adding all the products to equal the total value. Use the same strategy to solve Zelda's problem.

Zelda has 14 coins in her purse. She has twice as many nickels (N) as she has quarters (Q). The rest of the coins are dimes (D). If all the coins total $1.55, how many of each coin does Zelda have?

A   2Q, 8D, & 4N

B   3Q, 6D, & 5N

C   3Q, 5D, & 6N

D   4Q, 2D, & 8N

3. Ellen solved a problem similar to the one shown below. She let x represent the smaller number and $(n - x)$ represent the larger number (where n = the sum of the two numbers). Then she set up an equation showing how the two numbers are related. Apply the same strategy to solve the problem below.

The sum of two numbers is 21. The larger number is three more than twice the smaller number. What are the two numbers?

A   4 & 11

B   5 & 16

C   6 & 15

D   8 & 13

CHAPTER 12: GRAPHING STATISTICS FINAL QUIZ

Answers can be found on page 284–285.

1. Carlos's mother keeps a record of how many miles she travels and how much gasoline she uses. Carlos helped his mother construct a graph (shown below) of the data she recorded.

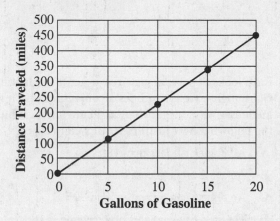

Based on the data in the graph, about how many miles does Carlos's mother travel per gallon of gasoline?

A   18

B   20

C   22

D   24

2. The density of a substance is its mass divided by its volume ($D = \dfrac{M}{V}$). Liquid mercury has a density of 13.5 g/ml (grams per milliliter). In the graph below, what would be the x and y values of the point designated by the arrow?

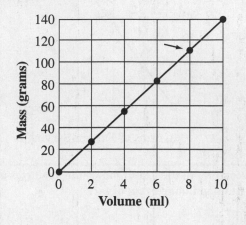

A   (8, 105)

B   (8, 108)

C   (105, 8)

D   (108, 8)

3. The graph below shows the relationship between the number of calories from fat contained in food and the number of grams of fat per serving.

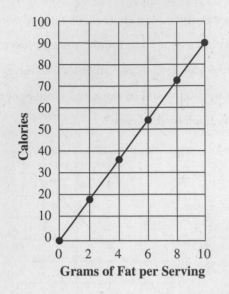

According to the graph, how many calories are contained in one gram of fat?

A   9

B   10

C   18

D   20

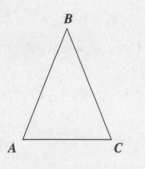

4. In △ABC ∠A is congruent to ∠C. Which statement is then true?

A   △ABC is an equilateral triangle.

B   △ABC is an isosceles triangle.

C   △ABC is an obtuse triangle.

D   △ABC is a scalene triangle.

5. For dessert, Angela and Karla each ate 1 piece of cake, and Vincenzo ate 2. If $\frac{3}{4}$ of the cake is left, into how many pieces was the cake cut?

A   4

B   8

C   12

D   16

6. Raffi looks at several pictures of acute angles and right angles. He formulates a conjecture that a right angle is always larger than an acute angle. Which of the following best justifies Raffi's conjecture?

A   All angles are less than 180°.

B   An acute angle is less than 90°.

C   An obtuse angle is more than 90°.

D   The sum of the angles of a triangle is 180°.

7. Of the 27 seniors on the girls' soccer team, 10 are taking AP Biology, 15 are taking AP English, and 6 are taking both. How many of the 27 girls are taking neither?

A   2

B   4

C   6

D   8

8. If the length of a rectangular prism is tripled, its height is doubled, and its width remains the same, which of the following statements is true?

   A The volume is double that of the original prism.

   B The volume is triple that of the original prism.

   C The volume is six times that of the original prism.

   D The volume is eight times that of the original prism.

9. Amy looked at several diagrams of quadrilaterals. She stated that if you know the measure of three angles in a quadrilateral, you can find the fourth angle. Which of the following best justifies Amy's statement?

   A An acute angle is less than 90°.

   B An obtuse angle is more than 90°.

   C All quadrilaterals have 4 sides.

   D The sum of the angles of a quadrilateral is 360°.

10. Using estimation, which of the following is closest to the value of $4,486.8 \div 9.2$?

   A 50

   B 500

   C 5,000

   D 50,000

6.75 in

$A = \pi r^2$

11. Using the formula $A = \pi r^2$, Andre calculated the area of the above circle to be 307.55 in². He wondered whether he had made an error, because he knew the right answer should be approximately

   A $3 \times 3.5 \times 3.5 = 36.75$

   B $9 \times 7 = 63$

   C $3 \times 7 \times 7 = 147$

   D $7 \times 7 \times 7 = 343$

12. Which of the following is the best estimate of 518×29.3?

   A 150

   B 1,500

   C 15,000

   D 150,000

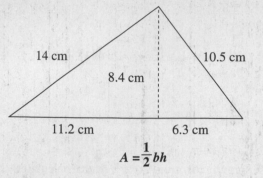

$$A = \frac{1}{2}bh$$

13. Heather used her calculator to find the area of the triangle shown above and got an answer of 91.875 cm². She recognized that she must have done something wrong because, before doing the calculations, she estimated that the area should be about

A $\frac{1}{2} \times 18 \times 8 = 72$

B $\frac{1}{2} \times 18 \times 14 = 126$

C $1 \times 18 \times 8 = 144$

D $1 \times 18 \times 14 = 252$

14. Using estimation, which of the following is closest to the value of 676.2 ÷ 39.5?

A   17

B   170

C   1,700

D   17,000

15. The graph below shows the average fuel rate, in miles per gallon, for passenger cars in the U.S. for 1994–2000.

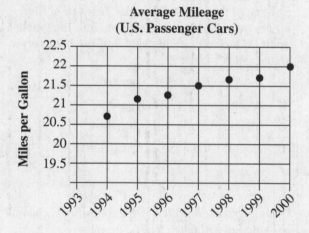

Based on the information in the graph, the average miles per gallon for-passenger cars in 1993 was most likely about

A   20.0

B   20.5

C   21.0

D   21.5

16. The U.S. Department of Labor has kept statistics on the number of working women since 1900. The graph below shows these statistics in 10-year intervals.

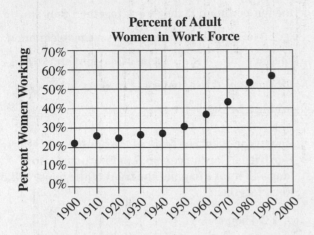

Percent of Adult Women in Work Force

According to the graph, what would have been the <u>probable</u> percentage of women working in the year 2000?

A   52%

B   55%

C   58%

D   62%

17. Which statement is the result of deductive reasoning?

A   Winter was mild this year, and in past years, the orange crop has been poor whenever the winter was mild, so the orange crop will not be good.

B   The orange crop needs at least a week of temperatures below freezing to be good, and this winter the temperature never went below freezing, so the orange crop will not be good.

C   Skiing was excellent this winter, and in winters that provided good skiing conditions, the orange crop was good, so the orange crop will be good.

D   Over the past twenty years, the orange crop has never been good after a mild winter, and this winter was mild, so the orange crop will not be good.

18. While putting gasoline in her car, Kristen stated the following:

If I do not add "dry gas" to my gas tank, the gas line will freeze.

If the gas line freezes, the car will not start.

If the car does not start, I will not get to school.

Which conclusion can be drawn?

A   If she gets to school, Kristen added "dry gas" to her gas tank.

B   If Kristen did not get to school, the gas line froze.

C   If she adds "dry gas" to her gas tank, Kristen will get to school.

D   If the gas line freezes, Kristen did not add "dry gas" to her gas tank.

19. Seth solved a problem like the one shown below. He let x represent the smallest angle, and $ax \pm b$ represent the other two angles. He then wrote an equation such that the sum of all the expressions equaled 180°. Use the same strategy to solve the problem below.

The middle angle of a triangle is five degrees less than three times the smallest angle. The largest angle is ten degrees more than three times the smallest angle. What is the measure of the smallest angle?

A   25°

B   30°

C   35°

D   40°

20. Georgia solved a problem similar to the one below. She let x represent the smaller side of the rectangle, and $(nx \pm b)$ represent the larger side. Then she used the formula for perimeter ($P = 2l + 2w$) to set up an equation. Use the same method to solve the problem below.

The length of a rectangle is three feet less than twice its width. If the perimeter is 48 feet, what are the dimensions of the rectangle?

A   8 ft $\times$ 6 ft

B   12 ft $\times$ 9 ft

C   15 ft $\times$ 9 ft

D   16 ft $\times$ 8 ft

21. Samantha let x represent the number of child tickets sold, and $(n - x)$ represent the number of adult tickets sold (n = total number of tickets sold). She then multiplied each expression by the cost for that type of ticket. Finally she wrote an equation in which the sum of the expressions equaled the total amount collected. Apply the same strategy to solve the problem below.

For a recent school play, 372 tickets were sold and $1,952 was collected. If an adult ticket cost $6.00 and the cost of a child ticket cost $3.50, how many child tickets were sold?

A   80

B   112

C   205

D   260

22. If a person can do a job in x hours, then he or she can do $\frac{1}{x}$ of the job per hour. If another person can do the job in y hours, then he or she can do $\frac{1}{y}$ of the job per hour. If they work together, they can do $\frac{1}{x} + \frac{1}{y}$ of the job per hour. Tina set up an equation so that $(\frac{1}{x} + \frac{1}{y}) \times t = 1$ (the whole job) and solved for the time, t. Use that same strategy to solve the problem below.

Robyn can paint the front of the house in six hours. Her friend Gordon can do it in four hours. How long will it take to paint the front of the house if they work together?

A   2.4 hours

B   3.2 hours

C   5 hours

D   10 hours

ANSWERS TO PRACTICE PROBLEMS

Ratios and Graphs
1. B
2. C

Verifying Results with Estimation
1. D
2. A

Inductive and Deductive Reasoning
1. C
2. D

Conjecture
1. D
2. D

Estimating With Graphs
1. C
2. C

Generalizing Results
1. B
2. C
3. C

Chapter 13
Answers and
Explanations to
Chapter Quizzes

CHAPTER 5

Arithmetic Final Quiz

1. **C** If you divide by an integer, unless the integer is 1, the number must get smaller. If you divide 1 by 100, you get 0.01 (the decimal moves two places to the left). If you divide 10 by 100 you get 0.1 (the decimal still moves two places to the left, get it?). So the answer must be C.

2. **D** Remember, a negative times a negative is a positive. A negative times a positive is a negative. If you raise a negative to an odd power (i.e., cube it), you are multiplying a negative times a negative (which becomes a positive) times another negative. So in the end, your result is a negative. So the answer must be D.

3. **C** If you multiply 10 by 0, you get 0. If you multiply 10 by 1 you get 10. So the answer must be a number somewhere between 0 and 10, which is choice C.

4. **D** If you divide the fractions, (denominator into numerator), you get a decimal, right? Multiply that decimal by 100 to get the equivalent percentage: $\frac{5}{8} = 0.625$. $0.625 \times 100 = 62.5\%$, and is therefore equivalent. D is correct.

5. **C** Since this problem only asks you to approximate, you can round 83 to 80 and 210 to 200 to make the math easier. To figure out percentage, it will help to write this like a proportion: $\frac{80}{200}$, which reduces to $\frac{2}{5}$ ($\frac{80}{200} = \frac{8}{20} = \frac{2}{5}$). Divide the numerator by the denominator and multiply by 100 to get the percentage: $\frac{2}{5} = .4$, which is 40%.

6. **A** This one is easy! Just put 15 over 100 and reduce. $\frac{15}{100} = \frac{3}{20}$.

7. **C** The total farm income in California increased by $6 billion dollars, from $20 billion to $26 billion, right? In order to figure out the percent change, just divide the difference by the original and multiply by 100. In this case, don't even worry about the billion part: 6 divided by 20 equals .3, which is 30%, answer choice C.

8. **B** You can figure out this percent change the same way you worked the last problem: Put the difference over the original value and multiply by 100 to find the percent change. So $1,173 - 1,020 = 153$. $153 \div 1,020 = 0.15$. 0.15 is 15%, answer choice B.

9. **C** You've probably guessed it by now! This is just like the previous two. Put the difference over the original value and multiply by 100 to find the percent change. Except you know what? These are some huge numbers. Dividing 4,172,000 (the amount the population increased) by 29,800,000 would take far too long. Let's set up a proportion to reduce these numbers to something manageable, but that will still give us the correct percent change: We can write our proportion like this: $\frac{4,172,000}{29,800,000}$, which reduces to $\frac{4,172}{29,800}$, which becomes $\frac{1,043}{7,450}$. That's still a really difficult number, isn't it? You could divide 1,043 by 7,450 longhand, and get 0.14, which works out to 14%, and you'd be right. But if you want to save some time, you could round and get approximations: 1,043 becomes 1,000, and 7,450 becomes 7,400. Now your proportion is $\frac{1,000}{7,400}$, which reduces to $\frac{10}{74}$, which reduces still further to $\frac{5}{37}$. That's a much easier number to divide, isn't it? Your result is something like 0.135135 and so on, which rounds up to 14%. Either of these methods will get you the correct answer, which is C.

10.   B   That's right! You're going to solve this just like the last three. Put the difference over the original value and multiply by 100 to find the percent change. Except this one doesn't even require you to do a lot of math. It should be pretty obvious that the amount of the senior citizen discount—$3.50— is 10% of $35.00. If you need to be sure, though, just do the math: $3.50 ÷ $35.00 = 0.10 = 10%, answer choice B.

11.   D   Look for the common denominator. What do 4 and 7 both divide into evenly? If you said 28, you're on the right track. You would multiply the fraction on the left by 4, to make the denominator 28, and the fraction on the right by 7, to get a denominator of 28. Remember that whatever we do to the numerator we must also do the denominator. So if you multiply the first denominator by 4, then you have to multiply the numerator as well, so that the value of the fraction does not change.

12.   B   The prime factors of 12 are 2,2, and 3. The prime factors of 16 are 2, 2, 2, and 2. So the lowest common denominator for both of the fractions in this problem is $2 \times 2 \times 2 \times 2 \times 3$, which is $2^4 \times 3$.

13.   A   Look for the common denominator. Remember that if you multiply the first denominator by 4, (the common denominator here is 24) then you have to multiply the numerator as well, so that the value of the fraction does not change.

14.   B   Look for the LCD here. It's 12, which is $2 \times 2 \times 3$.

15.   C   You don't even need to find the LCD here. You just need to find the prime factors of each denominator. The prime factors of 10 are 2 and 5. The prime factors of 8 are 2, 2, and 2. Together, the prime factors of the denominators can be expressed as $2 \times 2 \times 2 \times 5$, which is $2^3 \times 5$.

16.   B   Remember, when multiplying like bases, add the exponents. $5^2 \times 5^5 = 5^{2+5} = 5^7$.

17.   D   When *dividing* like bases, *subtract* the exponents: $4^3 \div 4^6 = 4^{3-6} = 4^{-3}$.

18.   C   When multiplying like bases, add the exponents: $2^5 \times 2^{-3} = 2^{5+(-3)} = 2^2$.

19.   B   When multiplying like bases, add the exponents. So $5^3 \times 5^{-4} = 5^{-1}$. When the exponent is negative, its base goes into the denominator, and when the exponent is 1, we don't have to write it. (Note that answer choice C is just a confusing way of writing 5.)

20.   B   When multiplying like bases, add the exponents: $3^{-5} \times 3^3 = 3^{-2}$.

21.   B   When dividing like bases, subtract the exponents: $4^{-2} \div 4^4 = 4^{-4-2} = 4^{-6}$.

22.   B   Separate the numerator into its prime factors—so that it will look like the denominator—and then cancel out like bases in the numerator and denominator: $\dfrac{6^4}{2^3 \times 3^3} = \dfrac{2^4 \times 3^4}{2^3 \times 3^3} = 2 \times 3 = 6$

23.   D   Cancel out like terms in the numerator and denominator and then combine terms. $\dfrac{2^4 \times 7^5}{7^3} - \dfrac{5^3 \times 3^4}{5^2}$ becomes $2^4 \times 7^2 - 5 \times 3^4$. Now just do the math—remember the order of operations! $2^4 \times 7^2 - 5 \times 3^4$ becomes $(16 \times 49) - (5 \times 81) = 784 - 405 = 379$.

24. **D** Separate numbers into their prime factors, and then cancel out like bases in the numerator and denominator and combine terms. Remember, a negative exponent can be written as a positive exponent in the denominator...so a negative exponent in the denominator can flipped, and turned into a positive exponent in the numerator. Which means that right away we can rewrite $\frac{3^{-2} \times 2^{-3}}{6^{-1} \times 2^{-4}}$ as $\frac{6 \times 2^4}{3^2 \times 2^3}$. This reduces to $\frac{2 \times 3 \times 2^4}{3^2 \times 2^3}$, which becomes $\frac{2 \times 2}{3}$, or $\frac{4}{3}$, or $1\frac{1}{3}$.

25. **B** Separate numbers into their prime factors, and then cancel out like bases in the numerator and denominator and combine terms. In other words, $\frac{4^2 \times 2^3}{2^4}$ becomes $\frac{4^2}{2}$, which is $\frac{16}{2}$ = 8. Then $\frac{6^2 \times 3^2}{3^4}$ becomes $\frac{6^2}{3^2}$, which is $\frac{36}{9}$, which is 4. From that point on, it's easy! 8 − 4 = 4.

26. **C** $\frac{2^4 \times 3^3}{9^1 \times 2^2}$ can be rewritten as $\frac{3^3 \times 2^4}{3^2 \times 2^2}$. This reduces to 3×2^2, which becomes 3×2^2, which is $3 \times 4 = 12$.

27. **A** Remember, any base with an exponent of 0 is equal to 1. So $\frac{4^{-1} \times 7^0}{2^{-3}}$ becomes $\frac{1}{4^1 \times 2^{-3}}$, which is also $\frac{1}{2^2 \times 2^{-3}}$, which equals $\frac{1}{2^{-1}}$ = 2. $\frac{2^5 \times 8^4}{8^5} = \frac{2^5}{8} = \frac{32}{8} = 4$. Then 2 + 4 = 6.

28. **B** Let's look at some common squares. $20^2 = 400$, so the number must be bigger than 20. That eliminates A. $25^2 = 625$, so the number must be less than that, which eliminates C and D. The number must between 25 and 30, so the answer must be B.

29. **C** Let's try some of the squares in the answers. Starting in the middle will give us a lot of information. $38^2 = 1,444$, so the number must be bigger than that, which eliminates A and B. $39^2 = 1,521$, so the answer must be C.

30. **B** Let's look at some common squares. $40^2 = 1,600$, so the number must be less than that. $35^2 = 1,225$, so the answer is B.

31. **C** Let's try some of the squares in the answers. Starting in the middle will give us a lot of information, just like in problem 29. $28^2 = 784$, so the number must be bigger than that. $29^2 = 841$, so the answer is C.

32. **A** Let's look at some common squares again. $20^2 = 400$, so the number must be less than that, which means answer must be A.

33. **B** Let's Plug In some of the squares in the answers. Again, we'll start in the middle to see if we can eliminate any answer choices right off the bat. $32^2 = 1,024$, so the number must be smaller than 32. $31^2 = 961$, so the answer is B.

34. **D** Remember that absolute value is the distance from 0 on a number line. T is the point furthest from 0.

35. **D** Absolute value is always stated positively, so the answer is D.

36. **D** Absolute value is always positive, so this expression becomes |2|.

37. **C** Absolute value is always stated positively, so the answer is C.

38. **C** Don't get confused by the W at −9! Absolute value is the distance from 0. Y is the closest to 0, so the answer is C.

CHAPTER 6

Applied Arithmetic Final Quiz

1. **C** 20% of $70 is 14. 70 × .2 = 14. But don't make the mistake of picking A! You've got to subtract $14 from $70 to get the sale price, which is $56.

2. **B** 25% of 1,100 is 275. $1,100 − $275 = $825.

3. **C** Remember *rate* × *time* = *distance*. If we plug our numbers into the formula, we get 225 × t = 300, so $t = \dfrac{300}{225} = \dfrac{4}{3}$.

4. **D** In this case, *rate* × *time* = *amount*. If we plug our numbers into the formula, we get 4 × 12 = 48, so our answer is D.

5. **C** We're using our *rate* × *time* = *distance* formula again. Plugging In our numbers gives us 1,440 × 1.5 = 2,160, which is C.

6. **D** This is another amount problem. If we plug into the formula, we get 0.5t = 20, so t = 40.

7. **B** The key here is to convert the 20 minutes to $\dfrac{1}{3}$ of an hour (since 20 min $\times \dfrac{1\,\text{hour}}{60\,\text{min}} = \dfrac{1}{3}$). If we plug into the formula, we get $r \times \dfrac{1}{3} = 8$, so r = 24 mph.

8. **C** Here we want to set up a proportion. $\dfrac{36}{100} = \dfrac{x}{250}$. If we cross multiply we get 9,000 = 100x, so x = 90g.

9. **C** Set up the equations. The fee for the snowmobile is 50 + 8.75h = 93.75. If we solve for h we get 8.75h = 43.75, so therefore h = 5.

10. **D** The key here is to add Tracy, Kevin, and Irene's rates to get the combined rate of all three working together. So 108 + 96 + 84 = 288. The area of the yard they need to sod is 36 × 48 = 1,728. So using our rate formula, *rate* × *time* = *amount*, we can plug in the number and solve for time. 288t = 1,728, so t = 6.

11. **A** Here we are looking at a variation on the percent mixture problem. Ms. Worthington needs 6 lb at $6/lb. So let's set up an equation, with x denoting the regular coffee, which means that (6 − x) will stand for the Arabican coffee: 4x$ + $10(6 − x) = $6(6). We'll use the distributive property to simplify the equation to 4x + 60 −10x = 36, which reduces to -6x + 60 = 36, and therefore -6x = -24. Divide both sides by -6 and we get x = 4. But what was the question again? How many pounds of *each* coffee were necessary. Well, Ms. Worthington needs 6 lb total, and we know that she has 4 lb of regular coffee, so 2 lb of the Arabican coffee are required, which makes the answer A.

12. **D** The key to this problem is to break it down into pieces. The first car will cover 80 miles in the first two hours (giving it an 80-mile head start). The second car will gain 20 miles every hour because it travels at 60 mph and the first car only travels at 40 mph (60 − 40 = 20). Therefore it will take 4 hours for the second car to close the 80-mile gap.

13. **A** Start with what you know. Maria is 9, and is 3 years younger than Lourdes, who must therefore be 12. Lourdes is 4 times as old as Ricky, so set up an equation: 12 = 4R (for Ricky), and therefore R = 3.

14. **D** The key here is to add 12 hours to the P.M. times; this gives the so-called "Army Time" (which uses a 24-hour clock), and then subtract the A.M. time for each flight. For instance, the flight leaving at 7:45 A.M. is getting in at 1:50 P.M., which would be 13:50. Then it's easy to see that the flight took 6:05, six hours and five minutes. Similarly, the flight that left at 9:30 A.M. and got in at 15:40 (i.e. 3:40 P.M.) lasted 6:10, six hours and ten minutes. The flight that left at 10:45 and got in at 16:35 only lasted 5:50. And lastly the flight that left at 11:55 and got in at 18:10 lasted 6:15, and was thus the longest flight.

15. **A** Here you must focus only on what's relevant. The number of balls per box is not relevant to the question, which was which container takes up less space. The dimensions of the container, not the number of balls, determine the amount of space it takes up.

16. **C** The key here is to try to see the pattern. How are we getting from one number to the next? From 1 to 1 to 2 to 3...wait, we're just adding the previous two numbers to get the next number. Then 13 + 21 = 34 and we have our answer. (Note: This is a special mathematical sequence called the Fibonacci sequence, which was featured in *The DaVinci Code*.)

CHAPTER 7

Measurements and Scientific Math Final Quiz

1. **C** To expand scientific notation, first remember that $10^2 = 100$. (You can easily calculate powers of 10—the exponent tells you how many 0's to put after the 1.) So $4.7 \times 100 = 470$.

2. **B** Scientific notation is always expressed as a number with only one digit to the left of the decimal, multiplied by a power of 10. For 0.000075, it will be a negative power of 10 (remember, all numbers less than 1 are expressed in scientific notation with a negative exponent). To calculate the power of 10 necessary, count how many places to the right we need to move the decimal to get 7.5×10^x. In this case we need to move the decimal 5 places, so the answer would be 7.5×10^{-5}.

3. **D** To expand scientific notation, first remember that $10^3 = 1,000$. So $1.6 \times 1,000 = 1,600$.

4. **C** If you remember that scientific notation is always expressed as a number with *only one* digit to the left of the decimal, you should notice right away that for this problem C is the only answer that could possibly be in scientific notation. But if you want to be absolutely sure this is correct, you can do the math: We know that we have to end up with 5.28×10^x. So we take 5,280 and count how many places to the left we need to move the decimal; this number is the number of the exponent. We need to move the decimal 3 places to the left, so the answer is 5.28×10^3.

5. **D** The exponent tells us how many places we need to move the decimal; the negative exponent tells us to move it to the left. So the answer would be $3.2 \times 10^{-2} = 0.032$.

6. **C** We know that we have to end up with 8.3×10^x. So we count how many places to the right we need to move the decimal; this number is the number of the exponent. We need to move the decimal 4 places to the right which also means that the exponent will also be negative, so the answer is C.

7. **B** The exponent tells us how many places we need to move the decimal; the positive exponent tells us to move it to the right. So the answer would be $9.1 \times 10^5 = 910,000$.

8. **D** We know that we have to end up with 2.5×10^x. So we count how many places to the left we need to move the decimal; this number is the number of the exponent. We need to move the decimal 6 places to the left, so the answer is D.

9. **C** Multiply the conversion factor (3.28 feet) by the distance to be converted (400 meters). So in this case that would be $3.28 \times 400 = 1{,}312$.

10. **D** You can solve this problem the same way. Multiply the conversion factor, 1.4 N-m by the amount of torque to be converted, 196 lb-ft. $1.4 \times 196 = 274.4$.

11. **C** Convert everything into one unit of measurement; then it will be easier to compare. Let's use square feet. If we imagine that the 12-square-yard piece is 1 yd × 12 yd and we convert those to feet, since there are 3 feet per yard we would get a piece that was 3 ft × 36 ft, which is 108 sq. ft. Note that the conversion for square yards into square feet is 9 (3^2), not 3! (So you could also have multiplied 12 by 9 to get 108.) Similarly, the conversion factor from square inches into square feet is $\frac{1}{144}$ not $\frac{1}{12}$, so that 15,840 sq. in. becomes $\frac{15{,}840}{144} = 110$ sq. ft. , so the answer is C.

12. **B** Multiply the conversion factor by the distance to be converted. So in this case that would be $0.62 \times 10 = 6.2$.

13. **D** Multiply the conversion factor by the amount to be converted. So in this case that would be $3.79 \times 12 = 45.8$, so the nearest answer is D.

14. **A** Multiply the conversion factor by the amount to be converted. Since the scale is 1 cm = 0.3 m, in this case that would be $0.3 \times 12.1 = 3.63$. Be sure your answer is reasonable—121 m would be longer than a football field!

15. **B** Since the scale is 1 in = 16 ft, our formula would be 16 ft. × 4.5 = 72.

16. **C** Since the scale is 1 in = 20 ft, in this case our formula would be $20 \times 4.25 = 85$.

17. **C** Take the equation that you've been given and plug in the given values. Since $D = \frac{M}{V}$, we get 10.5 g/cm³ $= \frac{M}{4cm^3}$. Solving for M we get (10.5 g/cm³)(4 cm³) = M and therefore M = 42 g. (Note that when you multiply the units together the cm³ cancels out, leaving g.)

18. **C** Take the equation that you've been given and plug in the given values. Since $E = P \times t$, we get E = 1.5 k-w × 30 hours, and so the answer is 45 kilowatt-hours.

19. **C** Multiply the rate by the time, given the formula *rate × time = amount*. So we get 360 cu. ft/min × 20 min = 7,200 cu. ft. Remember that the minutes cancel out.

20. **D** Set up a proportion. $\frac{24\ mi}{1\ gal} = \frac{X\ mi}{8\ gal}$. If we solve for X we get 192 miles.

21. **C** Picture a square inch, i.e. a square measuring one inch on each side. If we convert each side of that square to cm, using the formula given (1 in. = 2.54 cm) we get a square measuring 2.54 cm on each side. The area of that square would thus be 6.45 cm² ($2.54 \times 2.54 = 6.45$).

22. **C** The conversion of square yards to square feet would be $\frac{1\,sq.\,yd}{9\,sq.\,ft}$. So 43,560 sq. ft $\times \frac{1\,sq.\,yd}{9\,sq.\,ft}$ = 4,840 square yards.

23. **A**   It's easiest to convert the units into yards and then find the volume. Since the conversion is $\frac{1\,yd}{3\,ft}$, the new dimensions of the box would be $\frac{2}{3}\,yd \times 1\,yd \times 3\,yd$. When we use the formula $V = lwh$, we get a volume of 2.

24. **C**   The conversion of square feet to square inches would be $\frac{144\,in^2}{1\,ft^2}$. So 4 sq. ft $\times \frac{144\,in^2}{1\,ft^2} = 576$ sq. in.

25. **D**   Here we are given the conversion factor of the volume, so it's easiest to find the volume first and then do the conversion. The volume is $7.5 \times 14 = 30$. Since the conversion is $\frac{16.38cm^3}{1\,in}$, the new volume of the box would be 30 in³ $\times \frac{16.38cm^3}{1\,in^3} = 491.4$ in³.

CHAPTER 8

Algebra Final Quiz

1. **C**   The key skill here is turning words into math. Take the number (i.e., n), divide by 4 (i.e., $\frac{n}{4}$) then add three to the result and you get 8 (i.e., $\frac{n}{4} + 3 = 8$).

2. **A**   So H is (i.e. "$H =$") two more than (i.e. "$2 +$") twice the number of C (i.e., $2 \cdot C$). Put it all together and you have $H = 2 + 2 \cdot C$. This is just A shuffled around a bit.

3. **D**   If you multiply a number (n) by 5 ($5n$) and then subtract 7 (i.e. $5n - 7$) the result is 23: $5n - 7 = 23$.

4. **C**   So d is ($d =$) eight times the number of wolves, w (i.e. $8 \cdot w$). Put it all together and you get $d = 8 \cdot w$, which is just C re-shuffled.

5. **D**   When 1 is added ($1 +$) two times number ($2n$) the result is 15 ($= 15$). Put it all together and you get D.

6. **D**   Here we have to follow PEMDAS. There's nothing inside the parentheses we can do so we move on to exponents. We must use FOIL (First, Outer, Inner, Last) on the binomial. $(5x - 3)^2 = (5x - 3)(5x - 3) = 25x^2 - 15x + 9$, which is then multiplied by 2, so $2(25x^2 - 15x + 9) = 50x^2 - 60x + 18$, which is D.

7. **A**   There are no exponents and nothing inside the parentheses that we can combine, so it's time to multiply. Distributing the 4 and the -3 gives us $8x + 4 - 22 - 3x + 15$, and then we can combine terms to get $5x - 3$. Be sure to distribute the negative!

8. **C**   First we start with the exponents, since there's nothing in the parentheses we can combine. FOIL gives us $4(y^2 - 6y + 9) + 5(2y - 6)$. Then we distribute and get $4y^2 - 24y + 36 + 10y - 30$. Combining like terms leaves us with $4y^2 - 14y + 6$.

9. **C**   Here there is nothing to do in the parentheses and no exponents that need to be distributed, so we'll go straight to distributing the negative (we can think of it as multiplying the parentheses by -1), giving us $3a^2 - 5 - a^2 - a + 3$. Now we can combine terms to get $2a^2 - a - 2$.

10. **A**   Let's start with the exponent. $(x - 2)(x - 2) = (x^2 - 4x + 4)$. Now we'll distribute the -2 to get $9x^2 - 8x + 4 - 2x^2 + 8x - 8$. When we combine terms we're left with $7x^2 - 4$.

11. **B**   First thing to do here is to distribute the negative, leaving us with $5x^2 - 16x + 12 - 2x^2 + 8x + 8$. Combining like terms leaves us with $3x^2 - 8x + 4$.

12. **A**   The additive inverse will give a sum of 0 when added to the initial number, so it must have the same absolute value but the opposite sign. That would be A.

13.   **B**   One trick for solving this kind of problem is to look for *similar* roots. 6.25 doesn't look familiar, but 625 is the square of 25. So 2.5 squared would give us 6.25. Another approach is to see what numbers the square root of 625 must be between. $\sqrt{4} < \sqrt{6.25}$ $\sqrt{9}$, so $2 < \sqrt{6.25} < 3$. Then you can look more specifically at the remaining answers.

14.   **B** $4x^2 + 6 = 150$, so $4x^2 = 144$ and $x^2 = 36$ and therefore $x = 6$ or $x = -6$. Which means our set is $\{-6, 6\}$.

15.   **A**   Remember PEMDAS—we start with the parentheses. $\frac{(a^4b^{-3})^2}{a^2b}$ becomes $\frac{a^8b^{-6}}{a^2b}$ once we distribute the exponent on the top (remember to multiply exponents when raising a power to a power) and now we can divide like bases and subtract exponents, leaving $a^6b^{-7} = \frac{a^6}{b^7}$.

16.   **D**   The best thing to do here is to convert the mixed number to an improper fraction: $1\frac{1}{4} = \frac{5}{4}$. The reciprocal will give a product of 1 when multiplied by the original number, so the answer we're looking for is $\frac{4}{5}$.

17.   **B**   First isolate x. $1 - \frac{x}{5} = 3$, so $-\frac{x}{5} = 2$. and if we isolate x by multiplying both sides by -5 we get $x = -10$.

18.   **B** $3 - 2n = 7$, so $2n = 4$ and therefore $n = 1$.

19.   **D** $20 - 8d < 4$, so $-8d < -16$, and therefore $d > 2$. Remember to be sure to flip the sign if you multiply or divide an inequality by a negative number.

20.   **B**   Don't forget to change all the signs when you distribute a negative number! So $7y - 11 > 2y - 3(5 - y)$ is the same as $7y - 11 > 2y - 15 + 3y$.

21.   **D**   Let's go ahead and distribute. $4(2b + 1) = 17 - 3(2b - 5)$ would equal $8b + 4 = 17 - 6b + 15$. Don't forget to change the signs when you distribute a negative number.

22.   **B**   Distribute the 5, and $2n - 3 < 5(n - 1)$ becomes $2n - 3 < 5n - 5$.

23.   **A**   Here we need to cross-multiply. So $\frac{3}{x} = \frac{5}{x+4}$ becomes $3(x + 4) = 5x$, which is the same as A.

24.   **C**   Here we need to distribute and then combine terms. So $9a - 5(2 - a) \le 2(6a - 2)$ becomes $9a - 10 + 5a \le 12a - 4$ and therefore $14a - 10 \le 12a - 4$.

25.   **C**   This is just about distributing. $4m(2 - 1) = 5(m + 3 - 30)$ becomes $8m - 4m = 5m + 15 - 30$. You don't have to simplify the entire equation, notice. You just have to go as far as the answer choices do.

26.   **D**   Don't forget to change all the signs when you distribute a negative number! So $-h(1 - 6) = 6h - 10$ is the same as $-h + 6h = 6h - 10$, which when we combine terms becomes $5h = 6h - 10$.

27.   **D**   Since we're dealing with absolute value, we know that either $2b - 6 = 8$ or $2b - 6 = -8$. Sticking with the first possibility, we solve for b and see that $2b = 14$, so $b = 7$. Looking at the other possibility, we solve for b and find that $2b = -2$ so $b = -1$. So the solution set is $\{7, -1\}$.

28.   **C**   First thing is to isolate the variable. $15 - 4|n| > 3$ so $-4|n| > -12$. Be careful to flip the sign when you divide by the -4, leaving you $|n| < 3$. This tells us that either $n < 3$ or $n > -3$. Since n is an integer, C must be the answer.

29.   **A**   Again, we know that $h - 9 = 5$ or $h - 9 = -5$. When we solve for h we see that A is the answer.

30.   **B**   The absolute value tells us that $x - 1 \le 3$ and $x - 1 \ge -3$. So $-2 \le x \le 4$ and must be an integer, leaving B as the answer.

31.   **A**   First thing is to isolate the expression containing the variable. $2|y| = 6$ so $|y| = 3$ so our set is $\{-3, 3\}$.

32. **D** Again, isolate the expression containing the variable. $-|n| > -2$ so, being careful to flip the sign when dividing by a negative, we get $|n| < 2$, which tells us that $-2 < 2$. Since n is an integer, our answer must be D.

33. **B** $\dfrac{2^{-2}}{c^2} = \dfrac{1}{2^2} \times \dfrac{1}{c^2} = \dfrac{1}{4c^2}$. Remember that a negative exponent in the numerator moves the power to the denominator, and a negative exponent in the denominator moves the power to the numerator.

34. **C** $\dfrac{a^2 b^{-4}}{bc^{-2}} = \dfrac{a^2 b^{-4+1}}{c^{-2}} = \dfrac{a^2 b^{-3}}{c^{-2}} = a^2 \times \dfrac{1}{b^3} \times \dfrac{c^2}{1} = \dfrac{a^2 c^2}{b^3}$. Remember that a negative exponent in the numerator moves the power to the denominator, and a negative exponent in the denominator moves the power to the numerator.

35. **B** $\dfrac{1}{3x^{-2}} = \dfrac{1}{3} \times \dfrac{x^2}{1} = \dfrac{x^2}{3}$

36. **D** $(-3x^{-3}y)^2 = (-3)^2 x^{-6} y^2 = \dfrac{9y^2}{x^6}$

37. **C** $(5c^{-1})^2 d^2 = (25c^{-2})d^2 = 25 \times \dfrac{1}{c^2} \times d^2 = \dfrac{25d^2}{c^2}$

38. **B** Remember that $\dfrac{1}{z^4} = z^{-4}$, so $\dfrac{xy^2}{z^4} = xy^2 \times \dfrac{1}{z^4} = xy^2 z^{-4}$.

39. **C** Remember to distribute the square power to each of the factors inside the parentheses, and that when you're raising a power to a power you add the exponents. Right away you can eliminate B and D, because a negative times a negative gives you a positive. So $(-3xy^2z^3)^2$ becomes $-3^2 \times x^2 \times y^4 \times z^6$, which is $9x^2y^4z^6$.

40. **B** Remember that when you're dividing like bases you subtract the exponents. So $\dfrac{-15x^3y^5}{-3xy^2} = \dfrac{-15}{-3} \times \dfrac{x^3}{x} \times \dfrac{y^5}{y^2} = -5x^2y^3$.

41. **B** Remember that when you're multiplying like bases you add the exponents.

42. **A** Remember that when you're dividing like bases you subtract the exponents. If the resulting power is negative, it will be in the denominator of the new expression. $\dfrac{10x^2yz^2}{15xyz^3} = \dfrac{10}{15} \times \dfrac{x^2}{x} \times \dfrac{y}{y} \times \dfrac{z^2}{z^3} = \dfrac{2}{3} \times x^{2-1} \times y^{1-1} \times z^{2-3} = \dfrac{2}{3} \times x^1 \times y^0 \times z^{-1} = \dfrac{2}{3} \times x \times 1 \times \dfrac{1}{z} = \dfrac{2x}{3z}$

43. **D** Remember to distribute the square power to each of the factors inside the parentheses. Remember that when you're raising a power to a power you add the exponents.

44. **B** Remember that when you're dividing like bases you subtract the exponents.

45. **C** Here we want to isolate the variable, so we need to add 7 to both sides.

46. **D** Let's set up an equation. If the cost is $0.80 for the first three minutes, and remaining minutes cost $0.20, we can set up the equation $0.8 + 0.2m = 3.0$, where m is the number of minutes. Solving for m gives us 11. But this does not include the first three minutes! When we add those back we get 14.

47. **C** Distribute and combine terms. $2(3x + 11) + 5 = 3(4x - 7)$ so $6x + 22 + 5 = 12x - 21$. When we combine terms and isolate x we get $6x = 48$ so $x = 8$.

48. **A** Both sides contain the same terms, but they're grouped differently. This is an example of the associative property.

49. **A** The first thing you need to do is to isolate the expression containing the variable. Since it's inside the parentheses, you have to isolate the parentheses first. This means adding -3 to both sides.

50. **C** Just combine like terms. $5x^2 + 3x + 15 + x^2 - 16$ is $6x^2 + 3x - 1$.

51. **A** The area of a rectangle is represented by $A = lw$. If we plug in the values we have been given into that equation, we get $12x^4y^3 = l(4x^2y)$. Now we just solve for l. $\dfrac{12x^4y^3}{4x^2y} = l$ and therefore $l = 3x^2y^2$.

52. **D** The area of the parallelogram is $A = bh$. The height is $x + 4$ and the TOTAL base is $x + x + 5$, which equals $2x + 5$. So the area would be equal to $A = (2x + 5)(x + 4)$, which, if we use FOIL, gives us $A = 2x^2 + 8x + 5x + 20$, which simplifies to $A = 2x^2 + 13x + 20$.

CHAPTER 9

Geometric Shapes Final Quiz

1. **B** The key thing here is to find the area of the circle *minus* the area of the triangle. First, find the radius of the circle. Fortunately they tell us that the hypotenuse of the triangle is also the diameter of the circle. Since the hypotenuse is 10, the radius would be 5. Since the formula for the area of a circle is $A = \pi r^2$, the area of this circle would be $A = \pi \times 5^2$, or $25\pi = 25 \times 3.14 = 78.5$. The area of the triangle is $A = \dfrac{1}{2}bh = \dfrac{1}{2} \times 6 \times 8 = 24$. So the area of the shaded region is $78.5 - 24 = 54.5$.

2. **C** The base of the parallelogram is $6 + 5 = 11$ and the height is 8, so the area is $bh = 11 \times 8 = 88$.

3. **A** First calculate the areas of the circles. Since $A = \pi r^2$, the area of circle A is $\pi \times 5^2 = 25\pi$ and the area of circle B is $\pi \times 10^2 = 100\pi$, so the ratio of so the ratio of $\dfrac{Area\ A}{Area\ B} = \dfrac{25\pi}{100\pi} = \dfrac{1}{4}$.

4. **C** The key here is that corresponding parts of congruent triangles are congruent. The vertices of the triangles line up; if triangle ABC is congruent to triangle YZX, then then $\angle ABC \cong \angle YZX$

5. **B** The key here is to find a piece of information that we can use to prove congruency. We have one angle and one side. The side is opposite the angle, so we can't use SAS (Side-Angle-Side) or ASA (Angle-Side-Angle). But we could use AAS (Angle-Angle-Side) if we get another angle inside the triangle, which is what B gives us.

6. **A** Here we have to use the Pythagorean theorem, $a^2 + b^2 = c^2$, to find the height of the triangle. If we plug the numbers into the formula we get $6^2 + b^2 = 10^2$, so $b^2 = 64$ and $b = 8$. Now we can use $A = \dfrac{1}{2}bh$ to calculate $\dfrac{1}{2} \times 9 \times 8 = 36$.

7. **C** Here we have to use the Pythagorean theorem again, this time to find the height of the trapezoid. If we plug the numbers into the formula we get $18^2 + b^2 = 30^2$, which is $324 + b^2 = 900$, so $b^2 = 576$ and $b = 24$ (to find b, remember you can pick numbers in between 18 and 30 to try until you get the one that equals 576 when squared). Now we can use $A = \dfrac{1}{2}(b_1 + b_2)h$ to calculate $\dfrac{1}{2}(22 + 58)24 = 960$.

8. **C** Let's start with the area of the big triangle. $A = \dfrac{1}{2}bh$ so we get $A = \dfrac{1}{2}(8)(6)$. The area of the rectangle is just $A = lw$, so in this case it's $A = 5 \times 7 = 35$. But we need to subtract the area of the small triangle, so again using our formula we get $A = \dfrac{1}{2} \times 3 \times 4 = 6$. So the area of the whole figure is $24 + 35 - 6 = 53$.

9. **B** We can calculate the shaded region by determining the area of one of those triangles and then multiplying it by 4. The sides of the triangle will be 20 and 12.5 (i.e. 25 ÷ 2) so using $A = \frac{1}{2}bh$ we get $A = \frac{1}{2} \times 20 \times 12.5 = 125$. Multiplying that by 4 we get 500.

10. **C** The two semicircles together make a complete circle. If we find the area of the rectangle and then subtract the area of the circle, we'll get the area of the shaded region. The area of the rectangle is $A = bh$, so in this case it's $36 \times 20 = 720$. The area of the circle is $A = \pi r^2$ and the radius is 10 (half of the diameter of 20). So we get $A = \pi 10^2 = 100\pi = 100(3.14) = 314$. So the total area is $720 - 314 = 406$.

11. **D** Let's find the area of the triangle, then the area of the trapezoid, then add them together. First, the triangle is $A = \frac{1}{2}bh$ which in this case works out to $A = \frac{1}{2} \times 6 \times 16 = 48$. The trapezoid has an area of $A = \frac{1}{2}(b_1 + b_2)h$ which in this case works out to be $A = \frac{1}{2}(16 + 10)11 = 143$. When we combine them we get $48 + 143 = 191$.

12. **B** The circumference of the circle is also the width of the label, which in this case would be $C = \pi d = \pi 7$. The area of the label is therefore $A = bh = 3.14 \times 7 \times 10 = 219.8$, or roughly 220.

13. **C** If we let the length of a side of a cube be s, then the area of one face of a cube is s^2. Since there are 6 sides to a cube, the total surface area for a cube is $6s^2$. For Cube x the surface area is $6(4)^2 = 96$ and for Cube y it's $6(8)^2 = 384$. So $\frac{x}{y} = \frac{96}{384} = \frac{1}{4}$.

14. **D** If each small cube is 2 cm, then the edge of the big cube is 6 cm. The volume of the cube is $V = s^3$, so in this case the volume is 216.

CHAPTER 10

Geometric Graphs Final Quiz

1. **B** Look for where the solid line is above the dotted line, and draw a vertical line from those points down to the axis that has the months. The solid line is higher only from June to September.

2. **B** The equation $y = 3x^2$ is not a linear equation, because the x is raised to a power. This means it can't be A or D. The answer could be C, but C is a parabola that opens down, which would be fine if the equation were $y = -3x^2$, but it's not. This means it has to be B, which is an upward-opening parabola.

3. **A** This equation *is* a linear equation, meaning that the x does not have an exponent higher than 1. C is a parabola, and B and D are cubic functions. Only A is a linear equation.

4. **D** The slope formula is $\frac{y_2 - y_1}{x_2 - x_1}$. So in this case you can calculate the slope with $\frac{17 - 8}{4 - 1} = \frac{9}{3} = 3$

5. **A** The slope formula is $\frac{y_2 - y_1}{x_2 - x_1}$. So in this case you can calculate the slope with $\frac{7 - 3}{-2 - 0} = \frac{4}{-2} = -2$

6. **B** If you plot the coordinates on a piece of sketch paper you can see than in order to form a parallelogram the fourth point will have to be on the same horizontal as (-2, 2) and should be the same distance from that point that (4, 5) is from (0, 5). So the fourth point should be at (2, 2).

7.   **A**   C and D are reflections around the y-axis, not the x-axis. A true reflection reverses its orientation (like how left and right are reversed in a mirror), so A is the correct answer. A good way to see this is to folk the paper along the x-axis and see how the triangle is now projected onto the graph.

8.   **C**   To write the equation for a line, you should first determine the slope and then the y-intercept. The slope of this line will be $\dfrac{y_2 - y_1}{x_2 - x_1}$ which in this case equals $\dfrac{y_2 - y_1}{x_2 - x_1} = \dfrac{2-11}{-1-2} = \dfrac{-9}{-3} = 3$. The only answer with 3 as the slope is C.

9.   **B**   Plug the point into the equation for the line and solve for a. Since the equation is $2x - 6y = 14$, and -2 is our y-coordinate, that makes a our x-coordinate. if we plug in (a, -2) we get $2a - 6(-2) = 14$, which is $2a + 12 = 14$. $2a = 2$, and $a = 1$.

10.   **D**   Plug the points from the answer choices into the equation. Only D, (2, -1) works. $6(2) + 2(-1) = 10$. $12 - 2 = 10$.

11.   **A**   Plug the point into the equations from the answer choices. Only A, $x + y = 7$, works: $-2 + 9 = 7$.

12.   **B**   Plug the point $(3, n)$ into the equation $4x + 3y = 6$ and solve for n. $4(3) + 3n = 6$, so $12 + 3n = 6$. $3n = -6$, therefore $n = -2$

13.   **D**   Plug the points from the answer choices into the equation. Only D, $(10, -1)$ does not work. $2(10) + 5(-1) = 16$; $20 - 5$ certainly does not equal 16.

14.   **C**   You could make a linear equation in slope-intercept form (remember, $y = mx + b$) from the points $(-2, 1)$ and $(2, 9)$. However, you don't even have to do that. You have the points to plug into the slope formula. All you have to do is find the slope, then find the answer choice with the correct slope. The slope of this line will be $\dfrac{y_2 - y_1}{x_2 - x_1}$ which in this case equals $\dfrac{y_2 - y_1}{x_2 - x_1} = \dfrac{1-9}{-2-2} = \dfrac{-8}{-4} = 2$. C is the only answer with 2 as the slope.

15.   **C**   Plug the point $(q, -2)$ into the equation $9x + 3y = 21$ and solve for q. $9q + 3(-2) = 21$; $9q - 6 = 21$; $9q = 27$; $q = 3$.

16.   **B**   Re-state the equation in slope-intercept form: $y = mx + b$. The slope is given by the m value and the y-intercept by the b value. $3x - 5y = 15$ becomes $-5y = -3x + 15$. $y = \dfrac{3}{5}x - 3$ Therefore the y-intercept, the point where the line crosses the y-axis, is $(0,-3)$. Remember that the x-value is always 0 on the y-axis.

17.   **C**   The x-intercept is the point where the line crosses the x-axis. Remember that the y-value for that point will always be 0. Plug in 0 for y and solve for x and you have found the x-intercept: $5x + 2y = 20$; $5x + 2(0) = 20$; $5x = 20$; $x = 4$.

18.   **D**   The graph shows a line with a positive slope and a negative y-intercept. B and C have positive y-intercepts, so they're out. A has a slope of 1, which would be a line with at a 45° angle, and this line is steeper. D has a slope of 3 and a negative y-intercept—perfect.

19.   **D**   Let's put this one in slope intercept form: $y = mx + b$. The slope is given by the m value and the y-intercept by the b value. $5x - 3y = 15$; $-3y = -5x + 15$; $y = \dfrac{5}{3}x - 3$. So the y-intercept is $(0,-5)$.

20.   **B**   The x-intercept is the point where the line crosses the x-axis. Remember that the y-value for that point will always be 0. This can help us solve: plug in 0 for y and solve for x and you have found the x-intercept. $2y - 5x = 10$ becomes $2(0) - 5x = 10$; $-5x = 10$; $x = -2$. So the x-intercept is $(-2, 0)$.

21.   **A**   For this to be true, when you plugged the point $(0, 0)$ in for x and y in the equation, you should get a true statement. This only happens with A.

22. C The key here is that parallel lines have equal slopes. The slope of the line in question is 2, so the slope of the parallel line must be 2. Only C has a slope of 2.

23. D Let's put this one in slope intercept form: $y = mx + b$. $2x + y = 5$, so $y = -2x + 5$. So the slope must be -2. If you put all the answers in the slope-intercept form, only D has a slope of -2.

24. C Let's put this one in slope intercept form: $y = mx + b$. $3x - 4y = 16$; $-4y = -3x + 16$; $y = \frac{3}{4}x + 16$. So the slope is $\frac{3}{4}$, which must also be the slope of the parallel line.

25. B If we put all of the lines into slope-intercept form and compare their slopes to we see that they all also have a slope of 3 except for B, which has a slope of -3.

26. B Let's put this one in slope intercept form: $y = mx + b$. $2y - x = 14$; $y = \frac{1}{2}x - 7$, so the slope is $\frac{1}{2}$.

27. D Let's put this one in slope intercept form: $y = mx + b$. $3x + 2y = 12$, and $2y = -3x + 12$. The slope is given by the m value. So the slope is $y = \frac{-3}{2}x + 6$, so the slope is $-\frac{3}{2}$. The parallel line must have the same slope. If we put all the answers into slope-intercept form we find that only D has the same slope.

28. A Let's put this one in slope intercept form: $y = mx + b$. $6x + 3y = 15$; $3y = -6x + 15$; $y = -2x + 15$. So the slope of the line is -2 and the parallel line must have the same slope.

29. A Try plugging the answer choices into the inequality and seeing which ordered pair satisfies both. Only A does.

30. B Since the second equation says that $x = y - 1$, let's go ahead and substitute that into the first equation for x. So we get $3(y - 1) = 7y + 1$; $3y - 3 = 7y + 1$; $-4 = 4y$, therefore $y = -1$. Only B has a y value of -1.

31. C Since the second equation says that $y = 5x - 3$, let's go ahead and substitute that into the first one. So we get $3x + 5x - 3 = 5$, which becomes $8x = 8$, so $x = 1$. Only C has that as the x value.

32. C Since the second equation says that $x = 5 - y$, let's go ahead and substitute that into the first equation. So we get $2y + (5 - y) = 8$; $y + 5 = 8$; $y = 3$. Only C has that as the y value.

CHAPTER 11

Statistics Final Quiz

1. B Remember that the mean is the average. Rosa spent 11, 13, 8, and 12 hours watching TV in each of the four weeks. Add those up and divide by 4 and you get 11.

2. C First line up the set in order: 97, 98, 98, 99, 99, 99, 100, 100, 100, 100, 101, 101, 102. Then start crossing off one on each end of the list, until you get to the middle. The number left is 100.

3. D The mode is the most frequent number. If you examine the chart, 13 comes up more often than anything else.

4. A Here we're looking for something that might mislead us. American Motors has more total recalls, but Pacific-Rim makes less than half as many cars. So Pacific-Rim actually has the worse recall performance, even though it has fewer recalls.

5. D   If you notice, the bottom of the graph is not 0, but 7,500. This makes CAT wireless appear to be increasing at a greater rate, although it is actually at the same rate.

6. A   There are 8 wild cards out of 108 total. So $8 \div 108 \times 100 = 7\%$.

7. D   We want anyone *but* the Chargers. That leaves 31 other teams out of 32, so the answer is $\frac{31}{32}$.

8. C   There are 8 total gray squares and 1 checkerboard square, for a total of 9. There are 25 total squares, so $9 \div 25 = 0.36$.

9. A   Fill in the tree.

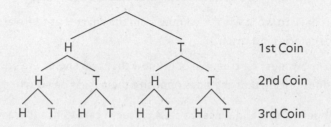

If you count up the paths that have two heads and one tails, there are three out of a total of 8 paths.

10. C   Once you take a book off the shelf, that reduces the number of books available for you to choose from. The other events are all independent of each other.

11. A   There are 3 comedies out of a total of 15 movies. So the chance she will pick a comedy at first is $\frac{3}{15}$. Then there are only 2 comedies out of 14. So the chance that she will pick two comedies is $\frac{3}{15} \times \frac{2}{14} = \frac{1}{35}$.

12. B   Not replacing the cards changes the number of cards available to choose from, and therefore these are dependent events. Dice, spinners, and coins are independent.

13. A   How many combinations can add to 12? Well, in this case it's only 6 and 6. So the only chance is to roll 2 sixes. The probability of that is $\frac{1}{6} \times \frac{1}{6} = \frac{1}{36}$.

14. D   From 1950−2000 the population tripled; nowhere else is the line that steep.

15. D   The population in 2,000 was actually 800,000,000. Read carefully!

16. D   There is no discernible shape to the scatter plot, and therefore there is no relationship between the variables.

17. C   The scatter plot slopes upward, indicating that as the dose goes up, so do the number of fainting episodes. There is a clear shape to the scatter plot so we can make a determination of relationship.

CHAPTER 12

Graphing Statistics Final Quiz

1. **C**   Let's choose an easy number to work with. Carlos's mom went 450 miles on 20 gallons of gasoline. So her miles per gallon (mpg) is $\frac{450}{20} = 22.5$.

2. **B**   Let's set up the equation. We know that $D = \frac{M}{V}$ and we're asked to find the coordinates of the point. Well the x is clearly 8, but the y is harder to read. Let's solve for it using the density of mercury. $13.5 = \frac{M}{8}$; $13.5(8) = M$; $M = 108$ So the coordinates would be (8, 108).

3. **A**   Pick a point that's easy to work with. We know from the chart that there are 90 calories in 10 grams, so there must be 9 calories in 1 gram.

4. **B**   Stick to what you know must be true. We only know that two angles are equal. That doesn't tell us a whole lot, but it does tell me that the sides opposite them must be equal, so the triangle is isosceles.

5. **D**   Between them, Angela, Karla, and Vincenzo ate 4 pieces of cake. Since there was $\frac{3}{4}$ left, they ate $\frac{1}{4}$. If $\frac{1}{4}$ of the cake is 4 pieces the cake must have originally been in 16 pieces.

6. **B**   Since a right angle = 90°, it would help Raffi's case if an acute angle were less than that. B helps us here.

7. **D**   If 10 are taking AP Bio and 6 are taking both, then 4 are taking AP Bio only. If 15 are taking AP English and 6 are taking both, then 9 are taking only AP English. Then we can find the number of girls taking neither by 4(Bio only) + 9(English only) + 6(Both) + n(Neither) = 27, so 19 + n = 27, so n = 8.

8. **C**   Let's say the original dimensions were $a \times b \times c$, so the original volume was $V = abc$. The new dimensions will be $3a \times 2b \times c$ so the new volume will be $V = 6abc$.

9. **D**   Something that told us that the angles of quadrilaterals had a fixed relationship would help prove Amy's hypothesis. And D gives us the sum relationship: Just like in a triangle where all the angles have to add up to 180°, in a quadrilateral, like a square for instance, all of the angles have to add up to 360°.

10. **B**   Here we want to approximate, so let's use easy numbers to get an idea. 4,500 ÷ 9 = 500.

11. **C** π is approximately 3, and 6.75 is roughly 7, so $3 \times 7 \times 7 = 147$.

12. **C**   Let's use simpler numbers. How about $520 \times 30 = 15{,}600$. C is closest.

13. **A**   The formula is $A = \frac{1}{2}bh$; here let's say $h = 8$ and $b = 18$. So we get $A = \frac{1}{2} \times 8 \times 18$.

14. **A**   Let's call it $\frac{676}{40} \approx 17$

15. **B**   Taking a look at the trend line, we see that 1993 value should be below the 1994 value of 20.75. But it won't fall sharply enough to go down to 20, so it's around 20.5.

16. **D**   The trend is definitely upwards, so the answer must be above 1990's value of 58%. 62% seems about right.

17. **B**   Remember that deductive reasoning is using a general principle to arrive at a specific result. The answer choices besides B all rely on observation, which would be inductive reasoning.

18. **A**   Remember your basic rules of logic. Kristen states that if she does not add dry gas, the line will freeze. Also, if the line freezes, then the car won't start. If the car does not start, she will not get to school on time. But if she got to school, none of those other things could have happened. Thus we see that A is correct. The others could be true but do not have to be—watch out for that!

19. **A**   Using Seth's strategy, let's make the little angle x. The middle angle would then be $3x - 5$. The largest angle would be $3x + 10$. The sum of all angles would be $x + (3x - 5) + (3x + 10) = 180$. $7x + 5 = 180$; $7x = 175$; $x = 25$.

20. **C**   Using Georgia's strategy, let's say that the width is w. The length would then be $2w - 3$. Since $P = 2l + 2w$ and we know the perimeter is 48, we can set up an equation: $48 = 2w + 2(2w - 3)$. When we solve for w we get $w = 9$ and therefore $l = 15$.

21. **B**   So using Samantha's strategy, x is the number of child tickets, and $372 - x$ will be the number of adult tickets. So the equation to solve would be $1,952 = 3.5x + 6(372 - x)$; $1,952 = 3.5x + 2,232 - 6x$; $-280 = -2.5x$; $112 = x$.

22. **A**   Using Tina's strategy, we find that Robyn can paint $\frac{1}{6}$ of the house per hour while Gordon can paint $\frac{1}{4}$ of the house per hour. So the equation to solve is $(\frac{1}{4} + \frac{1}{6}) \times t = 1$; $\frac{2+3}{12} \times t = 1$; $\frac{5}{12}t = 1$; $t = \frac{12}{5} = 2.4$ *hours*

INTRODUCTION TO THE PRACTICE TESTS

Congratulations! You've made it through the review section of this book, covering all the topics tested on the math portion of the California High School Exit Exam (CAHSEE). Now it's time to try your hand at a practice CAHSEE.

Each practice CAHSEE includes 92 multiple-choice questions, just like the real exam. Preceding each practice test is a bubble sheet. Tear or cut out this bubble sheet, and answer your questions on the practice test by filling in the bubbles accordingly. Use a #2 pencil, and take each practice test just as if you were taking the actual CAHSEE. That means you should sit at a desk without a television or stereo on. You should also turn off your phone so you won't get disrupted.

The CAHSEE is untimed, meaning you'll have as much time as you'll need to complete the test. It is given in two sessions of 46 questions each. You should try to take each session in one sitting, because you won't be allowed to take a break during sessions in the real CAHSEE. (Well, you can go to the bathroom if you need to.)

Calculators are not allowed on the CAHSEE. Therefore, you should certainly not take the practice CAHSEE with a calculator. You should get accustomed to working out the math by hand. Likewise, the CAHSEE will not provide you with some formulas, such as those for perimeter and area. If you don't know them yet, now would be a good time to memorize them. You *will* be allowed to use scratch paper, so keep some loose blank pages on the table for your practice test.

When you've completed the first practice test, check the answers and explanations for it on page 315. Make sure to read through the explanations to all the questions— even the ones you got right. The explanations can help you figure out different ways to solve certain problems. After taking the first test and checking your answers, take a break. (We recommend not taking both practice tests in the same day—give your brain time to rest!) The answers and explanations for the second practice test can be found beginning on page 360.

You will need approximately 43 points on the exam to receive a passing score. (That converts to a scaled score of 350.) Keep in mind that the passing rates and scaled-score conversion change from year to year.

When you're ready, cut out the bubble sheets on page 292 and get started on practice test #1. Good luck!

Part III
CAHSEE
Practice Tests
and Answers

Chapter 14
Practice Test 1

CAHSEE: Mathematics Practice Test #1 Answer Sheet

1. Ⓐ Ⓑ Ⓒ Ⓓ 2. Ⓐ Ⓑ Ⓒ Ⓓ 3. Ⓐ Ⓑ Ⓒ Ⓓ

4. Ⓐ Ⓑ Ⓒ Ⓓ 5. Ⓐ Ⓑ Ⓒ Ⓓ 6. Ⓐ Ⓑ Ⓒ Ⓓ

7. Ⓐ Ⓑ Ⓒ Ⓓ 8. Ⓐ Ⓑ Ⓒ Ⓓ 9. Ⓐ Ⓑ Ⓒ Ⓓ

10. Ⓐ Ⓑ Ⓒ Ⓓ 11. Ⓐ Ⓑ Ⓒ Ⓓ 12. Ⓐ Ⓑ Ⓒ Ⓓ

13. Ⓐ Ⓑ Ⓒ Ⓓ 14. Ⓐ Ⓑ Ⓒ Ⓓ 15. Ⓐ Ⓑ Ⓒ Ⓓ

16. Ⓐ Ⓑ Ⓒ Ⓓ 17. Ⓐ Ⓑ Ⓒ Ⓓ 18. Ⓐ Ⓑ Ⓒ Ⓓ

19. Ⓐ Ⓑ Ⓒ Ⓓ 20. Ⓐ Ⓑ Ⓒ Ⓓ 21. Ⓐ Ⓑ Ⓒ Ⓓ

22. Ⓐ Ⓑ Ⓒ Ⓓ 23. Ⓐ Ⓑ Ⓒ Ⓓ 24. Ⓐ Ⓑ Ⓒ Ⓓ

25. Ⓐ Ⓑ Ⓒ Ⓓ 26. Ⓐ Ⓑ Ⓒ Ⓓ 27. Ⓐ Ⓑ Ⓒ Ⓓ

28. Ⓐ Ⓑ Ⓒ Ⓓ 29. Ⓐ Ⓑ Ⓒ Ⓓ 30. Ⓐ Ⓑ Ⓒ Ⓓ

31. Ⓐ Ⓑ Ⓒ Ⓓ 32. Ⓐ Ⓑ Ⓒ Ⓓ 33. Ⓐ Ⓑ Ⓒ Ⓓ

34. Ⓐ Ⓑ Ⓒ Ⓓ 35. Ⓐ Ⓑ Ⓒ Ⓓ 36. Ⓐ Ⓑ Ⓒ Ⓓ

37. Ⓐ Ⓑ Ⓒ Ⓓ 38. Ⓐ Ⓑ Ⓒ Ⓓ 39. Ⓐ Ⓑ Ⓒ Ⓓ

40. Ⓐ Ⓑ Ⓒ Ⓓ 41. Ⓐ Ⓑ Ⓒ Ⓓ 42. Ⓐ Ⓑ Ⓒ Ⓓ

43. Ⓐ Ⓑ Ⓒ Ⓓ 44. Ⓐ Ⓑ Ⓒ Ⓓ 45. Ⓐ Ⓑ Ⓒ Ⓓ

46 Ⓐ Ⓑ Ⓒ Ⓓ   47 Ⓐ Ⓑ Ⓒ Ⓓ   48 Ⓐ Ⓑ Ⓒ Ⓓ

49 Ⓐ Ⓑ Ⓒ Ⓓ   50 Ⓐ Ⓑ Ⓒ Ⓓ   51 Ⓐ Ⓑ Ⓒ Ⓓ

52 Ⓐ Ⓑ Ⓒ Ⓓ   53 Ⓐ Ⓑ Ⓒ Ⓓ   54 Ⓐ Ⓑ Ⓒ Ⓓ

55 Ⓐ Ⓑ Ⓒ Ⓓ   56 Ⓐ Ⓑ Ⓒ Ⓓ   57 Ⓐ Ⓑ Ⓒ Ⓓ

58 Ⓐ Ⓑ Ⓒ Ⓓ   59 Ⓐ Ⓑ Ⓒ Ⓓ   60 Ⓐ Ⓑ Ⓒ Ⓓ

61 Ⓐ Ⓑ Ⓒ Ⓓ   62 Ⓐ Ⓑ Ⓒ Ⓓ   63 Ⓐ Ⓑ Ⓒ Ⓓ

64 Ⓐ Ⓑ Ⓒ Ⓓ   65 Ⓐ Ⓑ Ⓒ Ⓓ   66 Ⓐ Ⓑ Ⓒ Ⓓ

67 Ⓐ Ⓑ Ⓒ Ⓓ   68 Ⓐ Ⓑ Ⓒ Ⓓ   69 Ⓐ Ⓑ Ⓒ Ⓓ

70 Ⓐ Ⓑ Ⓒ Ⓓ   71 Ⓐ Ⓑ Ⓒ Ⓓ   72 Ⓐ Ⓑ Ⓒ Ⓓ

73 Ⓐ Ⓑ Ⓒ Ⓓ   74 Ⓐ Ⓑ Ⓒ Ⓓ   75 Ⓐ Ⓑ Ⓒ Ⓓ

76 Ⓐ Ⓑ Ⓒ Ⓓ   77 Ⓐ Ⓑ Ⓒ Ⓓ   78 Ⓐ Ⓑ Ⓒ Ⓓ

79 Ⓐ Ⓑ Ⓒ Ⓓ   80 Ⓐ Ⓑ Ⓒ Ⓓ   81 Ⓐ Ⓑ Ⓒ Ⓓ

82 Ⓐ Ⓑ Ⓒ Ⓓ   83 Ⓐ Ⓑ Ⓒ Ⓓ   84 Ⓐ Ⓑ Ⓒ Ⓓ

85 Ⓐ Ⓑ Ⓒ Ⓓ   86 Ⓐ Ⓑ Ⓒ Ⓓ   87 Ⓐ Ⓑ Ⓒ Ⓓ

88 Ⓐ Ⓑ Ⓒ Ⓓ   89 Ⓐ Ⓑ Ⓒ Ⓓ   90 Ⓐ Ⓑ Ⓒ Ⓓ

91 Ⓐ Ⓑ Ⓒ Ⓓ   92 Ⓐ Ⓑ Ⓒ Ⓓ

PRACTICE TEST 1

1. The table below displays the number of hours that three students spent on-line over a four-week period.

Hours Spent On-line

	Week 1	Week 2	Week 3	Week 4
Nelson	10	6	9	7
Marisol	7	8	10	11
Donald	9	6	7	9

What is the mean number of hours Marisol spent on-line per week?

A　7

B　8

C　9

D　10

Sports Injuries in 2001

Sport	Participants	Injuries
Baseball	37,500,000	475,000
Football	12,500,000	440,000

2. The local Board of Education considered dropping football as a varsity sport because too many players got hurt. At a recent board meeting, a spokesperson for the parents of football players, referring to the data in the chart above claimed, "Football has 7% fewer injuries per year than baseball." What is <u>deceptive</u> about the spokesperson's claim?

A　The average number of injuries <u>per 1,000 participants</u> is greater for baseball.

B　The spokesperson should have said, "one-third the number of injuries."

C　The spokesperson should have said, "thirty-five percent fewer injuries."

D　The average number of injuries <u>per 1,000 participants</u> is greater for football.

3. Four coins, a penny (P), a nickel (N), a dime (D), and a quarter (Q) are placed in a bag. Without looking, Hakeem picks one coin, replaces it, and then picks a coin again. The tree diagram shown below represents all the possible outcomes.

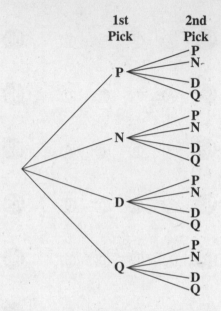

What is the theoretical probability that the total value of the coins Hakeem picks will be exactly $0.35?

A　$\dfrac{1}{16}$

B　$\dfrac{1}{8}$

C　$\dfrac{1}{4}$

D　$\dfrac{1}{2}$

4. An ink-jet printer has a suggested retail price of
    $150. This weekend, it is on sale for 30% off.
    How much does the printer cost during the sale?

    A $45

    B $105

    C $120

    D $195

5. The bubble gum machine shown above was just
    refilled with an equal number of red, green, blue,
    yellow, purple, and orange gumballs. What is the
    probability that the first gumball to come out will
    <u>not</u> be green?

    A $\frac{1}{6}$

    B $\frac{1}{2}$

    C $\frac{4}{5}$

    D $\frac{5}{6}$

6. Last year the Pacific Packing Co. lost 644 person-
    hours of work due to chronic back pain. If a normal
    day includes 8 hours of work, how many person-
    days of work did the company lose?

    A   80.5

    B   636

    C   652

    D   5,152

7. $1.8 \times 10^{-3} =$

    A   0.0018

    B   0.018

    C   180

    D   1,800

8. Which sum below is equal to a negative number?

    A   (5) + (−9) + (7)

    B   (−9) + (−5)

    C   (−5) + (9)

    D   (5) + (9)

9. One thousand is divided by a number between
    10 and 100. The resulting number must be

    A   less than 10.

    B   between 10 and 50 but not 25.

    C   between 10 and 100 but not 50.

    D   between 10 and 100.

10. Of the 652 students enrolled at Lincoln High School, 160 are of Hispanic descent. Approximately what percentage of the student enrollment is of Hispanic descent?

A   16%

B   25%

C   50%

D   160%

11. Given that *y* is an integer, what is the solution set for $5|y| = 20$?

A   {−4, 0}

B   {−4, 0, 4}

C   {−4, 4}

D   {0, 4}

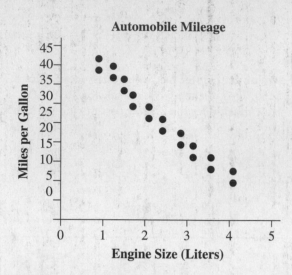

Automobile Mileage

12. For a project about energy conservation, Shana did some research on gas mileage attained by certain automobiles. The results of her research are shown in the scatter plot pictured above. What conclusion can Shana draw that is supported by her data?

A   The number of miles per gallon attained increases as the size of a car's engine increases.

B   The number of miles per gallon attained decreases as the size of a car's engine increases.

C   The number of miles per gallon attained remains the same as the size of a car's engine increases.

D   The number of miles per gallon attained has no relationship to the size of a car's engine.

13. Which inequality is equivalent to $2 + 5x < 4(x − 3)$?

A $2 + 5x < 4x − 3$

B $2 + 5x < 4x − 7$

C $2 + 5x < 4x − 12$

D $2 + 5x < 4x − 14$

14. Luh-Ling rolled a cube with faces numbered 1–6 three times, and each time she rolled an even number. If Luh-Ling rolls the number cube one more time, what is the theoretical probability that she will roll an odd number?

A $\dfrac{1}{6}$

B $\dfrac{1}{4}$

C $\dfrac{1}{2}$

D $\dfrac{3}{4}$

15. $3^2 \times 3^4 =$

A 3^6

B 3^8

C 9^6

D 9^8

16. Which of the expressions below shows the prime factorization of the least common denominator of $\dfrac{5}{12} + \dfrac{11}{18}$?

A $2 \times 2 \times 3$

B $2 \times 3 \times 3$

C $2 \times 3 \times 2 \times 3$

D 12×18

17. $\dfrac{3^5 \times 4^2}{3^3} + \dfrac{6^2 \times 2^7}{2^4} =$

A 140

B 180

C 252

D 432

18. One quart is equal to approximately 0.946 liter. About how many liters are equal to 4 quarts?

A 0.2365

B 0.546

C 1.346

D 3.784

19. Which number below shows the absolute value of –8?

A $\dfrac{1}{8}$

B –8

C $-\dfrac{1}{8}$

D 8

20. Carlos is thinking of a number. He says that if you divide the number by 3, and then add 5 to the result, the answer is 12.

Which equation below could be used to find the number that Carlos is thinking of?

A $\dfrac{n+5}{3} = 12$

B $5 = 12 + \dfrac{n}{3}$

C $\dfrac{n}{3} + 5 = 12$

D $\dfrac{n}{3} = 5 + 12$

21. For a certain hockey team traveling on the road, the number of sticks, *s*, equals 5 times the number of players, *p*.

Which of the following equations agrees with the information above?

A $5 \cdot p = s$

B $5 \cdot s = 5 \cdot p$

C $5 \cdot s = p$

D $s \cdot p = 5$

22. Evaluate the following expression.

$2(3x - 4)^2$

A $6x - 8$

B $12x + 16$

C $18x^2 - 48x + 32$

D $36x^2 - 96x + 64$

23. The line on the graph below represents which of the following equations?

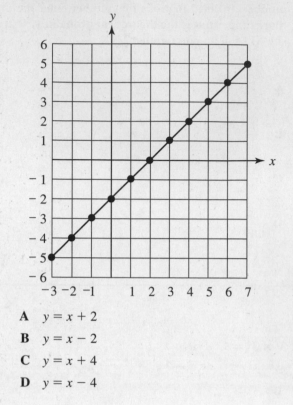

A $y = x + 2$

B $y = x - 2$

C $y = x + 4$

D $y = x - 4$

24. The graph below illustrates the total cost of bowling for one person at each of two bowling alleys.

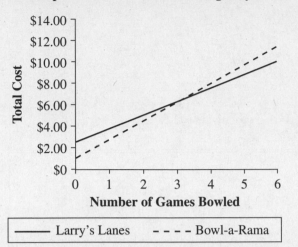

Larry's Lanes costs less than Bowl-a-Rama

A at all times.

B if a person bowls less than 3 games.

C if a person bowls 3 games.

D if a person bowls more than 3 games.

25. Simplify and evaluate $\dfrac{1}{5x^{-2}}$

A $\dfrac{x^2}{25}$

B $\dfrac{x^2}{5}$

C $5x^{-2}$

D $25x^2$

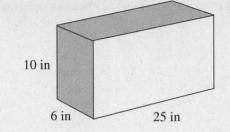

26. Find the volume, in cubic inches, of the box shown in the diagram above.

A 41

B 150

C 900

D 1,500

27. **Which graph shown below could be the graph of the equation $y = 2 + x^2$?**

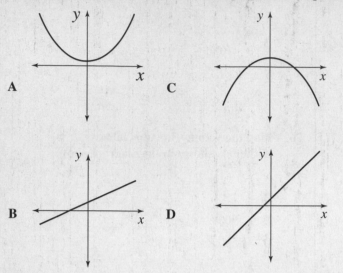

A

C

B

D

---

28. **Solve the following equation for a.**

$5a - 9 < 16$

A $a < 3$

B $a < 4$

C $a < 5$

D $a < 7$

29. **If $p = 7$ and $q = 3$, then $\dfrac{pq - 9}{4} + 4 =$**

A   4

B   7

C   8

D   17

30. Soledad is applying a water sealant to the deck around her pool at a rate of 12.5 square feet per minute. If the deck has a total surface area of 475 square feet, how long will it take to finish applying water sealant to the entire deck if she continues at this rate?

A   38 minutes

B   45 minutes

C   462.5 minutes

D   487.5 minutes

31. The slope of the line shown on the graph below is

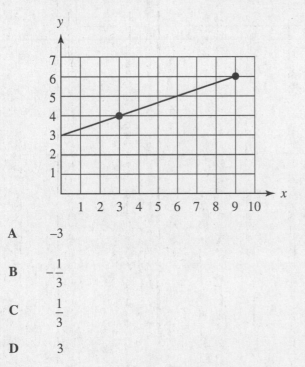

A   −3

B $-\dfrac{1}{3}$

C $\dfrac{1}{3}$

D   3

32. The density of a substance is equal to its mass divided by its volume ($D = \dfrac{M}{V}$). Ayeesha measured the mass and volume of six aluminum samples. Her data are plotted on the graph below.

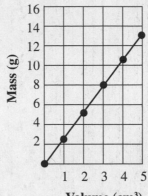

According to Ayeesha's data, what is the approximate density of aluminum?

A   1.4 g/cm³

B   2.7 g/cm³

C   3.2 g/cm³

D   5.8 g/cm³

33. The square root of 795 must be a number between

A   27 and 28.

B   28 and 29.

C   29 and 30.

D   30 and 31.

34. The diagram below shows a scale drawing of a soccer field.

The scale used for the drawing is 1 centimeter (cm) = 5 meters (m).

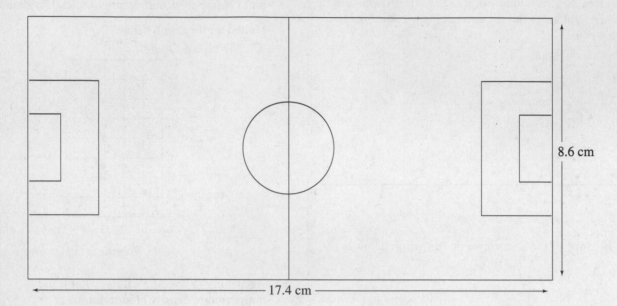

8.6 cm

17.4 cm

What is the length, in meters, of the soccer field?

A   87 m

B   105 m

C   122.5 m

D   174 m

35. The figure below shows a parallelogram drawn inside a rectangle. What is the area of the shaded portion of the rectangle? (Area of a triangle $= \frac{1}{2}bh$; Area of a parallelogram $= bh$)

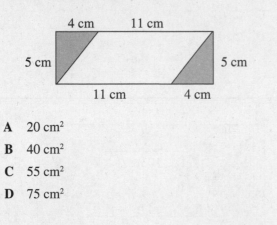

- **A**   20 cm²
- **B**   40 cm²
- **C**   55 cm²
- **D**   75 cm²

36. Which of the following pairs of events describes two **dependent** events?

- **A**   Flipping a coin that comes up heads; rolling a cube with faces numbered 1–6 and getting a 5
- **B**   Picking a spade from a standard deck of 52 cards without replacing it; picking another spade from the same deck of cards
- **C**   Drawing a vowel from a box of 26 different alphabet tiles and replacing it; drawing a consonant from the same box of alphabet tiles
- **D**   Picking a red jelly bean from a dish containing 20 each of eight assorted colors; picking a short straw from a hat containing 1 short straw and 9 long straws

37. A train in Japan travels a distance of 132 miles in three-quarters of an hour. What is the train's average speed?

- **A**   99 miles per hour
- **B**   176 miles per hour
- **C**   182 miles per hour
- **D**   184 miles per hour

38. Given the formula for the area of a triangle $(A = \frac{1}{2}bh)$, what is the area of the triangle in the figure below?

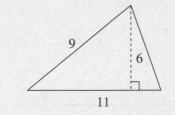

- **A**   27 square units
- **B**   33 square units
- **C**   54 square units
- **D**   66 square units

39. In the diagram shown below, Circle A has a radius of 4 in and Circle B has a radius of 8 in. What is the value of $\dfrac{\text{area of Circle } A}{\text{area of Circle } B}$? ($A = \pi r^2$)

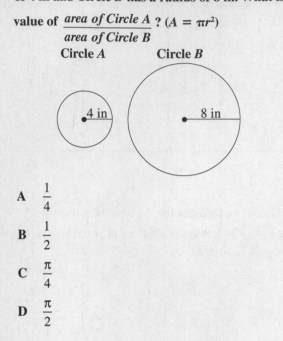

Circle A   Circle B

4 in   8 in

A $\dfrac{1}{4}$

B $\dfrac{1}{2}$

C $\dfrac{\pi}{4}$

D $\dfrac{\pi}{2}$

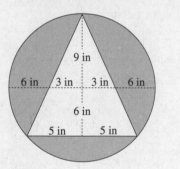

9 in

6 in   3 in   3 in   6 in

6 in

5 in   5 in

40. Migdalia is cutting out a triangular stencil from a gray circular piece of paper that measures 18 inches in diameter. Approximately how many square inches is the area of the remaining paper (the shaded portion of the diagram)?

(Area of a circle $= \pi r^2$; $\pi = 3.14$;

Area of a triangle $= \dfrac{1}{2}bh$)

A 84

B 179

C 198

D 254

41. The line whose equation is $3x + 2y = 8$ has a y-intercept whose coordinates are

A $(0, -3)$

B $(0, 4)$

C $(2, 0)$

D $(5, 0)$

10 ft

8 ft

4 ft   14 ft

8 ft   24 ft

10 ft

30 ft

42. Mr. Harris's backyard measures 30 feet by 24 feet and is covered with grass. He built a hexagonal gazebo (that is actually two identical trapezoids placed base to base) in the center of the yard as shown in the diagram above. What is the area of the grass that remains uncovered?

[Area of a trapezoid $= \dfrac{1}{2}(b_1 + b_2)h$]

A 224 ft²

B 496 ft²

C 528 ft²

D 608 ft²

43. What is the result of $(3x^3yz^4)(3xy^3z^3)$ if you simplify it?

A $6x^3y^4z^6$

B $9x^9y^3z^{12}$

C $9x^4y^4z^7$

D $9x^5y^4z^7$

44. Maria's bedroom measures 9 feet by 12 feet. The carpet store sells wall-to-wall carpeting by the square yard. How many square yards of carpet does Maria need to cover her bedroom?

A   7

B   12

C   36

D   108

45. The vertices of a quadrilateral are represented by the points (1, –2), (3, 3), (7, 3), and (5, –2). What kind of quadrilateral is it?

A   Parallelogram

B   Rectangle

C   Square

D   Trapezoid

46. In the diagram below, find the value of c.

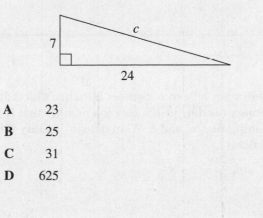

A   23

B   25

C   31

D   625

47. In the diagram below, $\angle A$ and $\angle D$ are both right angles, and C is the midpoint of $\overline{AD}$. Which of the following bits of information is needed to prove that $\triangle ABC \cong \triangle DEC$?

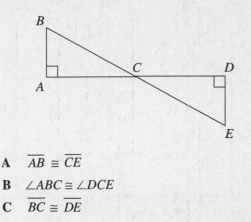

A $\overline{AB} \cong \overline{CE}$

B $\angle ABC \cong \angle DCE$

C $\overline{BC} \cong \overline{DE}$

D $\angle DCE \cong \angle BCA$

48. The table below lists the number of hours three students spent doing homework over a 4-week period.

Hours of Homework

	Week 1	Week 2	Week 3	Week 4
Raul	10	8	12	10
Daphne	8	12	9	12
James	7	6	11	9

What is the modal number of hours per week that Daphne spent doing her homework over the 4-week period?

A   9

B   10

C   11

D   12

49. The daily high temperatures for a city over a five-day period are shown in the graph below.

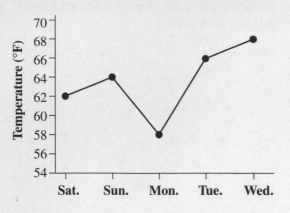

Which day's high temperature increased the most compared to the previous day?

A   Sunday

B   Monday

C   Tuesday

D   Wednesday

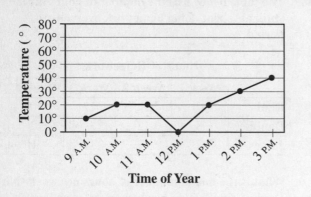

Time of Year

50. The above graph shows the temperature change over a period of a few hours. In which hour did the greatest increase in temperature occur?

A   9 A.M. to 10 A.M.

B   10 A.M. to 11 A.M.

C   11 A.M. to 12 P.M.

D   12 P.M. to 1 P.M.

51. A video game originally priced at $40.00 is reduced to $32.00. By what percent was the price decreased?

A   8%

B   20%

C   25%

D   80%

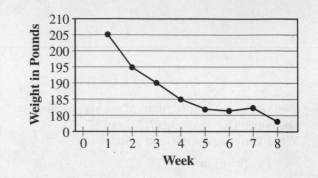

Week

52. Richard graphed his weight during an 8-week period. Based on the graph, which of the following statements is true?

A   Richard lost the most weight between weeks 1 and 2.

B   Richard ate ice cream during week 5.

C   Richard lost weight every week of the diet.

D   Richard lost a total of 10 pounds.

53. Moises was able to remember his sister's birthday because the date in January is a number that is a multiple of 3, 6, and 8. What date in January is her birthday?

A   12

B   18

C   24

D   30

54. A lollipop-manufacturing plant can produce 1,200 lollipops in one hour, and the plant receives $0.10 for every lollipop created. For every hour that the plant is operating, 10 employees receive $10 per hour each. If the manufacturing plant extended its day from 8 hours to 12 hours, how much more money would the plant make per day, considering the money received from the lollipops and the cost of the employees?

A $80

B $120

C $240

D $480

55. The schedule below indicates departure and arrival times for passenger trains running from Los Angeles (L.A.), California, to Phoenix, Arizona.

Departure L.A. Time	Arrival Phoenix Time
7:40 A.M.	6:50 P.M.
9:00 A.M.	8:25 P.M.
10:15 A.M.	9:35 P.M.
12:00 NOON	11:15 P.M.

Which train makes the trip in the shortest time?

A The train that departs at 7:40 A.M.

B The train that departs at 9:00 A.M.

C The train that departs at 10:15 A.M.

D The train that departs at 12:00 noon

56. In isosceles triangle *ABC*, the measure of the vertex angle is more than twice the measure of one of the base angles. Which of the following statements about △*ABC* is true?

A △*ABC* is an acute triangle.

B △*ABC* is an obtuse triangle.

C △*ABC* is an equilateral triangle.

D △*ABC* is a right triangle.

57. The coordinates of two points in a line are $(0, -1)$ and $(3, -3)$. What is the slope of this line?

A $-\dfrac{3}{2}$

B $-\dfrac{2}{3}$

C $\dfrac{2}{3}$

D $\dfrac{3}{2}$

58. The U.S. Department of Agriculture publishes statistics about diet trends. The graph represents the amount of whole milk consumed per person in the United States from 1965 to 1995.

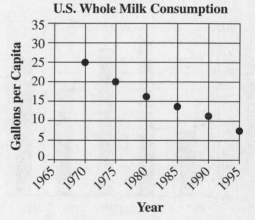

Based on this information, what was the **most likely** value for gallons of whole milk consumed per capita in 1965?

A 20

B 23

C 25

D 29

59. While getting ready to leave for school one rainy morning, Sherine stated the following:

If I do not take my umbrella, my hair will get wet.

If my hair gets wet, I will look silly.

If I look silly, I will not feel very good.

Which of the following conclusions can be drawn from Sherine's statements?

A   If she feels very good, Sherine took her umbrella.

B   If she does not feel very good, Sherine's hair got wet.

C   If she takes her umbrella, Sherine will feel very good.

D   If her hair gets wet, Sherine did not take her umbrella.

Home Run Totals, 1997–2001

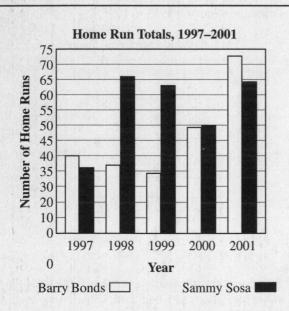

Barry Bonds ▢   Sammy Sosa ▮

60. The double-bar graph above compares the home run totals for Barry Bonds and Sammy Sosa in the years 1997 through 2001. In which years did Sammy Sosa hit more home runs than Barry Bonds?

A   1997 and 2001

B   1997, 2000, and 2001

C   1998 and 1999

D   1998, 1999, and 2000

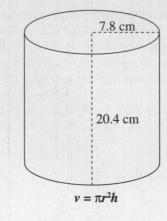

$$v = \pi r^2 h$$

61. Using her calculator, Seema found the volume of the cylinder shown above to be 389.7167 cm³. She immediately knew that she had made an error because the correct volume of the cylinder should be approximately

A $3 \times 3 \times 8 \times 20 = 1{,}440$

B $3 \times 8 \times 8 \times 20 = 3{,}840$

C $314 \times 8 \times 2 = 5{,}024$

D $8 \times 8 \times 8 \times 20 = 10{,}240$

---

62. Solve for x.

$$3x^2 + 5 = 152$$

A $\{-7, 7\}$

B $\{-5, 7\}$

C $\{-7, 5\}$

D $\{-5, 5\}$

63. Which of the following fractions is the equivalent of 40%?

A $\dfrac{1}{4}$

B $\dfrac{1}{3}$

C $\dfrac{2}{5}$

D $\dfrac{3}{5}$

Pressure (atm)	Volume (ml)
1.0	1,000
1.5	667
2.0	500
2.5	400
3.0	?

Table 1

64. Andrea found the unknown volume in Table 1 above by looking for a pattern. She noticed that the product of the pressure and the volume is always equal to 1,000. Therefore, when the pressure is 3 atm, the volume should be about 333 ml.

Temperature (°C)	Temperature (°F)
0	32
10	50
20	68
30	86
40	?

Table 2

Applying the same strategy, what value should Andrea get for the unknown temperature in Table 2 above?

A   98

B   100

C   104

D   120

$$\frac{14}{a} = \frac{5}{a+3}$$

65. Which equation below is equivalent to the one shown above?

A $a(a + 3) = 70$

B $14(a + 3) = 5a$

C $14a = 5(a + 3)$

D $19 = a + (a + 3)$

66. Which graph below represents the equation $2x = y - 2$?

A

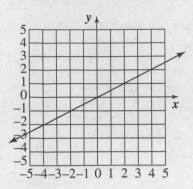

B

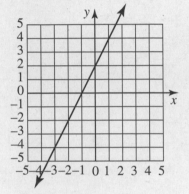

C

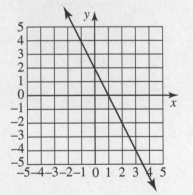

D

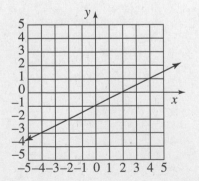

67. A dress that normally sells for $35.00 is on sale at 40% off. What is the price of the dress on sale?

　A　$14.00

　B　$21.00

　C　$25.00

　D　$49.00

$$3(x + 8) + 6 = 5(2x - 1)$$

68. To solve for x in the equation above, the first thing you should do is

　A　apply the distributive property.

　B　add −6 to each side.

　C　divide each side by 3.

　D　divide each side by 5.

69. In the figure below, $\angle LMN$ forms a 90-degree angle. What is the length of line $\overline{LM}$?

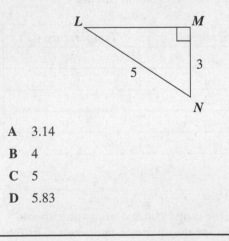

　A　3.14

　B　4

　C　5

　D　5.83

70. What is the x-intercept on the line $4x + 5y = 20$?

　A　(0, 4)

　B　(4, 0)

　C　(0, 5)

　D　(5, 0)

71. Which ordered pair below is the solution set for this system of equations?

$2x + y = 5$

$y = x - 4$

A $(-3, 1)$

B $(3, -1)$

C $(-5, 1)$

D $(5, 1)$

72. The set of numbers below displays the number of games won by each of 12 girls' volleyball teams in one division.

5, 15, 7, 4, 12, 7, 13, 9, 2, 7, 10, 15

What is the median of this set of data?

A 7

B 8

C 9

D 9.5

73. The line whose equation is $y = 3x - 4$ is parallel to the line whose equation is

A $y = \dfrac{1}{3}x - 4$

B $y = -\dfrac{1}{3}x - 4$

C $y = 3x + 1$

D $y = -3x + 1$

74. Point $(n, -2)$ lies on a line whose equation is $x - 3y = 7$. What is the value of n?

A -3

B 1

C 3

D 13

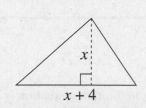

75. The base of the above triangle is 4 units longer than its height. Which of the following expressions could stand for the area of the triangle?

A $\dfrac{x^2 + 4x}{2}$

B $\dfrac{x^2 - 16}{2}$

C $\dfrac{x^2 + 4x + 4}{2}$

D $\dfrac{x^2 + 8x + 16}{2}$

76. While on vacation, Connor's parents rented a car for the weekend. Discount Rent-a-Car offers a special weekend rate: $99.00 plus $0.19 per mile driven. The total cost came to $134.72. Which of the following equations could be used to determine the number of miles they drove?

A $134.72 = .19n - 99$

B $19 = 134.72 + .99n$

C $.19n = 134.72 + 99$

D $99 + .19n = 134.72$

77. Which of these expressions is equal to a negative number?

A $(-3) \times (-3)$

B $(-3) \div (-3)$

C $(-3)^2$

D $(-3)^3$

$$2x + 5 = -1$$

78. The solution to the above equation is

A $x = -3$

B $x = -2$

C $x = 2$

D $x = 3$

---

79. A public pool holds 25,000 gallons of water. The directions on the outside of the pool say to add 2 large chlorine tablets for every 10,000 gallons of water. How many chlorine tablets should be added to the public pool water?

A 4

B 5

C 6

D 7

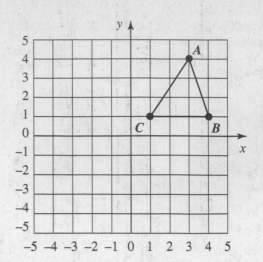

80. Triangle ABC is reflected across the x-axis. What are the coordinates of the image points of vertices A, B, and C?

A $A\,(-3, 4)$, $B\,(-4, 1)$, and $C\,(-1, 1)$

B $A\,(-4, -3)$, $B\,(-4, -1)$, and $C\,(-1, -1)$

C $A\,(3, -2)$, $B\,(4, 0)$, and $C\,(1, 0)$

D $A\,(3, -4)$, $B\,(4, -1)$, and $C\,(1, -1)$

---

81. Marta rolls a number cube with a different number—from 1 to 6—on each side. She rolls the cube twice. What is the probability that the two rolls will have a sum of 4?

A $\dfrac{1}{36}$

B $\dfrac{1}{18}$

C $\dfrac{1}{12}$

D $\dfrac{1}{9}$

Science Lab Scores

	Lab 1	Lab 2	Lab 3	Lab 4
Gail	6	8	8	7
Tanya	7	6	6	9
Martha	9	8	6	9

82. According to the above chart of science lab scores, what is Tanya's mean score?

A 6

B 6.5

C 7

D 8

83. A drawer was filled with knives, forks, and spoons. Alan reached into the drawer and took 1 knife, 3 forks, and 6 spoons. The utensils that Alan took were in proportion to their distribution in the drawer. If there were 25 utensils in the drawer to begin with, how many of them were not spoons?

A   5

B   10

C   15

D   20

84. Which of the following expresses 86,000 in scientific notation?

A 86×10^3

B 8.6×10^4

C 8.6×10^5

D 8.6×10^6

History Quiz Scores

	Quiz 1	Quiz 2	Quiz 3	Quiz 4	Quiz 5
Jacob	8	8	9	7	10
Diego	10	9	10	8	9
Clark	7	6	10	7	10

85. The above chart shows 3 students' scores on 5 history quizzes. What is the mode of Jacob's scores?

A   7

B   8

C   9

D   10

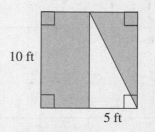

86. What is the area of the shaded region of the square shown above? (Area of a triangle = $\frac{1}{2} bh$)

A   25 ft^2

B   75 ft^2

C   100 ft^2

D   175 ft^2

87. What fraction is reduced to its lowest terms and is equal to 0.6?

A $\dfrac{3}{100}$

B $\dfrac{6}{10}$

C $\dfrac{3}{5}$

D $\dfrac{6}{5}$

88. $(6x^2y^5)(2x^3y)$ is equivalent to

A $6x^5y^6$

B $12x^6y^5$

C $12x^6y^6$

D $12x^5y^6$

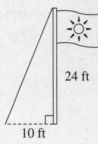

24 ft

10 ft

89. A 24-foot tall flagpole is supported by a cable. The cable is located 10 feet from the base of the flagpole. How long is the cable?

A 14 feet

B $\sqrt{476}$ feet

C 26 feet

D 34 feet

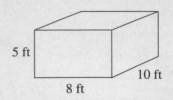

5 ft

8 ft

10 ft

90. The above rectangular prism is 8 feet wide, 10 feet long, and 5 feet high. What is its surface area?

A 170 ft²

B 180 ft²

C 340 ft²

D 400 ft²

91. What is the absolute value of –35?

A –35

B $\dfrac{1}{-35}$

C $\dfrac{1}{35}$

D 35

92. Some fifth graders were flying kites in the park. The wind took their kites to heights of 50, 36, 150, 45, 80, 45, 60, 100, and 90 feet. What was the median height at which the kites flew?

A 45 feet

B 50 feet

C 60 feet

D 73 feet

Chapter 15
Answers and
Explanations to
Practice Test 1

1. **C** *Standard SDAP 1.1*

This question asks you to find the mean number of hours that Marisol spent on-line over a four-week period. Look at the chart and find the row that shows the number of hours she spent on-line per week (cross out the rows for Nelson and Donald, they're just there to distract you). It says she spent 7 hours on-line during the first week, 8 hours on-line during the second week, 10 hours on-line during the third week, and 11 hours on-line during the fourth week. Remember that the "mean" is the average of a set of numbers. To find the mean, just add the numbers $(7 + 8 + 10 + 11)$ and divide by the number of weeks, 4 in this case. $36 \div 4 = 9$, so Marisol averaged 9 hours on-line over the four-week period.

2. **D** *Standard SDAP 2.5*

The spokesperson's claim that "Football has 7% fewer injuries per year than baseball" is deceptive, and you have to figure out why. If you can't tell from the chart given, look at the answer choices. Try **A** first: Is it true that the average number of injuries <u>per 1,000 participants</u> is greater for baseball? Well, there are almost as many football-related injuries, even though there are more than three times as many participants in baseball, so that can't be true. Likewise, there weren't one-third or 35 percent fewer injuries in football, so **B** and **C** aren't right either. That leaves **D** as the correct answer choice. Based on the chart, the average number of injuries <u>per 1,000 participants</u> is greater for football.

3. **B** *Standard SDAP 3.1*

This question is not as hard as it may first appear. Luckily, the tree diagram is extensive, and it presents all of Hakeem's 16 possible outcomes. The first step is to assign monetary values to each entry on the tree diagram. For instance, the first outcomes ("PP" and "PN") are worth $0.02 and $0.06, respectively. Go down the rest of the list and you will find the values $0.11, $0.26, $0.06, $0.10, $0.15, $0.30, $0.11, $0.15, $0.20, $0.35, $0.26, $0.30, $0.35, and $0.50. Because the question asks for the number of selections equal to $0.35, we count the two outcomes that yield such a value: QD and DQ. Two outcomes out of 16 possible outcomes is equivalent to $\frac{2}{16}$, which reduces to $\frac{1}{8}$. That makes **B** correct.

4. **B** *Standard NS 1.7*

This is one of those times it will help to create an equation to help solve the problem. Remember, 30% is equivalent to the decimal 0.30. So in order to find the amount saved, you can create the equation $150 \times 0.30 = x$. If you solve this equation accurately, you should find that the amount saved on the printer is $45, because $x = 45$. But don't stop there: The question is asking how much the printer *costs*, not how much the consumer saves. Now subtract $45 from $150 to find that $105, **B,** is the price of the printer.

5. **D** *Standard SDAP 3.3*

The question states that there are six different colors of gumballs and an equal number of each color. Therefore, if you were to choose one gumball, the probability of choosing a green gumball would be $\frac{1}{6}$, choice **A**. But the question is a bit sneakier than this. This question asks for the probability that you will not choose a green gumball. Remember that probability is always expressed as a number between 0 and 1. To find the probability that you will *not* pick a green gumball, subtract the probability of picking a green gumball from 1. $1 - \frac{1}{6} = \frac{5}{6}$. Since there are five equal ways out of six to not pick a green gumball, the probability is $\frac{5}{6}$, choice **D**.

6. **A**   *Standard MG 1.3*

This question uses some pretty complex ideas, but don't let that distract you! You don't have to know what a "person-hour" is to solve this problem. If you read the problem closely, you'll see that all you're being asked to do is convert from hours to days (days of a specific length: 8 hours). Again, it will help to create an equation. We'll need to divide 644 (the number of hours lost) by 8 (the number of hours in a workday): $644 \div 8 = 80.5$, choice **A**. Don't make the mistake, though, of multiplying 644×8, or of performing the operations of addition or subtraction, because the results of those are incorrect answer choices. Remember, there are 8 person-hours in one person-day, which means that there are going to be fewer person-days than hours!

7. **A**   *Standard NS 1.1*

Do you remember how negative exponents work? (If not, you might want to review Chapter 7 on scientific notation.) Remember, negative exponents mean the number is very small. To figure out what 10^{-3} is just move the decimal point three spaces to the left. This gives you 0.001. Now all you need to do is multiply 0.001×1.8, and you'll see that the answer is 0.0018, **A**.

8. **B**   *Standard NS 1.2*

The only way to solve this problem is to solve the math in each of the various answer choices. We're looking for a negative number, and **A** can be eliminated because the sum is equal to 3, a positive number. Choice **B** sums up to −14, so that certainly seems like the correct answer. It's always best to check the other answer choices, just in case. However, both **C** and **D** sum to positive numbers, so we can be sure that **B** is correct.

9. **D**   *Standard NS 1.2*

An easy way to solve this question is to try out a few simple division problems and see if you can settle on a general rule. If we divide 1,000 by 5 different numbers between 10 and 100, say 10, 20, 40, 50, and 100, we are left with 100, 50, 25, 20, and 10, respectively. Since all of these numbers are greater than or equal to 10, we can eliminate **A**. Also, some of the numbers are greater than 50, so we can eliminate B as well. We know for sure that all of the possible answers are between 10 and 100, but you need to confirm that 50 is one of them as well. This is proven when $1,000 \div 20 = 50$. **D** is correct.

10. **B**   *Standard NS 1.3*

For this problem, all you need to do is divide 160 by 652. Its result begins with 0.2453... As a percent this rounds easily to 25%, **B**. You can use POE to eliminate answer choice **D** immediately because that percentage would correspond to a number greater than the number of students in the entire school.

11. **C**   *Standard AI1 3.0*

The absolute value of a number is its distance from 0 on a number line. Therefore, the absolute value of a negative number is always written as a positive. For instance, the absolute value of −10 is 10, because −10 is 10 units away from 0. For this problem, you have to figure out what number's absolute value times 5 is equal to 20. The unknown number is represented by the variable y. Well, $5 \times 4 = 20$, so $|y| = 4$. Because the absolute value of −4 is also equal to 4, the solution set for y is equal to −4 and 4. You can quickly eliminate **A**, **B**, and **D** because if $y = 0$, its absolute value is still 0, and that does not solve the equation properly: $5(0) \neq 20$.

12. **B**   *Standard SDAP 1.2*

This question requires that you understand how to read a scatter plot. You'll notice that on this particular plot, there's not much scattering after all. Each point represents a particular automobile, and how many miles per gallon it achieves based on its engine size. Because the dots fall from left to right, the cars with larger engine sizes generally tend to achieve fewer miles per gallon than cars with smaller engine sizes. **B** is the only answer choice that supports this observation.

13. **C** *Standard AI1 4.0*

The order of operations will help you solve this problem. Luckily, you are not being asked to solve the inequality here; you're merely asked to determine which two inequalities are equivalent. Unfortunately, since the left side of the inequality is the same in all of the answer choices, POE won't really help you here. But if you multiply 4 by $(x - 3)$, the result will be $4x - 12$. **C** is correct.

14. **C** *Standard SDAP 3.3*

Since there are three even numbers on a number cube numbered 1 to 6, the probability of rolling an even number on a number cube is $\frac{3}{6}$, or $\frac{1}{2}$. No matter what the result of any previous experiment is, this is the theoretical probability at all times, so the answer is **C**.

15. **A** *Standard NS 2.1*

This question involves the multiplication of two numbers with exponents. One way to do this would be first to solve 3^2 and then to multiply the result by the solution of 3^4. Of course, then you would have to reduce it and convert the number back into exponent form. But why do all that work when there's a much easier solution? Since both numbers have the same base, 3, all you need to do is add the exponents together: $2 + 4 = 6$, so the answer is 3^6, choice **A**.

16. **C** *Standard NS 2.2*

Remember that the denominator is the bottom half of a fraction. Therefore, we can totally forget about the numerators 5 and 11 here. Now that those are out of the way, we're left with 12 and 18. What is the smallest number that both 12 and 18 go into evenly? It's 36. Now all you need to do is select the answer choice that produces 36. Since $2 \times 3 \times 2 \times 3 = 36$, **C** is correct.

17. **D** *Standard NS 2.3*

There are two ways to solve this question: the easy way and the hard way. The hard way is to figure out the value of every expression. 3^5, for instance is equivalent to $3 \times 3 \times 3 \times 3 \times 3$, or 243. If you simplify each of the expressions with exponents, and then perform the multiplication of the values in the numerators, you are left with the expression: $\frac{243 \times 16}{27} + \frac{36 \times 128}{16}$. Next is the multiplication stage, after which you will have $\frac{3,888}{27} + \frac{4,608}{16}$ to work with. If you reduce each fraction, you will then be left with the simple problem of $144 + 288$. Just add these together to get 432, choice **D**. We recommend using the easy way: canceling out the exponents in both fractions. Cancel the denominators out of the numerators so that $\frac{3^5 \times 4^2}{3^3} + \frac{6^2 \times 2^7}{2^4}$ simply becomes $(3^2 \times 4^2) + (6^2 \times 2^3)$. (Remember, when you divide numbers with exponents you subtract the exponents.) Then you've got $(9 \times 16) + (36 \times 8)$, which is $144 + 288 = 432$. That's much easier, right?

18. **D** *Standard MG 1.1*

If 1 quart = 0.946 liters, then 4 quarts must equal 4×0.946 liters. That equals 3.784, answer choice **D**. However, you may not even need to go this far. If you recognize that a quart and a liter are approximately the same amount, all you will need to do is look at the answer choices and see that 3.784 is closest to the number 4. (4 liters and 4 quarts are approximately the same amount.)

19. **D** *Standard SDAP 2.5*

Remember, absolute value is the distance a number is from 0 on the number line. So it doesn't matter if a nonzero number is negative or positive—its absolute value will be positive. Therefore, the absolute value of –8 is 8, choice **D**.

20. C *Standard AF 1.1*

This question requires that you convert a word problem into a mathematical equation. Take it step by step, and it should be pretty easy. Remember, you don't need to actually solve the equation; you just need to write it out. First off, Carlos is thinking of a number, which is represented by the variable n. The number is divided by 3, and then 5 is added to the result. That is key, because if you add 5 to the number n before you get the result, the equation will be totally different. So far, we should have $\frac{n}{3} + 5$. Because only one of the answer choices starts out with that expression, we know that **C** is correct.

21. A *Standard AF 1.1*

This question requires that you understand how to read an equation. You are told that a certain hockey team keeps an average of 5 sticks on hand for each player. The correct equation should display the number of players, p, being multiplied by the number 5. The equation, finally, should equal s. Only the equation in answer choice **A** uses the correct combination.

22. C *Standard AF 1.2*

Remember PEMDAS here! Before you multiply $(3x - 4)^2$ by 2, you need to solve for the exponent first. $(3x - 4)^2 = (3x - 4)(3x - 4)$. Use FOIL (First, Outside, Inside, Last) to solve this: $(3x)(3x) + (3x)(-4) + (-4)(3x) + (-4)(-4)$. That's $9x^2 - 12x - 12x + 16$, or $9x^2 - 24x + 16$. Now you can multiply this expression by 2, and you'll get $18x^2 - 48x + 32$—answer choice **C**.

23. B *Standard AF 1.5*

The easiest way to solve this question is to plug values into each answer choice and then use POE to determine which one works. For instance, one of the plotted points is (3, 1). Since the first number in the set represents the x-value and the second represents the y-value, plugging these values into the equation in choice **A** would yield the statement $1 = 3 + 2$. Clearly this is not true, so you can eliminate **A**. Choice **C** would yield $1 = 3 + 4$, and **D** would yield $1 = 3 - 4$, both of which are false. That eliminates **C** and **D**. Try the same process with choice **B**. Plugging in the values here yields the true statement $1 = 3 - 2$.

24. D *Standard AF 1.5*

This question asks you to compare two lines that are plotted on a single graph. Each line represents the cost of bowling at a given bowling alley. Depending on how many games are played, one alley costs more than the other. The point where the lines intersect is where the trend changes. At first, Bowl-a-Rama is less expensive, but once 3 games are played, the two lines intersect. Therefore, when 3 games are played, each alley charges an equal amount. However, once more than 3 games are played, Larry's Lanes costs less. That makes the statement in answer choice **D** correct.

25. B *Standard AF 2.1*

This question tests your understanding of negative exponents. Remember that $x^{-2} = \frac{1}{x^2}$? Well, using that same logic, $\frac{1}{x^{-2}} = x^2$. Therefore, since this problem has a negative exponent in the denominator, you can move it to the numerator and make it a positive exponent. That means $\frac{1}{5x^{-2}}$ is equal to $\frac{x^2}{5}$, answer choice **B**.

26. **D**   *Standard MG 2.3*

The volume for a cube or rectangular box is $V = lwh$. This is one of the formulas that you should make sure you have memorized by the time you take the CAHSEE. All you need to do is multiply the length of each side by the others. Since this figure has sides of lengths 10, 6, and 25 inches, multiply those three values to determine that **D**, 1,500 in^3, is the volume of the box. All of the answer choices give volumes that are too small for this rectangular prism.

27. **A**   *Standard AF 3.1*

This question is asking you to match an equation with a corresponding graph that has already been created. The equation in this question is $y = 2 + x^2$. The first thing to note is that x^2 can never be negative because $-1^2 = 1$, $-2^2 = 4$, and so on. So regardless of what the x-coordinate is in this graph, the y-coordinate will always be positive. Already you know that the correct answer choice must be **A**, because it's the only graph that doesn't show any points with negative values for the y-coordinate. Plug In some values to see if you're right. When $x = -4$, $y = 18$. When $x = 0$, $y = 2$. When $x = 4$, $y = 18$. That's about right for the graph in **A**.

28. **C**   *Standard AF 4.1*

You could solve this inequality by adding 9 to both sides. That means $5a - 9 < 16 = 5a - 9 + 9 < 16 + 9$, leaving you with $5a < 25$, which can then be reduced to $a < 5$ by dividing both sides by 5. That makes answer choice **C** correct.

29. **B**   *Standard AF 4.1*

In this question you are asked to plug two values into an expression. If $p = 7$ and $q = 3$, then $\frac{pq - 9}{4} + 4 = \frac{(7)(3) - 9}{4} + 4$. Remember the order of operations, and you will know to multiply 7×3 before subtracting 9, and then you will get $\frac{21 - 9}{4} + 4$, or $\frac{12}{4} + 4$. Since $\frac{12}{4}$ is equivalent to 3, and $3 + 4 = 7$, answer choice **B** is correct.

30. **A**   *Standard AF 4.2*

In this question you are asked to determine the total time a specific task will take. Remembering what we learned about rates in Chapter 6 is crucial here. Since you are trying to determine total *minutes*, you can use m as your variable. Construct the equation so that $12.5(m) = 475$. If you then divide each side of the equation by 12.5, you will see that the entire task should take Soledad 38 minutes, **A**. You could also set up a proportion so that $\frac{12.5 \text{ sq. feet}}{1 \text{ minute}} = \frac{475 \text{ sq. feet}}{m \text{ minutes}}$. Cross multiply to get $12.5x = 475$. Then divide both sides by 12.5 to isolate x. You'll get the same answer either way.

31. **C**   *Standard AF 3.3*

You will need to remember how to find the slope of a line in this problem. Remember, if a line is horizontal, its slope is 0. If the line goes up as it goes to the right, its slope is positive. If the line goes down as it goes to the right, its slope is negative. Knowing that will help you narrow down the answer choices to **C** and **D** because **A** and **B** are negative slopes and the line is clearly going up as it goes to the right. The slope of a line is its $\frac{rise}{run}$. Because this line is going up 2 units for every 6 units to the right, its slope is $\frac{2}{6}$, which is equal to $\frac{1}{3}$, answer choice **C**.

32. B *Standard AF 3.4*

The best way to solve this question would be to take a value set from the graph and plug it in to the equation $D = \frac{M}{V}$. Try it, for instance, with the point plotted near (3, 8). Since volume is represented by the x-axis, and mass is represented by the y-axis, we can rewrite the equation to read $D = \frac{8}{3}$. If you evaluate the fraction, you will recognize that $D = 2.6667$. Since this is approximately the same as 2.7, you can determine that **B** is correct. You could also use your own judgment. According to the graph, a volume of 5 cm³ is equal to a little less than 14 g. That means each cm³ is a little less than 3 g, eliminating **C** and **D** (because they're too heavy) and **A** (because it's too light).

33. B *Standard NS 2.4*

This problem asks you which two integers the square root of 795 lies between. Without a calculator, your best bet here is to Plug In the answer choices and find the one that fits. $28 \times 28 = 784$. That's too low, meaning the square root must be higher than 28. Cross off **A**, and then try 29. $29 \times 29 = 841$. Because 795 is between 784 and 841, its square root must be a number between 28 and 29, meaning that **B** is correct.

34. A *Standard MG 1.2*

The best way to solve this scale question is to set up an equation. The question states that 1 cm = 5 m in the scale drawing of a soccer field. Therefore, all you need to do is set up the equation $17.4 \times 5 = L$. Since the result is 87, you can determine that **A** is the correct answer. You can also set up a proportion so that $\frac{1\,cm}{5\,m} = \frac{17.4\,cm}{L\,m}$. Cross multiply, and you'll get the same answer: 87 *m*. The other answer choices are too large to be the actual length of the soccer field in this question.

35. A *Standard MG 2.1*

There are two ways to find the area of the shaded portion of the rectangle. You can calculate the area of the entire rectangle, and then subtract the area of the white parallelogram inside it, or you can just calculate the two shaded triangles. If you chose the former method, you should have gotten the area of the whole rectangle as 5 cm × 15 cm, or 75 cm². The area of the parallelogram is 11 cm ×5 cm, or 55 cm². 75 cm² − 55 cm² = 20 cm². If you calculate the area of the two triangles, you'll get $2 \times \frac{1}{2}$ (4 cm)(5 cm), which is also equal to 20 cm². Either way, **A** is it.

36. B *Standard SDAP 3.5*

This question requires you to be able to distinguish between dependent and independent events. Remember that dependent events are events that are related to each other; the result of one event influences the probability of the other event. Independent events have no relation to each other or their outcomes. Flipping a coin and then rolling a number cube are independent events because they don't influence each other's results. That makes **A** incorrect. Likewise, the events in answer choices **C** and **D** do not relate to each other. The events in **B** certainly do. There are 13 spades in a deck of 52 cards. If you remove one spade from the deck of 52 and don't replace it, the probability of picking another one goes down from $\frac{13}{52}$ to $\frac{12}{51}$. They're dependent events.

37. **B** *Standard MG 1.1*

It's best to write an equation or a proportion for this question. First, convert $\frac{3}{4}$ to decimal form, 0.75, and let h = hours. Because *distance = rate × time*, $132 = 0.75h$. Now divide both sides of the equation by 0.75 to determine the value of h. $132 \div 0.75 = 176$, so the train's average speed is 176 miles per hour, choice **B**. If you set up a proportion, it should look like $\frac{132 \text{ miles}}{0.75 \text{ hour}} = \frac{x \text{ miles}}{1 \text{ hour}}$. Cross multiply to get $132 = .75x$. It's the same equation, and it yields the same result.

38. **B** *Standard MG 2.1*

The diagram in this question already provides the length and the base of the triangle. That's all you need to know in order to find a triangle's area. Its height is 6 and its base is 11. Plug both values into the formula $A = \frac{1}{2}bh$ to determine the area of the triangle. $\frac{1}{2}(11)(6) = \frac{1}{2}(66)$, which is 33 square units.

39. **A** *Standard MG 2.1*

You can determine the area of each circle to solve this problem, but it's not entirely necessary. The question asks for the ratio of $\frac{area\ of\ circle\ A}{area\ of\ circle\ B}$. The formula for the area of a circle, as given, is $A = \pi r^2$. That means the fraction is now $\frac{\pi 4^2}{\pi 8^2}$. The π in the numerator cancels the π in the denominator, leaving you with $\frac{4^2}{8^2}$, which is $\frac{16}{64}$. You can simplify the fraction at this point, and you will discover that the answer is **A**, $\frac{1}{4}$.

40. **B** *Standard MG 2.2*

This question requires that you understand how to determine the area of a triangle, as well as the area of a circle. Once you have the area of each, you can subtract the area of the triangle from the area of circle. The remaining value will be the answer. Since the triangle's base is 10 in and its height is 15 in, multiply 10 in × 15 in × $\frac{1}{2}$ to determine the triangle's area. The result is 75 in². The circle's radius is 9 in. Using the formula $A = \pi r^2$, you can determine that the circle's area is approximately 3.14 × 9 in × 9 in or 254.34 in². Now, the questions says *approximately*, so let's round 254.34 to 254 to make it easier on ourselves. Finally, subtract 75 in² from 254 in² and you will find that 179, **B**, is the approximate area of the remaining paper.

41. **B** *Standard AI1 6.0*

You're asked for the coordinates of the point that lies on the *y*-axis of the line whose equation is $3x + 2y = 8$. Any point on the *y*-axis must have 0 for its *x*-coordinate. That means you can use POE to get rid of **C** and **D**—those points lie on the *x*-axis. Now you can just plug $x = 0$ into the equation to see what you get for *y*. $3x + 2y = 8$ then becomes $3(0) + 2y = 8$, or $2y = 8$. At that point you can divide both sides of the equation by 2 to see that the *y*-coordinate of the point must be 4. That's (0, 4), answer choice **B**.

42. **B** *Standard MG 2.2*

This question can be solved using a similar method to question 40. However, you are required here to determine the area of a hexagon—which is like two trapezoids connected at the base. Mr. Harris's backyard, in total, measures 24 ft × 30 ft, or 720 ft². Since you're looking for the area of the backyard *minus* the area of the hexagonal gazebo, you know it must be less than 720 ft². Use POE to cross off **D**, and you're down to three possible answer choices. You can calculate the area of each identical trapezoid, using the formula $\frac{1}{2}(b_1 + b_2)h$. That translates to $\frac{1}{2}(10\text{ ft} + 18\text{ ft})(8\text{ ft})$, or $\frac{1}{2}(28\text{ ft})(8\text{ ft})$, which is equal to 112 ft². Each trapezoid is 112 ft², which makes the hexagon's area 112 ft² × 2, or 224 ft². So the area of the uncovered grass is 720 ft² – 224 ft², which comes out to 496 ft², answer choice **B**.

43. **C**   *Standard AF 2.2*

This question asks you to multiply two algebriac expressions and to simplify the answer. Remember that when you *multiply* exponents with the same base, you just *add* the exponents together. Therefore, the z^4 and z^3 in this problem would multiply to z^7. (Knowing that, you can already cross off **A** and **B**.) Multiply the like terms: $3 \times 3 = 9$; $x^3 \times x = x^4$; $y \times y^3 = y^4$; $z^4 \times z^3 = z^7$. Put all of those terms together, and you'll get $9x^4y^4z^7$, answer choice **C**.

44. **B**   *Standard MG 2.4*

Before you answer this question you will first need to determine the area of Maria's room. Multiply 9×12 to determine that it is 108 square feet. Now you will need to convert from square feet to square yards. 1 square yard is equivalent to 9 square feet (3 ft × 3 ft); now just divide 108 by 9 to get the final answer: $108 \div 9 = 12$, answer choice **B**.

45. **A**   *Standard MG 3.2*

Plotting the given points on a piece of scratch paper may help you visualize the shape of the unknown quadrilateral in this question. The top and bottom sides are horizontal and therefore parallel. One line stretches from 1 to 5, the other from 3 to 7, so they are the same length. However, because the top and bottom lines don't create 90° angles with the sides, the shape can't be a square or a rectangle. And because the top and bottom lines are the same length, the shape must be a parallelogram.

46. **B**   *Standard MG 3.3*

Do you remember the Pythagorean theorem? Since this is a right triangle, we can use it to determine the answer. Because $a^2 + b^2 = c^2$, $7^2 + 24^2 = c^2$. This converts to $49 + 576 = c^2$, or $625 = c^2$. Now all you need to do is determine the square root of 625. If you're not sure, Plug In the numbers in the answer choices. Does $23 \times 23 = 625$? No, so try 25. Does $25 \times 25 = 625$? Yes, so 25 is the length of side c. **B** is correct.

47. **D**   *Standard MG 3.4*

The question tells us that $\angle A$ and $\angle D$ are both right angles, and are therefore congruent. It follows that if C is the midpoint of $\overline{AD}$, then $\overline{AC}$ and $\overline{CD}$ must be congruent also. So you already know that one corresponding angle and one corresponding side of $\triangle ABC$ are congruent to $\triangle DEC$. Answer choices **A**, **B**, and **C** don't give two corresponding sides or angles, so they won't help prove congruency between the two triangles. But if you know that $\angle DCE \cong \angle BCA$, then you can use angle-side-angle (ASA) to prove congruency. That makes **D** correct.

48. **D**   *Standard SDAP 1.1*

Remember, the mode is the value in a data set that appears most often. (If you didn't know what "modal" meant, you could probably guess that this question was looking for the *mode*, because the two words are similar.) In Daphne's row of the diagram, it says that she studied 8 hours once, 9 hours once, and 12 hours twice. Since Daphne studied for 12 hours more than any other value, the modal number of hours per week of time spent on her homework was 12, as in **D**.

49. **C** *Standard SDAP 1.1*

This question requires you to compare each day listed in the graph to the previous day of the week. You have to pick the day in which the temperature increased the most from the previous day. Be careful: You're not looking for the hottest day, just the day when the temperature increased the most from the previous day. If you compare Sunday to Saturday you will see a jump of about 2 degrees. Comparing Monday to Sunday actually shows a decrease in temperature, so we can rule out choice **B**. Comparing Tuesday to Monday shows a rise of about 8 degrees, and comparing Wednesday to Tuesday show a rise of about 2 degrees. Based on this reading, the temperature increased most from Monday to Tuesday, choice **C**.

50. **D** *Standard SDAP 1.1*

This question is a lot like the last one, isn't it? Again, be careful. You're not looking for the highest temperature, which occurred at 3 P.M. Instead, you're looking for the largest rise in temperature from one hour to the next. From 12 P.M. to 1 P.M., answer choice **D**, the temperature rose 20°, which is the greatest increase in temperature shown between two consecutive points on the graph.

51. **B** *Standard NS 1.7*

This question is really asking you what percent $8.00 is of $40.00 because $8.00 is being taken off of the original price. All you need to do to solve this is divide 8 by 40. $8 \div 40 = 0.2$. That means that **B**, 20%, is correct because 0.2 is equivalent to 20%.

52. **A** *Standard SDAP 1.1*

This question requires you to read each answer choice and compare it to the data in the graph. Answer choice **A** states that Richard lost the most weight between weeks 1 and 2. According to the graph, Richard lost 10 pounds between weeks 1 and 2, the biggest weekly loss. So, the statement in answer choice **A** is true. But check the other answer choices to be sure that choice **A** is the best answer. The graph doesn't show anything about what Richard ate, so answer choice **B** is not true. If you compare answer choice **C** to the data in the graph, you see that this choice is false. Richard weighed more in week 6 than in week 5. Answer choice **D** states that Richard lost a total of 10 pounds. Again, check each answer choice against the graph. Richard lost over 20 pounds, so answer choice **D** is false.

53. **C** *Standard MR 1.1*

Moises certainly has an interesting way of remembering things! To answer this question, though, all you need to find is a multiple of 6 and 8 that is less than 31 (because there are 31 days in January). You don't have to worry about the 3, because 6 is already a multiple of 3. First, determine all of the multiples of 8 that are lower than 31 (8, 16, and 24). Then you can determine that 24 is the only one that's also a multiple of 6. That means that January 24, answer choice **C**, is Moises's sister's birthday.

54. **A** *Standard MG 1.3*

This is a rather complicated problem, so it's important to keep your work organized. The first thing to do is find out how much money the plant makes in an hour. Multiply 1,200 by $0.10 to determine this figure. $1,200 \times \$0.10 = \$120$. Now subtract the combined salary of the employees from $120 to see how much profit the plant generates per hour. Ten employees earning $10 per hour is $10 \times \$10$, or $100. $120 – $100 is a difference of $20; that's the hourly profit of the plant. Therefore, in an 8-hour day, the plant makes 20×8, or $160 in profit. In a 12-hour day, the plant would make 20×12, or $240—an extra $80 profit for 4 extra hours. Answer choice **A** is the one you want.

55. **A** *Standard MR 1.1*

The best way to answer this question is to determine the duration of each trip listed and then choose the one that has the shortest travel time. Remember that an hour has 60 minutes, not 100, a common oversight in these types of problems. Since the first train makes the trip in only 11 hours, 10 minutes, you can determine that **A** is correct.

56. **B** *Standard MR 1.2*

Remember that an obtuse triangle is one that has an angle greater than 90°. (An obtuse angle is more than 90°, an acute angle is less than 90°.) Also remember that the two base angles of an isosceles triangle are equal. Since triangles have angles that add up to 180° in total, and an obtuse angle is more than 90° (meaning more than half of 180°), an obtuse triangle has an angle whose measure is more than two times the measure of one of the base angles. You know this for sure because the base angles in an isosceles triangle are equal. If the obtuse vertex angle is more than 90°, the other angles must be less than 45°. Answer choice **B** is correct.

57. **B** *Standard AF 3.3*

In order to answer this question you must remember how to find the slope of a line. You can use the equation $\frac{y_2 - y_1}{x_2 - x_1}$. Since you know the coordinates of two points, plug them into the formula to get $\frac{-1-(-3)}{0-3}$ which reduces to $\frac{-1+3}{-3}$ and then $-\frac{2}{3}$. If you sketched the line on scratch paper, perhaps you noticed that the line is going down as it moves to the right. That means the line has a negative slope. That would eliminate **C** and **D**, because the slopes in those answer choices are positive.

58. **D** *Standard MR 2.3*

The best way to answer this question is to look at the graph and determine any kind of visible trend. Clearly it appears that whole milk consumption has gone down steadily every five years. Therefore, it is reasonable to expect that in 1965 the figure was higher than it was in 1970. That means it is most likely that the figure is higher than 25, **C**, based on how steady the trend is. **D**, 29, seems to be the best choice.

59. **A** *Standard MR 2.4*

In Sherine's statement she claims, "If I do not take my umbrella, my hair will get wet. If my hair gets wet, I will look silly. If I look silly, I will not feel very good." From these statements, you can deduce that if she feels very good, she must have taken an umbrella, so **A** seems like a good choice. However, some other choices also seem reasonable. Choice **B** proposes that if Sherine does not feel good it is because her hair got wet. While that may be true, there are other reasons that Sherine may not feel good that are completely unrelated. Choice **C** is incorrect for the same reason. **D** is a bit more tricky. It's certainly possible, however, for Sherine's hair to get wet even if she takes her umbrella. (But if she doesn't take an umbrella, it most certainly will get wet!) **A** is correct because Sherine states that she will not feel good if she forgets her umbrella.

60. **D** *Standard SDAP 1.1*

In order to answer this question, you will need to compare the black bars with the white bars and correctly identify the years in which Sammy Sosa hit more home runs than Barry Bonds. According to the key, Sammy Sosa's home runs are represented by black bars. So, you are looking for the years in which the black bars are higher than the white bars. On the graph, the black bars are higher than the white bars in the years 1998, 1999, and 2000. You can therefore eliminate answer choices **A** and **B**. Although answer choice **C** lists the years 1998 and 1999, it is not the correct answer because it doesn't list the year 2000. Answer choice **D** is the correct answer.

61. **B**   *Standard MR 2.1*
Seema clearly has a very good eye for detail! When solving this problem, don't get distracted by the wrong answer that Seema got, though. Since you only need to find the approximate volume of the cylinder, you can estimate the volume, like Seema did, by multiplying 3 (for π) times 8 (an estimate of the radius) times 8 (because it's squared) times the height, which is about 20 cm. That's $3 \times 8 \times 8 \times 20$, answer choice **B**.

62. **A**   *Standard AI1 2.0*
This question presents an equation where the variable x has two possible values. To solve $3x^2 + 5 = 152$, subtract 5 from both sides of the equation to get $3x^2 = 147$. Then you can divide both sides by 3 to get $x^2 = 49$, meaning $x = \sqrt{49}$. At this point you should be aware that the variable x can be equal to either 7 or –7. (Both numbers squared equal 49.)

63. **C**   *Standard NS 1.3*
Can you think of a fraction that is the equivalent of 10%? It's $\frac{1}{10}$. Since $\frac{1}{10}$ is equivalent to 10%, $\frac{4}{10}$ must be equivalent to 40%. $\frac{4}{10}$ reduces to $\frac{2}{5}$, which is answer choice **C**. Another way to solve this problem would be to divide the numerator by the denominator in each answer choice. Eventually, you will find that $2 \div 5 = 0.40$, which is the same thing as 40%. Answer choice **C** is correct.

64. **C**   *Standard MR 3.3*
The best way to solve this problem is to find a pattern in the data. For the first four sets of data in Table 2, the temperature in °F has gone up 18° from the previous temperature. Therefore, it is most reasonable to deduce that when the temperature in °C rises from 30 to 40, the temperature in °F will again increase by 18°F. Because $86 + 18$ is 104, **C** is the correct answer.

65. **B**   *Standard AI1 4.0*
This question is best solved by using cross multiplication. Remember, though, that you are not required to solve for a, so don't waste your time trying! All you need to do is identify the equation that you would have after the first two steps of multiplication. First, multiply 14 by $a + 3$ to get $14(a + 3)$. Since only one answer choice, **B**, has that included as part of it, you can determine that **B** is correct. (The right side of the equation in answer choice **B** is also the second step of the cross multiplication process.)

66. **B**   *Standard AF 1.5*
This question is similar to question 23; however, you now need to determine which line matches up to a predetermined equation. The easiest way to solve it is to Plug In values from each answer choice into the equation to determine which one works. For instance, one of the plotted points in choice **B** is (1, 4). Since the first number in the set represents the x-value and the second represents the y-value, plugging these into the equation would yield the statement $2 \times 1 = 4 - 2$, or $2 = 2$. Try the same process with a point from each graph. Once you have done so, you will see that choice **B** is correct, because those values will create a true equation.

67. **B**   *Standard NS 1.7*
All you need to do to solve this problem is multiply $35 by 40%, and then subtract that result from $35. 40% converts to a decimal value of 0.4, and $35 \times 0.4 = 14. $35 – $14 = 21, the right answer. Since the price of the dress is decreasing by 40%, it is retaining 60% of its original value. Therefore, you could also multiply $35 by 60%, or 0.6, to find the sale price of the dress: $35 \times 0.6 = 21.00, answer choice **B**.

68. **A** *Standard AI1 5.0*

This question involves deciding what strategy to use before you approach a complex equation. It also makes sure that you're familiar with the distributive property and the order of operations (it's PEMDAS, all over again). When you're faced with the kind of problem, $3(x + 8) + 6 = 5(2x - 1)$, it's important to distribute the first number over the set of numbers that it's multiplying. So the 3 should get multiplied by the x and the 8; the 5 should get multiplied by the $2x$ and the -1. Since you're distributing the numbers around, it's a process of the distributive property. You shouldn't add or divide anything until you've done that. So **A** is the correct answer choice.

69. **B** *Standard MG 3.3*

Since this is a right triangle, we can use the Pythagorean theorem to determine the answer. Because $a^2 + b^2 = c^2$, $3^2 + b^2 = 5^2$, since line $\overline{LN}$ is the hypotenuse. This converts to $9 + b^2 = 25$. Subtract 9 from each side to yield $b^2 = 16$. Now all you need to do is determine the square root of 16, which is 4. Therefore, 4, answer choice **B**, is the length of line $\overline{LM}$.

70. **D** *Standard AI1 6.0*

Remember, the x-intercept must have a y-value of 0. You can therefore eliminate choices **A** and **C** because each ordered pair has a value for y other than 0. Now you must decide between (4, 0) and (5, 0). If you plug the value 4 for x and 0 for y into the equation $4x + 5y = 20$ you are left with $16 + 0 = 20$, so **B** is incorrect. The values for choice **D**, however, yield the equation $20 + 0 = 20$, which of course proves that choice **D** is correct. You could also have figured out the coordinates by inserting 0 as the line's y-coordinate. $4x + 5(0) = 20$ is equivalent to $4x = 20$. Divide both sides of the equation by 4, and you'll see that the x-coordinate is indeed 5.

71. **B** *Standard AI1 9.0*

The best way to solve this question is to Plug In the values from the ordered pairs in the answer choices into the equations. Go through each answer choice, starting with **A**. $(-3, 1)$, when used in the first equation, yields the statement $-6 + 1 = 5$. That's not right. Try **B** next. Using the ordered pair $(3, -1)$, $2x + y = 5$ becomes $2(3) - 1 = 5$, which works. Don't forget to try the second equation too! (Some pairs will work for one equation but not both!) Does $y = x - 4$ if $x = 3$ and $y = -1$? Well, $-1 = 3 - 4$, so yes, it works. Choices **C** and **D** are incorrect because their pairs do not correctly satisfy both equations in the system. **B** is the correct answer.

72. **B** *Standard SDAP 1.1*

Remember that the median of a data set is the number that lies exactly in the middle of the set. The first thing you need to do to solve this is put the numbers in the set in numerical order. So your data set now reads 2, 4, 5, 7, 7, 7, 9, 10, 12, 13, 15, 15. Since there is an even number of values in the set, you will have to take the average of the two numbers that fall in the middle. In this case, the two numbers in the middle are 7 and 9, and their average is 8. (If it helps to find the median, you can always cross off the lowest and highest numbers in a set until you're left with one or two numbers.)

73. **C** *Standard AI1 8.0*

One way to solve this question is to plot 2 or 3 points for each equation onto scratch paper and determine which one yields a line parallel to the line yielded by the equation. But that requires a lot of work. Remember that parallel lines have the same slope. You can easily figure out which answer choice lists a parallel slope to the line whose equation is $y = 3x - 4$ if you remember that the formula for lines in this situation is always given in the form $y = mx + b$, and m is the slope of the line. The slope of the line in the question here is 3. Now all you have to do is find the equation of the line in the answer choice that also has 3 in the slope position. The only one that has the same slope is the equation in answer choice **C**.

74. **B** *Standard Al1 7.0*

This question requires that you understand how an equation relates to the line that it plots. Since n in this ordered pair represents the x-value, plug in –2 for the y-value in the equation. $x - 3y = 7$ then becomes $n - 3(-2) = 7$, which is equal to $n + 3(2) = 7$, $n + 6 = 7$. Subtract 6 from both sides of the equation, and n would therefore equal 1, making **B** correct.

75. **A** *Standard Al1 10.0*

Remember, the formula for determining the area of a triangle is $A = \frac{1}{2}bh$. You're not given exact values for the dimensions, but you know that the base is $x + 4$ and the height is x. That means that the area of this triangle could be determined by the statement $\frac{1}{2}(x + 4)x$, or $\frac{1}{2}(x^2 + 4x)$. When divided by 2, the expression $(x^2 + 4x)$ would be the numerator, with 2 as the denominator, as in choice **A**.

76. **D** *Standard Al1 15.0*

This question requires you to understand how to create an equation based on a word problem. Since the total cost of the rental was \$134.72, one side of the written equation should equal this amount. Therefore, you can eliminate choices **B** and **C** because neither equation equals \$134.72. The proper equation will also multiply .19 by a variable—n, for instance—with n representing the number of miles driven. Finally, the proper equation will add 99 to the expression .19n, because the \$99 fee is in addition to the per-mile fee. Only choice **D** meets all of these criteria.

77. **D** *Standard NS 1.2*

Remember, a negative multiplied by a negative equals a positive, so you can eliminate choices **A** and **C**. Choice **B** can be eliminated as well, because $-3 \div -3 = 1$. **D** is correct, because a negative times a negative times a negative equals a negative. (A negative squared is always positive, but a negative to the third power is negative.)

78. **A** *Standard AF 4.1*

All this question is asking you to do is to solve for x. You can do this by subtracting 5 from both sides of the equation to get $2x = -6$. Then you can divide by 2 to find that $x = -3$. Another strategy is to plug each answer choice into the equation until you find the one that yields the statement $-1 = -1$. If you plug in –3, you produce the equation $2 \times -3 + 5 = -1$. This converts to $-6 + 5 = -1$, or $-1 = -1$. **A** is therefore correct because all of the other choices yield false equations.

79. **B** *Standard AF 4.2*

Two tablets must be added for every 10,000 gallons of water, which is the same as 1 tablet for every 5,000 gallons. Since there are 25,000 gallons of water in the pool, divide 25,000 by 5,000 to determine that the pool needs 5 tablets, as in choice **B**. You can also set up a proportion so that $\frac{10,000}{2} = \frac{25,000}{x}$. Cross multiply, and you'll find that $10,000x = 50,000$, giving $x = 5$.

80. **D** *Standard MG 3.2*

The reflection of an image is similar to the reflection you see when you look in a mirror: it's the complete opposite. When reflecting across the x-axis, the x-value of each point remains constant, but the y-values change to their opposites. The best way to solve this is to first determine where each point of the triangle would reflect individually. Point A, for instance, at (3, 4) reflects to (3, –4). Because **D** is the only answer choice that includes these coordinates for point A, **D** is correct. If you're still not sure, go ahead and find the coordinates for the reflected points B and C—they're (4, –1) and (1, –1), respectively.

81.　**C**　*Standard SDAP 3.3*
For this problem it will probably help to draw a diagram.

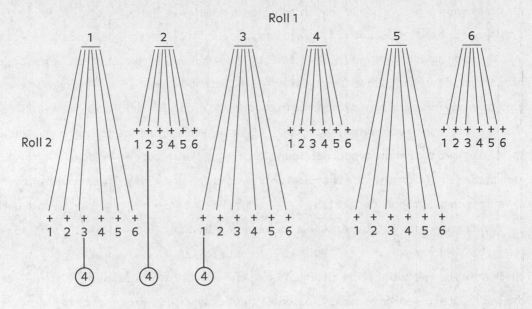

Marta rolls the cube twice. You can see from the diagram we drew that there are 36 possible outcomes. (You could also have multiplied 6 times 6 to get this: 6 possible outcomes for each cube.) Count all possible pairs of numbers that have a sum of 4. Then you should see that there are 3 favorable outcomes with a sum of 4: 1 + 3, 2 + 2, and 3 + 1. That's 3 possible outcomes out of 36. Since we can write probability as a fraction, that becomes $\frac{3}{36}$, which simplifies to $\frac{1}{12}$, answer choice **C**.

82.　**C**　*Standard SDAP 1.1*
To answer this question, you need to know how to compute the mean, or average. You do that by adding the data points and then dividing the total by the number of individual data points. To determine Tanya's mean score, locate Tanya's name on the chart, add up the scores in her row, and then divide by 4, which is the number of individual scores in her row. The mean is 7.

83. **B** *Standard SDAP 3.5*

You need to determine how many utensils in the drawer were not spoons. Because the utensils that Alan took were in proportion to their distribution in the drawer, the best way to approach this question is to set up the proportion of forks and knives to spoons in Alan's handful and then translate that into the total amount of utensils. Alan had a total of 4 forks and knives. He also had 6 spoons. The proportion of forks and knives to spoons is $\frac{4}{6}$, which can be simplified to $\frac{2}{3}$. Now we need to find out how many forks and knives compared to spoons that proportion translates into out of 25. Notice that the total number of utensils Alan took is 10, and the numbers of our proportion, 4 and 6, total to 10. We need to find the proportion equivalent to $\frac{2}{3}$ whose numbers add up to 25. Now let's just Plug In the values from the answer choices until we find one that works. Starting with answer choice **A** we'll set up our proportions like this: $\frac{2}{3} = \frac{5}{x}$, which doesn't work, because $5 + x$ has to equal 25, but $\frac{5}{20}$ reduces to $\frac{1}{4}$, not $\frac{2}{3}$. Cross off **A**. For answer choice **B** we get $\frac{2}{3} = \frac{10}{x}$. Now, $10 + x$ has to equal 25, remember, which means that $x = 15$. Does $\frac{10}{15}$ reduce to $\frac{2}{3}$? Yes! So **B** is probably our answer. Let's check the other two choices first, though. $15 + x$ has to equal 25, which means $x = 10$. but $\frac{15}{10}$ certainly doesn't reduce to $\frac{2}{3}$ so cross out **C**. Cross out **D**, too, because if 15 doesn't work, then 20 won't either. Choice **B** is our answer.

84. **B** *Standard NS 1.1*

Remember that scientific notation is written in the form of *a number less than 10* multiplied by a power of 10. Although the product in answer choice **A** equals 86,000, it is not in proper scientific notation because 86 is not less than 10. The product in answer choice **B** is also equal to 86,000; and 8.6 is less than 10, so this is the correct answer. The decimal point in 8.6 is moved 4 places to the right, which equals 86,000.

85. **B** *Standard SDAP 1.1*

Remember that the mode is the most frequently occurring value in a sequence of numbers. Locate Jacob's name in the chart and compare the scores listed in his row. Jacob scored an 8, 8, 9, 7, and 10. Because 8 occurs the most frequently in the data set of Jacob's scores, 8 is the mode.

86. **B** *Standard MG 2.2*

The question asks you to find the area of only the shaded region. First, determine the area of the entire square. $10 \times 10 = 100$ ft². Then, find the area of the unshaded region (the triangle), and subtract the unshaded region from the area of the entire square. The area of the unshaded region (the triangle) is $\frac{1}{2} \times 5 \times 10 = \frac{5 \times 10}{2} = 25$ ft². Now, subtract the area of the triangle from the area of the square: 100 ft² – 25 ft² = 75 ft². The difference is the area of the square's shaded region, answer choice **B**.

87. **C**   *Standard NS 1.3*

Note that the question asks you for a fraction that is reduced to its lowest terms. This means that no number can be divided into both the numerator and denominator. To answer the question, first convert 0.6 into the fraction $\frac{6}{10}$. Be careful! Although answer choice **B**, $\frac{6}{10}$, is equal to 0.6, it is not fully reduced. Answer choice **B** is therefore not the correct answer. You have to reduce the fraction to $\frac{3}{5}$, answer choice **C**.

88. **D**   *Standard AF 2.1*

When multiplying variables raised to different powers, remember the rules of exponents. $x^a \times x^b = x^{a+b}$, not x^{ab}. For this question, just add the exponents: $x^2 \times x^3 = x^{2+3} = x^5$. To find the answer, you might want to break down the terms and plug in the rest of the numbers from the question: $6 \times 2 = 12$, $x^2 \times x^3 = x^5$, and $y^5 \times y = y^6$. The final answer is $12x^5y^6$, answer choice **D**.

89. **C**   *Standard MG 3.3*

As you can see from the diagram, the cable is basically the hypotenuse of a right triangle. To answer this question, you just have to remember the Pythagorean theorem: $a^2 + b^2 = c^2$. Plug the numbers from the diagram into the formula: $10^2 + 24^2 = c^2 = 676$. To figure out which of the answer choices is the square root of 676, just multiple each answer choice by itself until you find the one that equals 676. $26 \times 26 = 676$, so answer choice **C** is correct.

90. **C**   *Standard MG 2.3*

To find the surface area, calculate the area of each face of the rectangular prism and add them together. Remember that there are 6 faces, and opposite faces are congruent. Find the area of each of the 3 unique faces of the rectangular prism, double them, and find their sum: $2(5 \times 8) + 2(8 \times 10) + 2(5 \times 10) = 340$ ft^2.

91. **D**   *Standard NS 2.5*

One way to think about absolute value is as a measure of distance. The absolute value of a number is how far that number is from 0 on the number line. You can't have a negative distance. Therefore, you can eliminate answer choices **A** and **B** because they are negative numbers. Also, because –35 is a whole number, you can eliminate answer choices that are fractions. Thus, the absolute value of –35 must be 35, answer choice **D**.

92. **C**   *Standard SDAP 1.1*

Remember that the median is the middle number in a set of data when the data is ordered from least to greatest. If there is an even number of items of data in a set, the median is the mean, or average, of the two middle numbers. In this question, you need to arrange the numbers from least to greatest and then find the middle value. The middle value of the 9 heights is 60 feet, answer choice **C**.

Chapter 16
Practice Test 2

CAHSEE: Mathematics Practice Test #2 Answer Sheet

1 Ⓐ Ⓑ Ⓒ Ⓓ   **2** Ⓐ Ⓑ Ⓒ Ⓓ   **3** Ⓐ Ⓑ Ⓒ Ⓓ

4 Ⓐ Ⓑ Ⓒ Ⓓ   **5** Ⓐ Ⓑ Ⓒ Ⓓ   **6** Ⓐ Ⓑ Ⓒ Ⓓ

7 Ⓐ Ⓑ Ⓒ Ⓓ   **8** Ⓐ Ⓑ Ⓒ Ⓓ   **9** Ⓐ Ⓑ Ⓒ Ⓓ

10 Ⓐ Ⓑ Ⓒ Ⓓ   **11** Ⓐ Ⓑ Ⓒ Ⓓ   **12** Ⓐ Ⓑ Ⓒ Ⓓ

13 Ⓐ Ⓑ Ⓒ Ⓓ   **14** Ⓐ Ⓑ Ⓒ Ⓓ   **15** Ⓐ Ⓑ Ⓒ Ⓓ

16 Ⓐ Ⓑ Ⓒ Ⓓ   **17** Ⓐ Ⓑ Ⓒ Ⓓ   **18** Ⓐ Ⓑ Ⓒ Ⓓ

19 Ⓐ Ⓑ Ⓒ Ⓓ   **20** Ⓐ Ⓑ Ⓒ Ⓓ   **21** Ⓐ Ⓑ Ⓒ Ⓓ

22 Ⓐ Ⓑ Ⓒ Ⓓ   **23** Ⓐ Ⓑ Ⓒ Ⓓ   **24** Ⓐ Ⓑ Ⓒ Ⓓ

25 Ⓐ Ⓑ Ⓒ Ⓓ   **26** Ⓐ Ⓑ Ⓒ Ⓓ   **27** Ⓐ Ⓑ Ⓒ Ⓓ

28 Ⓐ Ⓑ Ⓒ Ⓓ   **29** Ⓐ Ⓑ Ⓒ Ⓓ   **30** Ⓐ Ⓑ Ⓒ Ⓓ

31 Ⓐ Ⓑ Ⓒ Ⓓ   **32** Ⓐ Ⓑ Ⓒ Ⓓ   **33** Ⓐ Ⓑ Ⓒ Ⓓ

34 Ⓐ Ⓑ Ⓒ Ⓓ   **35** Ⓐ Ⓑ Ⓒ Ⓓ   **36** Ⓐ Ⓑ Ⓒ Ⓓ

37 Ⓐ Ⓑ Ⓒ Ⓓ   **38** Ⓐ Ⓑ Ⓒ Ⓓ   **39** Ⓐ Ⓑ Ⓒ Ⓓ

40 Ⓐ Ⓑ Ⓒ Ⓓ   **41** Ⓐ Ⓑ Ⓒ Ⓓ   **42** Ⓐ Ⓑ Ⓒ Ⓓ

43 Ⓐ Ⓑ Ⓒ Ⓓ   **44** Ⓐ Ⓑ Ⓒ Ⓓ   **45** Ⓐ Ⓑ Ⓒ Ⓓ

46 (A) (B) (C) (D)   47 (A) (B) (C) (D)   48 (A) (B) (C) (D)

49 (A) (B) (C) (D)   50 (A) (B) (C) (D)   51 (A) (B) (C) (D)

52 (A) (B) (C) (D)   53 (A) (B) (C) (D)   54 (A) (B) (C) (D)

55 (A) (B) (C) (D)   56 (A) (B) (C) (D)   57 (A) (B) (C) (D)

58 (A) (B) (C) (D)   59 (A) (B) (C) (D)   60 (A) (B) (C) (D)

61 (A) (B) (C) (D)   62 (A) (B) (C) (D)   63 (A) (B) (C) (D)

64 (A) (B) (C) (D)   65 (A) (B) (C) (D)   66 (A) (B) (C) (D)

67 (A) (B) (C) (D)   68 (A) (B) (C) (D)   69 (A) (B) (C) (D)

70 (A) (B) (C) (D)   71 (A) (B) (C) (D)   72 (A) (B) (C) (D)

73 (A) (B) (C) (D)   74 (A) (B) (C) (D)   75 (A) (B) (C) (D)

76 (A) (B) (C) (D)   77 (A) (B) (C) (D)   78 (A) (B) (C) (D)

79 (A) (B) (C) (D)   80 (A) (B) (C) (D)   81 (A) (B) (C) (D)

82 (A) (B) (C) (D)   83 (A) (B) (C) (D)   84 (A) (B) (C) (D)

85 (A) (B) (C) (D)   86 (A) (B) (C) (D)   87 (A) (B) (C) (D)

88 (A) (B) (C) (D)   89 (A) (B) (C) (D)   90 (A) (B) (C) (D)

91 (A) (B) (C) (D)   92 (A) (B) (C) (D)

1. The table below shows the number of points three players scored in the first four basketball games of the season.

Number of Points Scored

	Game 1	Game 2	Game 3	Game 4
Ellen	6	7	10	4
Karla	9	6	5	8
Cherisse	5	8	6	9

What is the mean number of points Karla scored per game?

A   6

B   7

C   8

D   9

2. The volume of a gas under constant pressure varies directly with its temperature in Kelvin. If a container of 250 ml of nitrogen gas at 275 Kelvin is heated under constant pressure to 440 Kelvin, what is the new volume of the gas?

A   156 ml

B   400 ml

C   415 ml

D   484 ml

3. Denesh rolls two number cubes with faces numbered 1–6. The table shown below represents all the possible outcomes for the sum of the two number cubes.

Sums of Two Number Cubes

1st Cube	2nd Cube					
	1	2	3	4	5	6
1	2	3	4	5	6	7
2	3	4	5	6	7	8
3	4	5	6	7	8	9
4	5	6	7	8	9	10
5	6	7	8	9	10	11
6	7	8	9	10	11	12

What is the theoretical probability that the sum of the two number cubes will equal 9?

A $\dfrac{1}{18}$

B $\dfrac{1}{9}$

C $\dfrac{5}{36}$

D $\dfrac{1}{6}$

4. Given that n is an integer, what is the solution set for $4|n| = 24$?

A $\{0, 6\}$

B $\{-6, 0, 6\}$

C $\{-6, 6\}$

D $\{0, 96\}$

5. Which of the following pairs of events describes two <u>independent</u> events?

A   Picking a pair of white socks from a drawer that contains 5 white pairs and 3 gray pairs; picking another pair of white socks from the drawer

B   Drawing an ace for a standard deck of 52 cards without replacing it; drawing a king from the same deck of cards

C   Picking a girl from a class of 16 girls and 14 boys; picking a boy from a different class of 12 girls and 17 boys

D   Drawing a black marble from a bag that contains 1 black and 9 white; drawing a white marble from the same bag of marbles

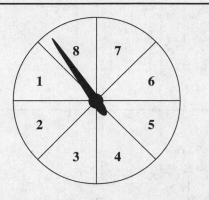

6. A fair spinner is illustrated in the diagram above. If Victor spins one time, what is the theoretical probability that the number the spinner stops on is <u>not</u> 3?

A $\dfrac{1}{8}$

B $\dfrac{1}{4}$

C $\dfrac{3}{4}$

D $\dfrac{7}{8}$

7. $7.8 \times 10^3 =$

A   7.8000

B   78

C   780

D   7,800

8. Which mathematical expression below has a negative value?

A $(5) - (8)$

B $(-5) - (-8)$

C $(8) - (5)$

D $(5) - (-8)$

9. If a number between 1 and 10 is divided by 1,000, the answer must be

A   less than 0.

B   between 0 and 0.01.

C   between 0.01 and 0.1.

D   between 0.1 and 1.

10. Of the 203 cars parked in a parking lot, 150 were made in the United States. About what percentage of the cars were made in the United States?

A   15%

B   50%

C   75%

D   150%

11. What is 80% expressed as a fraction?

   A $\dfrac{1}{8}$

   B $\dfrac{5}{8}$

   C $\dfrac{3}{4}$

   D $\dfrac{4}{5}$

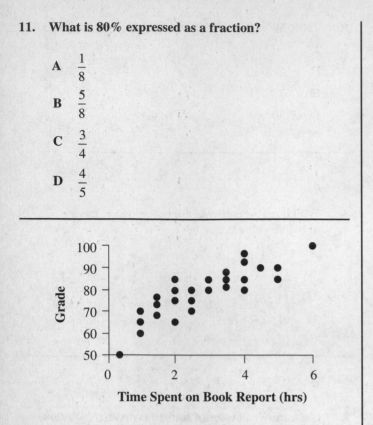

Time Spent on Book Report (hrs)

12. After grading her students' book reports, Ms. Reuben asked the students how much time they had spent researching and writing them. She then constructed a scatter plot to show the results. What conclusion can be inferred from the data on the scatter plot?

   A   In general, as more time is spent on the book report, the grade gets higher.

   B   In general, as more time is spent on the book report, the grade does not change.

   C   In general, as less time is spent on the book report, the grade gets higher.

   D   In general, the time spent on the book report and the grade are unrelated.

13. The regular price of a pair of sneakers is $60.00. The store is having a sale for the next week, and sneakers are 30% off. What is the price of the sneakers while they are on sale?

   A $18.00

   B $42.00

   C $48.00

   D $78.00

14. Which inequality is equivalent to $3 + 3x > 2(x - 5)$?

   A $3 + 3x > 2x - 5$

   B $3 + 3x > 2x - 7$

   C $3 + 3x > 2x - 10$

   D $3 + 3x > 2x - 11$

15. $5^2 \div 5^5 =$

   A 5^{-3}

   B 5^{-7}

   C 25^{-3}

   D 25^{-7}

16. Jill wants to find the sum of $\frac{5}{12} + \frac{3}{8}$. If she writes the prime factorization of the least common denominator, what will the result will be?

A 4×1

B $3 \times 2 \times 2$

C $3 \times 2 \times 2 \times 2$

D 8×12

17. $\dfrac{3^2 \times 5^4}{5^3} - \dfrac{4^5 \times 2^6}{4^7} =$

A 29

B 37

C 41

D 43

18. When a particular whole number is squared, the result is a number between 800 and 900. Therefore, the original whole number must be between which two integers?

A 20 and 25

B 25 and 30

C 30 and 35

D 35 and 40

19. The following scatter plot shows the number of albums sold and the number of concerts performed by a dozen of the world's most popular bands.

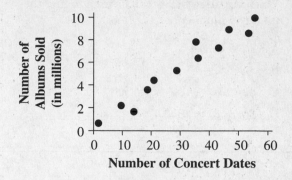

Based on the information in the scatter plot, what can you conclude about the relationship between the number of albums sold in relation to the number of concerts performed?

A In general, the number of album sales and the number of concerts performed do not have any relation.

B In general, the number of album sales decreases as the number of concerts performed increases.

C In general, the number of album sales increases as the number of concerts performed decreases.

D In general, the number of album sales increases as the number of concerts performed increases.

20. If you multiply a number by 3 and then subtract 8, the resulting number is 13.

Which equation below can be used to find the unknown number?

A $3n = 8 - 13$

B $3n - 8 = 13$

C $8 = 13 - 3n$

D $3(n - 8) = 13$

21. In isosceles triangle *DEF*, the measure of the vertex angle is exactly twice the measure of one of the base angles. Which of the following statements about Δ*DEF* is true?

A Δ*DEF* is an acute triangle.

B Δ*DEF* is an obtuse triangle.

C Δ*DEF* is an equilateral triangle.

D Δ*DEF* is a right triangle.

22. Evaluate the following algebraic expression:
$5(3x + 2)^2$

A $15x + 10$

B $30x + 20$

C $45x^2 + 60x + 20$

D $90x^2 + 120x + 40$

23. The line shown on the graph below represents which of the following equations?

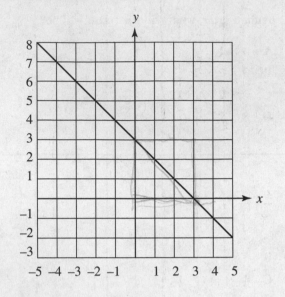

A $y = x + 3$

B $y = x - 3$

C $y = 3x$

D $y = 3 - x$

24. The graph below shows the total monthly cost to subscribers for time spent on-line with each of two Internet service providers.

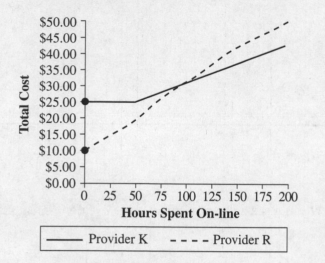

The monthly cost to subscribers with Provider R is less than that with Provider K

A if the subscriber spends exactly 100 hours on-line.

B if the subscriber spends fewer than 100 hours on-line.

C if the subscriber spends more than 100 hours on-line.

D no matter how many hours the subscriber spends on-line.

25. Simplify the following algebraic expression: $9x^{-2}$

A $\dfrac{9}{x^2}$

B $\dfrac{1}{9x^2}$

C $\dfrac{81}{x^2}$

D $(9x)^{-1}(9x)^{-1}$

26. One ounce is equal to approximately 28.4 grams. Given that information, about how many grams are equal to 4 ounces?

A 7.1

B 24.4

C 32.4

D 113.6

27. Which of the graphs below could be the representation of the equation: $y = -(x^2)$?

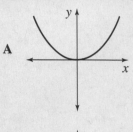

A

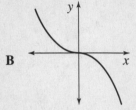

B

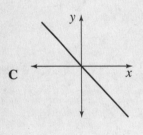

C

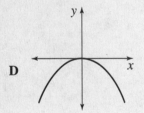

D

28. Solve the following inequality for t.

$$6t + 32 > 56$$

A $t > 4$

B $t > 5$

C $t > 6$

D $t > 7$

29. If $q = 2$ and $r = -6$, then $\dfrac{r^2 - 4q}{2} + r =$

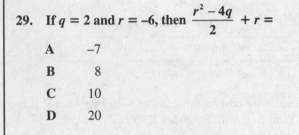

A   −7

B   8

C   10

D   20

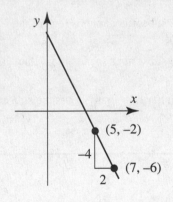

30. The slope of the line shown on the graph above is

A   −2

B $-\dfrac{1}{2}$

C $\dfrac{1}{2}$

D   2

31. Eric's homework assignment for his social studies class is to count how many cars pass by a certain exit sign on the parkway between 4:00 and 4:05 P.M. If 208 cars pass by during that time, about how many cars should pass by in 1 hour?

A   1,000

B   1,500

C   2,000

D   2,500

32. Keyshawna works part-time after school and on Saturdays at a video store. Last week she worked five days. The number of hours she worked and her salary for each day are plotted on the graph below.

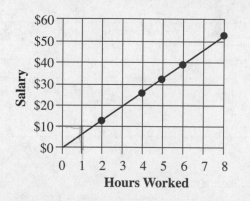

Approximately how much does Keyshawna get paid per hour of work?

A $5.00

B $6.50

C $8.00

D $9.50

33. At a recent stock-car race, the winning driver covered the race's 400-mile distance in $2\frac{1}{2}$ hours. What was her average speed?

A   160 miles per hour

B   200 miles per hour

C   625 miles per hour

D   1,000 miles per hour

34. The diagram below is a scale drawing of an ice hockey rink. The scale used is
1 inch (in) = 22 feet (ft).

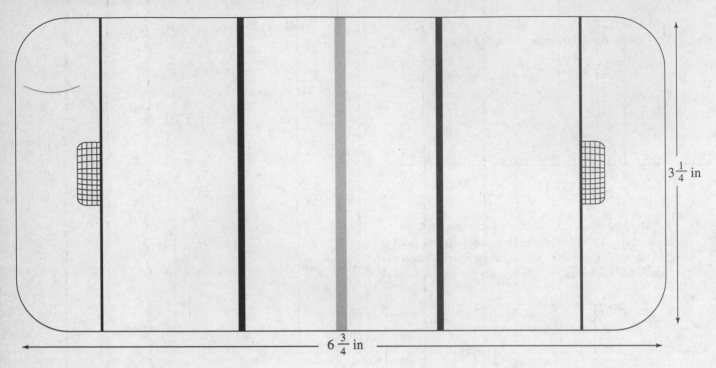

$6\frac{3}{4}$ in

$3\frac{1}{4}$ in

The actual length, in feet, of the ice hockey rink is

A   126.5 ft

B   143.0 ft

C   148.5 ft

D   154.0 ft

35. Simplify $\dfrac{15x^3y^2z^5}{-3xy^2z^3}$.

   A $-12x^2yz^2$

   B $-5x^2z^2$

   C $-5x^2yz^2$

   D $-45x^4y^4z^8$

---

36. In the figure below, what is the area of the shaded portion?

(Area of a triangle $5\ \dfrac{1}{2}\ bh$)

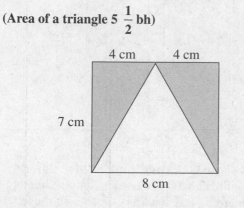

   A 14 cm²

   B 28 cm²

   C 42 cm²

   D 56 cm²

37. Given the formula for the area of a trapezoid $[A = \dfrac{1}{2}(b_1 + b_2)h]$, what is the area of the trapezoid shown in the diagram below?

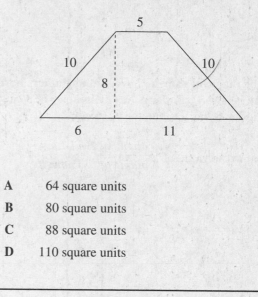

   A   64 square units

   B   80 square units

   C   88 square units

   D   110 square units

---

38. The density of lead is 11.3 grams per cubic centimeter $(\dfrac{g}{cm^3})$. What is the approximate volume of a 1-ounce lead fishing sinker, given that 1 ounce = 28.4 grams?

   A   2.5 cm³

   B   3.0 cm³

   C   25 cm³

   D   321 cm³

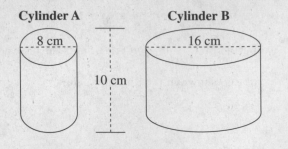

Cylinder A   Cylinder B

8 cm   16 cm

10 cm

39. In the diagram shown above, both cylinders have the same height. Cylinder A has a diameter of 8 cm, and Cylinder B has a diameter of 16 cm.

What is the value of $\dfrac{Volume\ of\ Cylinder\ A}{Volume\ of\ Cylinder\ B}$?

$(V = \pi r^2 h)$

A $\dfrac{1}{8}$

B $\dfrac{1}{4}$

C $\dfrac{1}{2}$

D $\dfrac{\pi}{8}$

40. The area of a 3-foot-by-3-foot piece of cardboard is 9 square feet. How many square inches are in 9 square feet?

A   108

B   324

C   648

D   1,296

41. Three of the vertices of a rectangle are the points (2, 2), (2, 6), and (8, 6). What are the coordinates of the fourth vertex?

A   (2, 8)

B   (6, 2)

C   (8, 2)

D   (8, 8)

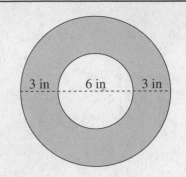

3 in   6 in   3 in

42. Gladys is making large iron-on letter *O*s for Oakmont High School T-shirts. Approximately how many square inches is the area of the letter *O*, represented by the shaded portion of the figure above? ($A = \pi r^2$ and $\pi \approx 3.14$)

A   28

B   85

C   113

D   226

43. In the diagram below, a triangle is added to a rectangle to form an irregular pentagon. What is the area of the entire pentagon?
(Area of a triangle = $\frac{1}{2}bh$)

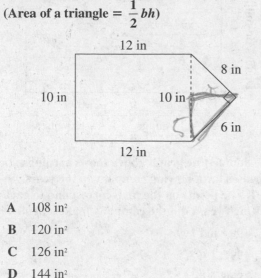

12 in

8 in

10 in

10 in

6 in

12 in

A 108 in²

B 120 in²

C 126 in²

D 144 in²

44. Evaluate the expression: $|-5|$

A -5

B $-\dfrac{1}{5}$

C $\dfrac{1}{5}$

D 5

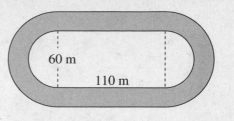

60 m

110 m

45. The school running track is composed of a gray all-weather surface oval that surrounds a region covered with grass. The grassy region in the middle is a rectangle that measures 110 meters by 60 meters. The grassy region at either end is a semicircle that measures 60 meters in diameter. What is the area, in square meters, of the grassy region (the portion that is not shaded)? (Area of a circle 5 πr^2 and $\pi \approx 3.14$)

A 6,600 m²

B 8,013 m²

C 9,426 m²

D 17,904 m²

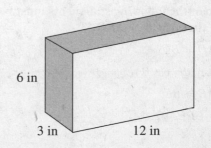

6 in

3 in

12 in

46. In order to determine the size of the label needed to cover the box shown above, the area of all 6 faces must be calculated. What is the total surface area of the box?

A 108 square inches

B 126 square inches

C 216 square inches

D 252 square inches

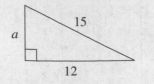

47. Find the value of *a* in the right triangle shown above.

   A   7

   B   9

   C   11

   D   13

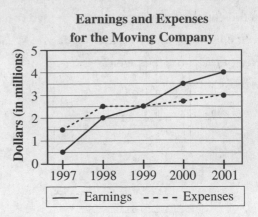

Earnings and Expenses for the Moving Company

50. The double-line graph above shows earnings and expenses for a moving company in the years 1997 to 2001. The points on the map correspond to each year. In which years did the company make a profit?

   A   1997 and 1998

   B   1997, 1998, and 1999

   C   1999 only

   D   2000 and 2001

48. In the diagram above, ∠ADC is congruent to ∠BCD. Which of the following statements must be true to prove that $\triangle ACD \cong \triangle BDC$?

   A $\overline{AD} \cong \overline{BC}$

   B $\angle ABE \cong \angle BAE$

   C $\overline{AE} \cong \overline{BE}$

   D $\angle CBE \cong \angle DAB$

Budget for Fall Dance

51. The entire budget for the fall dance was $1,000. Based on the above graph, about how much money was spent on hiring a DJ for the dance?

   A $400

   B $250

   C $100

   D $50

49. At a recent hockey game, the price of a general admission seat was lowered from $18.00 to $15.00 for students with a valid ID. By about what percent was the price lowered?

   A   3%

   B   17%

   C   20%

   D   83%

52. $(\frac{3}{5})^4(\frac{3}{5})^6 =$

A $(\frac{3}{5})^{10}$

B $(\frac{3}{5})^{24}$

C $(\frac{9}{25})^{10}$

D $(\frac{9}{25})^{24}$

---

53. A plane traveling at a constant speed from New York City to Boston covers 200 miles in 40 minutes. If the same plane traveled the same constant speed from L.A. to San Francisco, a distance of 380 miles, how long would it take?

A 38 minutes

B 1 hour, 3 minutes

C 1 hour, 16 minutes

D 1 hour, 26 minutes

$$\frac{12}{y} = \frac{3}{y-3}$$

54. Which equation is equivalent to the one above?

A $y(y-3) = 36$

B $12(y-3) = 3y$

C $12y = 3(y-3)$

D $15 = y + (y-3)$

---

55. The start time and finish time for four baseball games is shown in the table below.

Game	Start Time	Finish Time
1	7:30 P.M.	10:41 P.M.
2	1:30 P.M.	4:27 P.M.
3	5:00 P.M.	7:55 P.M.
4	6:30 P.M.	9:22 P.M.

Which game took the shortest amount of time to play?

A Game 1

B Game 2

C Game 3

D Game 4

---

56. In a school's science laboratory, the number of lab stations, l, is equal to 4 times the number of sinks, s.

Which of the following equations contains the same information about the school's science laboratory?

A $l \cdot s = 4$

B $4 \cdot s = 4 \cdot l$

C $4 \cdot l = s$

D $4 \cdot s = l$

---

57. The coordinates of three points on a graph are (−1, 5), (0, 1), and (1, −3). What is the slope of the line created by these three points?

A   −4

B   −1

C   1

D   4

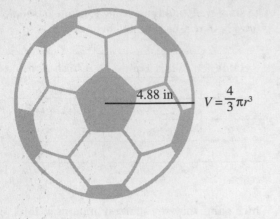

4.88 in

$$V = \frac{4}{3}\pi r^3$$

58. Brittney used her calculator to find the volume of the soccer ball shown above. When she saw her answer was 99.7 cubic inches, she knew immediately that she had done something wrong. She knew this because she had estimated that the volume should be approximately

A $\frac{4}{3} \times 3 \times 5 \times 5 = 100$

B $3 \times 5 \times 5 \times 5 = 375$

C $\frac{4}{3} \times 3 \times 5 \times 5 \times 5 = 500$

D $31 \times 5 \times 5 \times 5 = 3{,}875$

59. The National Center for Education Statistics released information about the average salaries paid to full-time professors at United States colleges and universities. The graph below displays the information for the years 1990 to 1994.

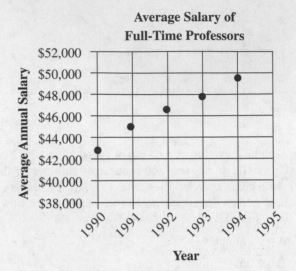

Average Salary of Full-Time Professors

Based on this information, what was the most likely average salary paid to full-time professors at United States colleges and universities in 1995?

A $53,000

B $51,500

C $49,000

D $2,000

60. While getting ready to study for her final exam in English, Wendy, a senior at Jefferson High School, stated the following:

If I do not study for my English final, I will fail the exam.

If I fail the exam, I will have to go to summer school.

If I have to go to summer school, I will not graduate with my class.

Which of the following conclusions can be drawn from Wendy's statements?

A   If she graduates with her class, Wendy studied for her English final.

B   If she did not graduate with her class, Wendy failed her exam.

C   If she studies for her English final, Wendy will graduate.

D   If she fails her exam, Wendy did not study for her English final.

61. A bag holds 3 blue marbles, 9 red marbles, and 5 yellow marbles. Ahmad removes 1 marble from the bag. Without replacing the first marble, he then removes a second marble. What is the probability that both marbles Ahmad removes are red?

A $\dfrac{9}{34}$

B $\dfrac{9}{17}$

C $\dfrac{35}{34}$

D $\dfrac{2}{9}$

62. Two perpendicular lines that both cross through (0, 1) on a graph have

A   the same slope and the same x-intercept.

B   slopes of opposite signs and different x-intercepts.

C   slopes of opposite signs but the same y-intercept.

D   the same slope and the same y-intercept.

63. Solve for x: $4x^2 - \sqrt{81} = 55$

A $\{-3, 3\}$

B $\{-4, 4\}$

C $\{3, -4\}$

D $\{-8, 8\}$

64. A standard deck of cards contains 13 spades, 13 hearts, 13 diamonds, and 13 clubs. From a standard deck of cards, Samantha picked a card at random four times, replacing the card after each pick. Each time she picked a heart and puts it back. If Samantha picks a card one more time, what is the theoretical probability that she will pick a heart?

A $\dfrac{1}{16}$

B $\dfrac{1}{8}$

C $\dfrac{1}{4}$

D $\dfrac{1}{2}$

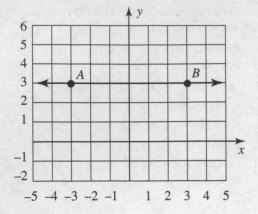

65. If you were to graph the equation $x + 3 = y$ on the graph above, at what point would the new line intersect with AB?

A $(0, 3)$

B $(1, 3)$

C $(0, 4)$

D $(1, 4)$

Albert bought two new shirts for the summer. They were on sale at 25% off their regular price of $30.00 each. This is $15.00 less than Albert paid for his favorite shirt. What was the total price paid by Albert for his new shirts?

66. What information is given in the problem that is <u>not</u> needed to find the answer?

A The number of new shirts bought

B The regular price of the new shirts

C The percent off for the sale

D How much less Albert paid for his favorite shirt

67. Beginning next month, the price of a year's subscription to a magazine will be increased by 15%. If the current price is $20.00 a year, what will be the price next month?

A $3.00

B $17.00

C $23.00

D $35.00

68. Which of these expressions is equal to a negative number?

A $(-4) \times (-2)$

B $(-4) \div (-2)$

C $(-4)^2$

D $(-4)^3$

69. The line whose equation is $2x - 5y = 15$ has what coordinates for its y-intercept?

A $(0, -3)$

B $(0, -5)$

C $(0, 3)$

D $(2, 0)$

70. Which ordered pair is the solution set for the following system of equations?

$$y = 2x + 10$$
$$y = 1 - x$$

A $(-3, 4)$

B $(3, -2)$

C $(10, -9)$

D $(-9, 10)$

Day	Sunrise	Sunset
Mon.	7:09 A.M.	6:16 P.M.
Tues.	7:07 A.M.	6:18 P.M.
Wed.	7:05 A.M.	6:20 P.M.
Thurs.	7:03 A.M.	6:22 P.M.
Fri.	7:01 A.M.	?

Table 1

71. Laurita figured out the unknown time in Table 1 for sunset on Friday by looking for a pattern. She noticed that with each new day, sunrise occurs two minutes earlier and sunset occurs two minutes later. Accordingly, sunset should occur at 6:24 P.M. on Friday.

Noble Gas	Boiling Point (°C)
helium	−269
neon	−246
argon	−186
krypton	−153
xenon	−108
radon	?

Table 2

Above is a table of the six noble gases, labeled from lightest to heaviest. Using the same strategy, what is a good estimate Laurita could use for the unknown boiling point in Table 2?

A −130°C

B −62°C

C 2°C

D 22°C

72. What is the x-intercept of the line $5x + 3y = 15$?

A (0, 3)

B (3, 0)

C (0, 5)

D (5, 0)

English Test Scores

	Test 1	Test 2	Test 3	Test 4	Test 5
Tim	88	89	92	91	88
Sue	88	81	83	86	81
Mao	85	88	91	88	82

73. The above chart shows the English test scores of three students. What is the mode of Mao's scores?

A 81

B 83

C 84

D 88

74. Alex went bowling with his friends after school. The bowling alley has a discount price for students from 4:00 to 6:00 P.M. It charges $1.50 to rent shoes, and $2.50 per game bowled. If his total cost for the outing was $11.50, which of the following equations could be used to determine how many games Alex bowled?

A $11.50 = 2.50n - 1.50$

B $2.50n + 1.50 = 11.50$

C $11.50 + 1.50 = 2.50n$

D $1.50n = 11.50 + 2.50$

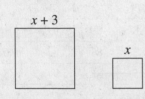

75. In the diagram above, a side of the larger square is 3 units longer than a side of the smaller square. Which of the following algebraic expressions could stand for the area of the larger square?

A $2x + 6$

B $x^2 + 9$

C $x^2 + 3x + 3$

D $x^2 + 6x + 9$

76. Point $(3, p)$ lies on a line whose equation is $y = 8x - 14$. What is the value of p?

A -6

B -3

C 2

D 10

Mathematics

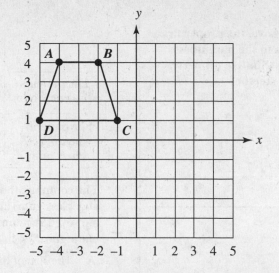

77. Trapezoid *ABCD* is reflected across the *x*-axis. Which of the following shows the result of that reflection?

A

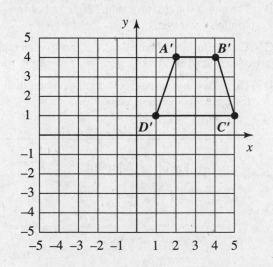

B

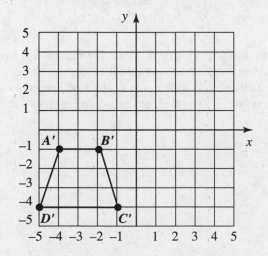

C

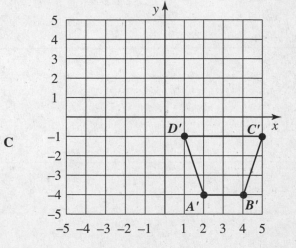

D

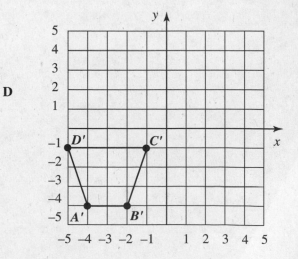

$2(y + 7) - 5 = 3(4 \times 3) + 3^3$

78. To solve for y in the equation above, the proper first step would be to solve the math in the parentheses, factoring it out by using the distributive property. What would the proper second step be?

A Add 5 to each side.

B Divide each side by 2.

C Solve for the exponent 33.

D Apply the distributive property.

$3x - 4 > 5$

79. The solution to the above inequality is

A $x > -1$

B $x > 1$

C $x > 3$

D $x > 9$

	Dentists who recommend *NixGum*	Dentists who do *NOT* recommend *NixGum*
For patients who chew gum	1,350	150
For patients who do *NOT* chew gum	86	1,414

80. The company that makes *NixGum* (a brand of sugarless gum) claims, "Ninety percent of dentists surveyed recommend *NixGum* for their patients who chew gum." What is misleading about this claim?

A The size of the sample of dentists surveyed was too small.

B The claim should have said, "eight out of ten dentists surveyed."

C The claim should have said, "eighty-five percent of dentists surveyed."

D The data suggest that most dentists prefer that their patients not chew gum.

Favorite Color Ink

81. The above circle graph shows the results of a survey asking students to name their favorite color ink. Approximately how many of the 1,000 students surveyed chose green as their favorite color ink?

A 100

B 250

C 400

D 500

athematics

Mathematics Test Scores

	Test 1	Test 2	Test 3	Test 4
Mai	5	8	9	10
Damon	10	8	10	8
Sasha	6	6	9	7

82. The above chart shows the mathematics test scores of three students. What is Sasha's median score?

   A   6

   B   6.5

   C   7.5

   D   8

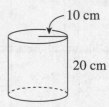

83. The above cylinder has a height of 20 centimeters and a radius of 10 centimeters. What is the surface area of the cylinder?
    (Area of a circle = πr^2; lateral area of a cylinder = $2\pi rh$, $\pi = 3.14$)

   A   1,570 cm²

   B   1,884 cm²

   C   3,768 cm²

   D   6,280 cm²

84. Marvin rolls a number cube with a different number—from 1 to 6—on each side. He rolls the cube twice. What is the probability that the two rolls will have a sum of 7?

   A $\dfrac{1}{36}$

   B $\dfrac{1}{12}$

   C $\dfrac{1}{9}$

   D $\dfrac{1}{6}$

85. $(\dfrac{3}{4})^2(\dfrac{3}{4})^0 =$

   A $(\dfrac{3}{4})0$

   B $(\dfrac{3}{4})^2$

   C $(\dfrac{9}{16})^0$

   D $(\dfrac{9}{16})^2$

86. What is the absolute value of $\dfrac{1}{6}$?

   A -6

   B $\dfrac{-1}{6}$

   C $\dfrac{1}{6}$

   D   6

87. What is $\dfrac{x^2y^3 \times x^4y^2}{x^3y^2}$?

A x^3y^3

B x^5y^4

C $x^2y^{\frac{5}{2}}$

D $x^{\frac{8}{3}}y^3$

10 in

6 in

88. What is the area of the shaded region in the above figure?

(Area of a triangle = $\dfrac{1}{2}$ bh)

A 15 in²

B 30 in²

C 45 in²

D 90 in²

89. What is 0.2 expressed as a fraction in its lowest terms?

A $\dfrac{2}{100}$

B $\dfrac{20}{100}$

C $\dfrac{2}{10}$

D $\dfrac{1}{5}$

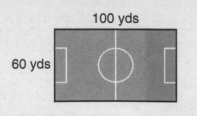

100 yds

60 yds

90. To the nearest yard, what is the diagonal distance across the soccer field represented above? (The Pythagorean theorem: $c^2 = a^2 + b^2$)

A 80 yards

B 94 yards

C 105 yards

D 117 yards

91. Which of the following choices expresses 63,000,000 in scientific notation?

A 63×10^6

B 6.3×10^7

C 6.3×10^8

D 6.3×10^9

Vocabulary Test Scores

	Test 1	Test 2	Test 3	Test 4
Olivia	12	15	11	14
Julie	13	11	10	14
Kimberly	12	13	14	15

92. The above chart shows the vocabulary test scores of three students. What is Olivia's mean score?

A 11

B 12

C 13

D 14

Chapter 17
Answers and
Explanations to
Practice Test 2

1. **B**   *Standard SDAP 1.1*

   This question asks you to find the mean number of points that Karla scored per game. Remember that the mean of a set of numbers is its average. So if you look at the points Karla scored in the first four games of the season, you'll see 9, 6, 5, and 8. Add them up and divide by 4 to get the mean. $28 \div 4 = 7$, making **B** the correct answer choice.

2. **B**   *Standard AF 4.2*

   Don't worry about all the scientific stuff in this problem. Just set up a proportion with the numbers given. Since you're told that the volume of a gas varies directly with its temperature in Kelvin, and that at 275 Kelvin, a gas's volume is 250 ml, the first part of the proportion is $\frac{250}{275}$. Then you can set up the second part of the proportion with the unknown volume over the new temperature: $\frac{250}{275} = \frac{?}{440}$. Cross multiply, and you'll get $250 \times 440 = 275 \times$ the unknown volume. $250 \times 440 = 110,000$. To solve $110,000 = 275 \times$ the unknown volume, just divide 110,000 by 275 to get the unknown volume. It's 400!

3. **B**   *Standard SDAP 3.1*

   Read the table carefully. It shows the possible outcomes of rolling two number cubes. Since each number cube has six sides, there are 636, or 36, possible outcomes. Since the table only lists 12 once, there is only one way to get a sum of 12—by rolling a 6 and a 6. Since the table lists 11 twice, there are two ways to get a sum of 11—by rolling a 6 and a 5, or by rolling a 5 and a 6. This question asks for the probability that the sum of the two dice will equal 9. Count the number of times that the number 9 appears in the table. It appears 4 times. 4 out of the possible 36 outcomes reduces to $\frac{1}{9}$, and that's the answer.

4. **C**   *Standard AI1 3.0*

   Go back to Chapter 5 if you don't remember how to solve absolute value problems. Just remember that the absolute value of a number is its distance from 0 on a number line. Since distance can never be negative, absolute values are always positive. Therefore, the absolute value of $n \times 4$ must equal 24. What times 4 equals 24? 6, right? But if the absolute value of –6 is also 6, then –6 is also a solution to $4|n| = 24$. So our solution set so far is {6, –6}. If $n = 0$, then $4|0|$ cannot equal 24, so **A**, **B**, and **D** are all incorrect.

5. **C**   *Standard SDAP 3.5*

   Remember from Chapter 11 that independent events do not influence the odds of another event occurring. For example, answer choice **A** does not show independent events because if you pick a pair of white socks from a drawer that contains white and gray pairs and don't replace it, there will be a lesser chance of picking a white pair again. Those events are dependent, just like in answer choice **D**. The events in answer choice **B** may seem independent, but they're not. The probability of picking an ace from a deck of 52 cards is $\frac{4}{52}$. Without replacing the ace, the probability of picking a king from the remaining 51 cards increases to $\frac{4}{51}$. The events in **C** are independent because the boy and the girl are from *different* classes. The first event won't alter the probability of the second event. (Different is the key word here.)

6. **D**   *Standard SDAP 3.5*

The spinner in this problem has an equal chance of landing on any of the 8 possible numbers. That means the probability of landing on any one number is exactly $\frac{1}{8}$. But wait—before you pick **A**, make sure you read the question carefully! It asks for the probability that the spinner will <u>not</u> stop on 3. That's $1 - \frac{1}{8}$, or $\frac{7}{8}$.

7. **D**   *Standard NS 1.1*

This question tests your knowledge of scientific notation. All you have to do is move the decimal point. Since 7.8 is being multiplied by 10^3, you simply move the decimal point three spaces to the right. (You create 0s for the empty spaces.) If you're careful, you'll end up with 7,800, making **D** correct. **B** would be correct if the question asked for 7.8×10^1; **C** would be correct if the question asked for 7.8×10^2.

8. **A**   *Standard NS 1.2*

To answer this question, simply solve the math in each of the answer choices. Whichever one gives you a negative result is the correct answer choice. Remember that subtracting a negative number is equivalent to adding a positive number! If you're careful with the negative signs, you'll get –3 for **A**, which is the only answer choice that yields a negative number.

9. **B**   *Standard NS 1.2*

For questions like this, plug in your own number to see what fits the answer choices. The question asked what the result of a number between 1 and 10 divided by 1,000 would be. Well, take 5, for example, and divide it by 1,000. You should get 0.005. That satisfies the conditions only in answer choice **B,** so that's it!

10. **C**   *Standard NS 1.3*

This question isn't asking for an exact figure, it just wants to know if you can make rough estimates for percentages. If 150 out of 203 cars in a parking lot were American, what percentage would that be? Well, it's clearly more than half of them, so you can get rid of **A** and **B**. And it's not more than 100% of the cars (that's not possible!), so it must be **C**. 150 out of 203 is about 75%. In fact, it's about 73.9%—but you don't even need to know that.

11. **D**   *Standard NS 1.3*

If you weren't sure that 80% is equal to $\frac{4}{5}$, you could always prove it by dividing. $4 \div 5 = 0.8$, which is the same as 80%. (To convert a decimal to a fraction, just move the decimal two places to the right.) Using simple division, you can tell that $\frac{1}{8}$ is equal to 12.5%, $\frac{5}{8}$ is equal to 62.5%, and $\frac{3}{4}$ is equal to 75%.

12. **A**   *Standard SDAP 1.2*

Take a good look at the scatter plot in this question. It shows the grades of 27 students' book reports—which ranged from 50 to about 98—in respect to the time spent on the reports. Look at the worst grade in the class. One student received a 50. That point is also very close to the 0 hrs marker of the time spent, meaning he or she probably didn't spend much more than 20 minutes on it. Now look at the best grade in the class. According to the scatter plot, that student spent 6 hours on the book report. Do you see a pattern? In general, this scatter plot shows that as more time is spent on the book report, the higher the grade.

13. **B**   *Standard NS 1.7*

To answer this question, just multiply the price of the sneakers ($60.00) by the sale (30%), and subtract the money saved from the original price. To multiply with a percent, convert it to a decimal first. 30% changes to 0.30, and 0.30 × 60 = 18. Be careful not to choose **A**! The <u>discount</u> is $18, but the question asks for the price of the sneakers during the sale. That's $60.00 – $18.00, or $42.00.

14. **C**   *Standard AI1 4.0*

This question is asking you to find the answer choice that is equivalent to $3 + 3x > 2(x – 5)$. Well, all you have to do is figure out what $2(x – 5)$ is equal to, and then you'll be able to answer the question correctly. If you picked **A**, you probably forgot about the distributive property—you need to multiply the coefficient of the parentheses (2) through *both* of the terms in the parentheses. $2(x – 5)$ is equal to $2(x) – 2(5)$, which is $2x – 10$. Therefore, $3 + 3x > 2(x – 5)$ is the same as $3 + 3x > 2x – 10$, making **C** correct.

15. **A**   *Standard NS 2.1*

You add the exponents if you're multiplying two exponents with the same base, and you subtract them if you're dividing two exponents with the same base. Therefore, $5^2 \div 5^5$ is equal to 5^{2-5}, which is 5^{-3}.

16. **C**   *Standard NS 2.2*

The least common denominator (LCD) is the least common multiple (LCM) of the denominators of the fractions. Prime factorization can be used to find the LCM of a set of numbers. A common multiple contains *all* the prime factors of each number. The LCM contains *each* factor the greatest number of times it appears. Look at the denominator in $\frac{5}{12}$: 12 = 4 × 3 = 2 × 2 × 3. For $\frac{3}{8}$, the denominator is 8: 8 = 4 × 2 = 2 × 2 × 2. The 2 appears three times for 8. The greatest number of times 2 appears for any single number is three times, so the LCM or LCD = 2 × 2 × 2 × 3.

17. **C**   *Standard NS 2.3*

Don't let the exponents in this question scare you—just remember to cancel the exponents in the fractions. For example, the 5^3 cancels out in the first fraction, $\frac{3^2 \times 5^4}{5^3}$, leaving you with only $3^2 \times 5^1$. ($5^1 = 5$.) The second fraction, $\frac{4^5 \times 2^6}{4^7}$, also reduces—by canceling the 4^5. So $\frac{4^5 \times 2^6}{4^7}$ is equal to $\frac{2^6}{4^2}$. Now it's easier to solve. The first fraction, which is now $3^2 \times 5$, reduces to 9 × 5, or 45. The second fraction, which is now $\frac{2^6}{4^2}$, is equal to $\frac{64}{16}$, which reduces to 4. Now the problem is 45 – 4, which equals 41. You could have solved this problem without canceling the exponents, but it would have taken more time and left more room for mistakes.

18. **B**   *Standard NS 2.4*

The best way to answer this question is to Plug In the numbers in the answer choices to see if they fit the specifications given. For example, the question says that when a whole number is squared, its result is between 800 and 900. Try the numbers in **A** first: 20 squared is 400, and 25 squared is 625. Our mystery number *can't* be between 20 and 25 because 25 squared is 625—and that's too small. Try **B** next: If you square 30, you will get 900. Since 25 squared is 625 and 30 squared is 900, and we're looking for the number whose square is between 800 and 900, our number must be between 25 and 30. 30 squared is 900, so no number above 30 when squared would be between 800 and 900, eliminating **C** and **D**.

19. **D** *Standard SDAP 1.2*

This scatter plot shows the relationship between album sales and the number of concerts performed by a dozen popular bands. Don't be too concerned with the individual points on the plot—just look for the general trend. The points seem to be going upward as they go to the right. That means that more albums are sold as more concerts are performed for each band. That makes **D** the best answer choice.

20. **B** *Standard AF 1.1*

This question is asking you to find an appropriate mathematical equation for the word problem given. Take it piece by piece to solve it. "If you multiply a number by 3" is equivalent to $n \times 3$ or $3n$. "And then subtract 8" is equivalent to $- 8$. So the first part of the problem is $3n - 8$. Since the resulting number is 13, the last part of the equation is $= 13$. Now you already know that the answer is choice **B**, but you can check to be sure by solving the equation. If $3n - 8 = 13$, then $3n = 21$. That means n must be 7. Fit that into the original word problem to see if it works. It does!

21. **D** *Standard MR 1.2*

In an isosceles triangle, two sides and two angles are congruent, and the vertex is the point opposite the base. You are told that the vertex angle is twice the measure of one of the base angles. So you've got two identical base angles and one vertex angle that's twice the measure of one base angle. Remember that the angles in any triangle add up to 180°. The only possible solution to this triangle is that the base angles are each 45° and the vertex angle is 90°. Since there is a 90° angle in the triangle, it's a right triangle.

22. **C** *Standard AF 1.2*

To simplify $5(3x + 2)^2$, you have to use the correct order of operations. Remember that exponents get evaluated before multiplication. That means you should expand $(3x + 2)^2$ before you multiply by 5. $(3x + 2)^2 = (3x + 2)(3x + 2)$. Use FOIL (First, Outside, Inside, Last) to multiply the two expressions: $(3x \times 3x) + (3x \times 2) + (2 \times 3x) + (2 \times 2)$. Now reduce: $9x^2 + 6x + 6x + 4 = 9x^2 + 12x + 4$. Now multiply $(9x^2 + 12x + 4)$ by 5 to get the final answer. $5(9x^2) + 5(12x) + 5(4) = 45x^2 + 60x + 20$. That's **C**.

23. **D** *Standard AF 1.5*

Look at the line on the graph. The line crosses the y-axis at 3 and also crosses the x-axis at 3. That means that when $x = 0$, $y = 3$ and when $y = 0$, $x = 3$. Use the equations in the answer choices to see which one represents the line. Try the equation in **A** first. If $x = 0$, does $y = 3$? $3 = 0 + 3$, so yes! But if $y = 0$, does $x = 3$? $0 \neq 3 + 3$, so no, **A** doesn't work. Try **B**: If $x = 0$, does $y = 3$? Well, $3 \neq 0 - 3$, so **B** is incorrect too. Next, try **C**: If $x = 0$, does $y = 3$? $3 \neq 3(0)$, so **C** isn't it. Already you know **D** must be correct, but check it to be certain. $0 = 3 - 3$ and $3 = 3 - 0$, so it works!

24. **B** *Standard AF 1.5*

The graph shows the respective monthly costs of two Internet providers—Provider K and Provider R. You're asked to find when the monthly cost to subscribers is less for Provider R than it is for Provider K. The key tells you that the solid line in the graph represents the costs for Provider K. Internet access costs $25.00 per month until it reaches the 50-hour point, and then it slowly gets more expensive. Provider R starts at $10.00, and then immediately gets more expensive with every hour spent on-line. The two lines cross at the 100-hour mark, meaning they cost the exact same amount (somewhere between $25.00 and $30.00). After 100 hours per month Provider R is more expensive. Based on this information, **B** is correct: Provider R is less expensive than Provider K if the subscriber spends less than 100 hours on-line per month.

25. **A**   *Standard AF 2.1*

This question tests your knowledge of negative exponents. Remember that $x^2 = \dfrac{x^2}{1}$, and $x^{-2} = \dfrac{1}{x^2}$. This problem is asking you to simplify $9x^{-2}$. Exponents get solved first so the question could be simplified to $9\left(\dfrac{1}{x^2}\right)$. That's the same as $\dfrac{9}{x^2}$, which is answer choice **A**. Try it with a real number to prove it. For example, if you make $x = 3$, you will get 1 as the final answer in both **A** and the question.

26. **D**   *Standard MG 1.1*

If 1 ounce is equal to about 28.4 grams, then 4 ounces would be equal to about 4×28.4 grams, or 113.6 grams. You didn't even need to perform the math to solve this problem; answer choice **D** gives the only reasonable answer.

27. **D**   *Standard AF 3.1*

You have to pick the graph that represents the equation $y = -(x^2)$. Plug in some values for x to see how the graph should look. If $x = 0$, then $y = -(0^2)$, or 0. Well, all four graphs pass through $(0, 0)$, so that doesn't eliminate any answer choices. If $x = 1$, then $y = -(1^2)$, or –1. If $x = 2$, then $y = -(2^2)$, or –4. As x goes up, y will go down exponentially (–1, –4, –9, –16, –25, etc.) because of the exponent. Because of the negative sign, the y coordinate will always be negative. For example, if $x = -1$, $y = -(-1^2)$, which equals –1; if $x = -2$, then y will equal $-(-2^2)$, or –4. The only graph that does not show any points with a positive y-coordinate is **D**.

28. **A**   *Standard AF 4.1*

To solve the inequality in this question, you need to isolate t on one side. The first step is to move 32 to the right side of the inequality, just like it was an equation. If $6t + 32 > 56$, then $6t + 32 - 32 > 56 - 32$. That simplifies to $6t > 24$. To isolate t at this point, divide both sides of the inequality by 6. $\dfrac{6t}{6} > \dfrac{24}{6}$ becomes $t > 4$. That's answer choice **A**.

29. **B**   *Standard AF 4.1*

Plug the values for q and r into the equation, and you'll end up with the correct answer. If $q = 2$ and $r = -6$, then $\dfrac{r^2 - 4q}{2} + r = \dfrac{-6^2 - 4(2)}{2} + -6$. Take the math one step at a time. $\dfrac{36 - 8}{2} - 6$. That comes to $\dfrac{28}{2} - 6$, which is equal to $14 - 6 = 8$. That's the answer.

30. **A**   *Standard AF 3.3*

The first thing you should notice about the line on this graph is that it points downward. That means the slope is negative. Since the slope is negative, **C** and **D** can't be correct. Right away you've eliminated two answer choices! You're given two points on the line: $(5, -2)$ and $(7, -6)$. You can see from the diagram that the line goes down four units for every two units to the right. Put those numbers in a fraction with the rise over the run: $\dfrac{-4}{2} = -2$. That's the slope, and it makes **A** correct.

31. **D**   *Standard AF 4.2*

You know that Eric counted 208 cars passing by an exit sign in five minutes. Based on that information, you have to estimate how many cars will pass by that exit sign in one hour. You can answer this question in several ways. First, if you know that 5 minutes is $\dfrac{1}{12}$ of an hour, (because $\dfrac{5}{60}$ reduces to) $\dfrac{1}{12}$ you can just multiply 208 by 12 to get 2,496. That's very close to 2,500, answer choice **D**. You could also set up a proportion so that $\dfrac{\text{minutes}}{\text{cars}} = \dfrac{\text{minutes}}{\text{cars}}$. It should look like $\dfrac{5}{208} = \dfrac{60}{x}$. Cross multiply to get $5x = 12,480$. To isolate x, divide both sides of the equation by 5, and you'll get the same answer, which is 2,496. **D** is the best choice.

32.　**B**　*Standard AF 3.4*

The line graph for this question shows how much Keyshawna gets paid based on how many hours she worked. A point is marked for the five different numbers of hours that she worked on five days. The first point is marked at two hours. Look to the vertical axis to see how much she earned—between $10 and $15. (It's difficult to tell exactly.) At four hours she earned between $25 and $30, at five hours she earned slightly more than $30, at six hours she earned almost $40, and at eight hours she earned a little more than $50. What rate is that? You can use the answer choices to help. If she earned $5 per hour, **A**, she would get about $40 for eight hours. That's too low. **B**, $6.50 per hour, seems to work. If she worked six hours she would make $39. If she worked eight hours she would make $52. The salaries listed in **C** and **D** are too high. **B** is it.

33.　**A**　*Standard MG 1.1*

The winning driver of a stock-car race traveled 400 miles in $2\frac{1}{2}$ hours. You need to figure out the average speed of this winning car in miles per hour. You can set up a proportion so that $\frac{\text{miles}}{\text{hours}} = \frac{\text{miles}}{\text{hours}}$. Filling in what we know, we've got $\frac{400}{2.5} = \frac{x}{1}$. (*x* represents the number of miles traveled in one hour.) Cross multiply to get $2.5x = 400$. Divide by 2.5, and you'll get $x = 160$. You could have used POE to eliminate answer choices **C** and **D**, because if the car traveled 400 miles in 2.5 hours, it couldn't have averaged more than 400 miles per hour!

34.　**C**　*Standard MG 1.2*

The drawing in this question shows a scale drawing of an ice hockey rink. You are told that 1 inch = 22 feet. The question asks for the actual length of the ice hockey rink. Since the drawing shows the length as $6\frac{3}{4}$ inches, you can just multiply $6\frac{3}{4}$ by 22 to get the right answer. (It's easier if you convert the fraction to a decimal: $6\frac{3}{4} = 6.75$.) $6.75 \times 22 = 148.5$. That's answer choice **C**. You could also set up a proportion so that $\frac{1\,\text{inch}}{22\,\text{feet}} = \frac{6.75\,\text{inches}}{x\,\text{feet}}$. You'll end up with the same answer—148.5 feet.

35.　**B**　*Standard AF 2.2*

The fraction $\frac{15x^3y^2z^5}{-3xy^2z^3}$ looks terribly confusing, but you can simplify it easily by taking it one step at a time. For example, notice that there is a y^2 in both parts of the fraction. That means they cancel out, leaving no *y* in the fraction at all. (Already that leaves only **B** as a correct answer choice!) Divide 15 by –3, and you will get –5. You can cancel one *x*, leaving x^2 in the numerator. The z^3 cancels, leaving a z^2 in the numerator. Altogether, $\frac{15x^3y^2z^5}{-3xy^2z^3}$ simplifies to $-5x^2z^2$.

36.　**B**　*Standard MG 2.1*

To find the area of the shaded portion of the drawing in this problem, you can either calculate the area of the two shaded triangles or subtract the area of the white triangle from the entire rectangle. Either method will give you the right answer. Use the given formula to help you. Let's calculate the area of the two shaded triangles—that's probably easier. If the base is 4 cm and the height is 7 cm, and the area for each one is $\frac{1}{2}bh$, then each triangle's area is $\frac{1}{2}(4\,\text{cm})(7\,\text{cm})$. That's $\frac{1}{2}(28\,\text{cm}^2)$, or 14 cm². But wait—don't forget that you have to add the area for both shaded triangles together. 14 cm² + 14 cm² = 28 cm², which is answer choice **B**.

37. **C** *Standard MG 2.1*

All you have to do here is plug the numbers from the diagram into the formula given in the question. The top base is 5 and the bottom base is $6 + 11 = 17$. Because the height is 8, the area of the trapezoid is $\frac{1}{2}(5 + 17)(8)$, or $\frac{1}{2}(22)(8)$. The trapezoid's area is $(11)(8)$, or 88 square units, answer choice **C**.

38. **A** *Standard MG 1.3*

This question is a bit tricky, but don't get thrown by the scientific nature of it. The density of lead is 11.3 grams per cm^3. You have to figure out the approximate volume of a lead weight that weighs 1 ounce, or about 28.4 grams. Set up a proportion so that $\frac{11.3g}{1\,cm^3} = \frac{28.4\,g}{x\,cm^3}$. If you cross multiply and divide, you'll get $11.3x = 28.4$. Divide 28.4 by 11.3 to get your answer. It's about 2.5, making A, $2.5\,cm^3$, the best answer choice.

39. **B** *Standard MG 2.1*

You could work out the volumes of both cylinders to solve this problem, but it would be easier simply to figure out the proportion that they have. You know that the radius of Cylinder *A* is 4 cm and the radius of Cylinder *B* is 8 cm. (Each radius is half the diameter.) Since the volume of a cylinder is $\pi r^2 h$, the value of $\frac{Volume\ of\ Cylinder\ A}{Volume\ of\ Cylinder\ B}$ is $\frac{\pi(4^2)(10)}{\pi(8^2)(10)}$. The 10 and the π cancel out in the fraction, leaving only $\frac{4^2}{8^2}$, which is the same as $\frac{16}{64}$. That reduces to $\frac{1}{4}$, which is the final answer.

40. **D** *Standard MG 2.4*

The information in the first sentence is not necessary to solve the question. All you need to know to solve this problem is that there are 12 inches in a foot—and 12×12, or 144, *square* inches in a *square* foot. If you forgot to square the number 12, you probably ended up mistakenly picking **A**. Once you know that there are 144 square inches in a square foot, you can just multiply that number by 9 to get your answer. $144 \times 9 = 1,296$.

41. **C**   *Standard MG 3.2*

It might help to draw a sketch for this problem.

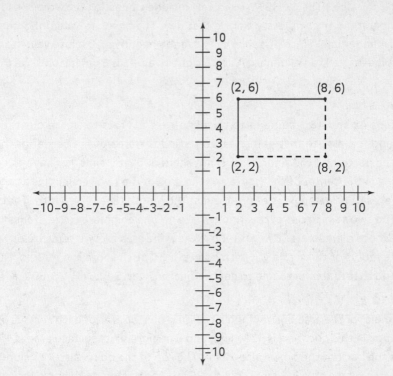

You can see from the sketch that the points (2, 2) and (2, 6) create a vertical line. The point (8, 6) creates a horizontal line with (2, 6). The missing point is in the lower right corner of the rectangle, and it must create a horizontal line with (2, 2) and a vertical line with (8, 6). That's eight units to the right and two up, which can be identified as the coordinates (8, 2). If you weren't sure of the correct answer choice, you could have eliminated **B** and **A**. A rectangle must have two pairs of two vertices on the same *x*- and *y*-axes.

42. **B**   *Standard MG 2.2*

You have to find the shaded area of the figure in this question—the *O* that Gladys is going to use on the T-shirts. You aren't given the formula for the area of an *O*, but you are given the area for a circle. To compute the area for the *O*, you can simply subtract the area of the white circle from the entire figure. The diameter of the outer circle is 6 in + 3 in + 3 in, or 12 inches. That means its radius is 6 in and its area is $\pi \cdot 6^2$, or 36π. The diameter of the white inner circle is 6 in, meaning its radius is 3 in and its area is $\pi \cdot 3^2$, or 9π. Therefore, the area of the shaded *O* figure is $36\pi - 9\pi$. Use 3.14 for π and see what you get: 36(3.14) – 9(3.14) = 113.04 – 28.26 = 84.78. The result is closest to 85, answer choice **B**.

43. **D**   *Standard MG 2.2*

To figure out the area of the entire pentagon, you need to combine the areas of the rectangle and the right triangle. The area of a rectangle is determined by multiplying its length by its width. In this case that's 12 in × 10 in, or 120 in². The area of a triangle is $\frac{1}{2}$ times its base times its height. It may look like this right triangle doesn't have a base, but you just have to look at it from another angle. (Turn the page 45 degrees clockwise, and 6 inches will become the base. Then 8 in will become the height. That makes the area $\frac{1}{2}$ (6 in)(8 in), or $\frac{1}{2}$ (48 in²), which reduces to 24 in². Add the areas of the rectangle and the triangle to get the final answer: 120 in² + 24 in² = 144 in².

44. **D**   *Standard NS 2.5*

This question tests your knowledge of absolute value. (Vertical bars surrounding an expression represent absolute value.) The CAHSEE will surely include a question or two on absolute value, so make sure you understand it completely before test day. The absolute value of a number is its distance from 0 on a number line. Since distance can never be negative, absolute value can never be negative either. That means you can eliminate **A** and **B** right away. –5 is 5 units from 0 on the number line, so **D** is correct.

45. **C**   *Standard MG 2.2*

Like questions 42 and 43, you need to calculate several areas to figure out the area of the region you're looking for. Notice that you're asked to find the area of the center part of the track, represented by the portion of the figure that is not shaded. That means you have to calculate the area of the rectangle in the center of the figure and the area of the two semicircles at either end of the rectangle. The area of a rectangle is easy—it's just the length times the width. That's 110 m × 60 m, or 6,600 m². The two semicircles in this figure make up one complete circle. So just figure out the area for a circle whose diameter is 60 m, and you'll know the area for two semicircles with diameters of 60 m. Since the radius of this circle you've made up is 30 m, the area is $\pi \cdot 30^2$, or 900π, which is about 2,826 m². Add that to the rectangle to get the final answer: 2,826 m² + 6,600 m² = 9,426 m².

46. **D**   *Standard MG 2.3*

Use the formula for the area of a rectangle to figure out the area of each surface of the box. The front side of the box in this question is 12 in long and 6 in high, so its surface area is 12 in × 6 in, or 72 in². That means the back of the box is also 72 in². The top of the box is also 12 in long but only 3 in wide. That means its surface area is 12 in × 3 in, or 36 in². The bottom of the box must therefore also be 36 in². The sides of the box are each 3 in long and 6 in tall, making their surface areas 3 in × 6 in, or 18 in². In total, the six sides of the cube are 72 in² + 72 in² + 36 in² + 36 in² + 18 in² + 18 in². That adds up to 252 in².

47. **B**   *Standard MG 3.3*

The Pythagorean theorem says that in a right triangle, the square of the hypotenuse equals the sum of the squares of the two other sides. In this case, $12^2 + a^2 = 15^2$. Then just simplify the equation: $144 + a^2 = 225$. Subtract 144 from both sides of the equation to get $a^2 = 81$. Now if you take the square root of both sides, you'll get $a = 9$.

48. **A**   *Standard MG 3.4*

The measure of $\angle ADC$ is the same as $\angle BCD$. That means you already know that one side and one angle are congruent in both $\triangle ACD$ and $\triangle BDC$. (The side $\overline{CD}$ is shared by both triangles, so it must be the same!) To know for sure that $\triangle ACD \cong \triangle BDC$, you need to know if another side is congruent. (That creates side-angle-side, or SAS, congruency.) If the two lines $\overline{AD}$ and $\overline{BC}$ are congruent, that would prove it. That's **A**. None of the other answer choices would prove it.

49. **B**   *Standard NS 1.6*

There are several ways to figure out the percentage that the price was lowered in this problem. You could multiply the values in the answer choices by $18.00 to see which one is closest to $3.00, the discount on the price of a seat. Be careful not to pick **D**, though. 83% is the reduced cost, meaning that the price was lowered by 17%. That's answer choice **B**.

50. **D** *Standard NS 1.1*

Refer to the graph and its key when answering this question. The graph shows both earnings (the solid line) and expenses (the dotted line). The question asks you in which years the company made a profit. Be careful! Don't just look for the years with the highest earnings. For a company to make a profit, its earnings must be more its expenses. So, you need to find which years the earnings were greater than the expenses. On the graph, look for the years in which the solid line is higher than the dotted line. The solid line is higher than the dotted line in the years 2000 and 2001.

51. **B** *Standard NS 1.1*

Refer to the circle graph to estimate how much money was spent on hiring a DJ. First, it is clear that the cost of renting a hall was half of the budget. Because the costs of decorations, refreshments, and the DJ take up the second half of the budget, you can assume that *less* than one-half of the budget was spent on the DJ. According to the circle graph, the cost of the DJ actually takes up one-quarter of the budget. Dividing the $1,000 budget by 4 (because a quarter is one-fourth of the whole) will give you $250, answer choice **B**. You can also multiply $1,000 by $\frac{1}{4}$ to get $250.

52. **A** *Standard NS 2.3*

Remember the rule for multiplying numbers with exponents? If the bases are the same, add the exponents and leave the bases alone. In this question, the bases of the two numbers are the same. Therefore, you should carry the base of $\frac{3}{5}$ to the other side of the equal sign. Then, add the exponents of the two numbers, 4 + 6, and write their sum as a new exponent on the base you carried over. The correct answer is $(\frac{3}{5})^{10}$, answer choice **A**.

53. **C** *Standard MG 1.3*

If the plane traveled 200 miles from New York City to Boston in 40 minutes, then its rate of speed is $\frac{200 \text{ miles}}{40 \text{ minutes}}$. To figure out how long it would take a plane traveling at the same speed to cover 380 miles, you should set up a proportion so that $\frac{200 \text{ miles}}{40 \text{ minutes}} = \frac{380 \text{ miles}}{x \text{ minutes}}$. Cross multiply, and you'll get $200x = 15,200$. Divide both sides of the equation by 200 to find x. $15,200 \div 200 = 76$. $x = 76$. 76 minutes is the same as one hour, 16 minutes. You should have eliminated A right away. If the plane traveled 200 miles in 40 minutes, it must have taken longer than 38 minutes to travel 380 miles.

54. **B** *Standard AI1 4.0*

This equation is set up a lot like the proportion in the problem you just did, isn't it? You can solve it the same way you solved that one. Cross multiply the two fractions in the equation: $\frac{12}{y} = \frac{3}{y-3}$ is equivalent to $12 \times (y - 3) = y \times 3$. That's the same as $12(y - 3) = 3y$. You don't even have to simplify it more than that. Answer choice **B** already shows this new equation.

55. **D** *Standard MR 1.1*

The best way to solve this question is to calculate the playing time of each game. The one with the shortest difference between start and end times is the right answer. Game 1 started at 7:30 and ended at 10:41. That's a difference of 3 hours and 11 minutes. Game 2 started at 1:30 and ended at 4:27—3 minutes short of exactly 3 hours. Since Game 2, **B**, took 2 hours and 57 minutes, you know Game 1, **A**, can't be the shortest game. Cross it off. Game 3 started at 5:00 and ended at 7:55. That's 2 minutes faster than Game 2. Cross off **B**. Game 4 started at 6:30 and ended at 9:22, making it only 2 hours and 52 minutes. It was the quickest game, making **D** the correct answer choice.

56. **D** *Standard AF 1.1*

Read this word problem carefully. It says that the number of lab stations, which is represented by the variable *l*, is equal to the 4 times the number of sinks, represented by the variable *s*. That's $l = 4 \times s$. **D** shows that same equation backwards. None of the other choices show a proper way to translate the problem. Plug in real numbers if you need to. For example, say that there are 3 sinks. There must then be 3×4, or 12, lab stations. Plug those numbers into the answer choices, and only **D** will work.

57. **A** *Standard AF 3.3*

Sketch this line on a piece of scrap paper if it helps you visualize the line created by the coordinates $(-1, 5)$, $(0, 1)$, and $(1, -3)$. You should see that the line goes downward at a steep angle. That means -4 is the best answer choice. You can use the formula for the slope of a line ($\frac{y_1 - y_2}{x_1 - x_2}$ or $\frac{\text{rise}}{\text{run}}$) to determine exactly which answer choice is correct. You may use any two of the three given points. Using the first two coordinates, $y_2 - y_1 = 5 - 1$, or 4. $x_2 - x_1 = -1 - 0$, or -1. $\frac{4}{-1} = -4$.

58. **C** *Standard MR 2.1*

The volume of a sphere is given by the formula $V = \frac{4}{3}\pi r^3$. The soccer ball in the question is shown to have a radius of about 5 inches. Remember that to find the volume of a three-dimensional object, you must take its radius to the third power—meaning you multiply it by itself three times. Therefore, using a rough estimate of 3 for π, the volume of the soccer ball should be about $\frac{4}{3} \times 3 \times 5 \times 5 \times 5$. That's answer choice **C**.

59. **B** *Standard MR 2.3*

Follow the graph as it goes upward. At the beginning of the graph, 1990, full-time professors were paid an average of between $42,000 and $44,000. Every year following 1990 the average salary appears to increase by almost $2,000. By 1994 the average salary had almost reached $50,000. You have to use the graph to predict the approximate average salary for full-time professors in 1995. $53,000 is too much of an increase, based on the previous years. $49,000 is actually a decrease in pay, and $2,000 is the approximate increase in salary—not the actual salary. $51,500, **B**, is the best answer choice.

60. **A** *Standard MR 2.4*

This question gives you three statements from which to deduce a reasonable conclusion. If Wendy doesn't study, she will fail. If she fails, she will go to summer school. If she goes to summer school, she won't graduate with her class. Look at the conclusions in the answer choices. Start with **A**. If Wendy graduates with her class, does that mean she studied for her final? Well, if she didn't study, then she could not have passed and couldn't graduate with her class, according to the three initial statements. So yes, **A** seems right, but try the other ones to be sure. **B** is not necessarily true because Wendy might not be able to graduate with her class for other reasons than failing her exam. Likewise, Wendy could still have failed her exam even if she studied for it. But she can't pass it if she doesn't study for it. That makes **D** incorrect. **C** is not true because while you know she won't pass if she doesn't study, you can't know if she *will definitely pass* if she *does* study. They're not the same things.

61. **A** *Standard SDAP 3.5*

Break the problem down into a few steps to find the probability that both marbles Ahmad removes from the bag are red. First, find the probability that the first marble chosen is red. The probability that the first marble is red is $\frac{9}{17}$, because there are 9 red marbles and 17 total marbles. Next, find the probability that the second marble chosen is also red. The probability that the second marble is red is $\frac{8}{16} = \frac{1}{2}$, because there are 8 red marbles left and 16 total marbles left. Then, multiply the two values together to find the probability that both marbles are red. The probability that both marbles chosen are red is therefore $\frac{9}{17} \times \frac{1}{2} = \frac{9}{34}$.

62. **C** *Standard AI1 8.0*

First of all, remember that perpendicular means "at right angles to each other." It might help to sketch two perpendicular lines that go through the (0, 1) point on a graph. Use scratch paper to do this. You'll notice that the slopes are clearly different. For example, if one line goes steadily up with a slope of 1, passing through (0, 1), then a perpendicular line must have a slope of –1, also passing through (0, 1). Since both lines pass through (0, 1), they must have the same y-intercepts—1 for both. And because they have slopes of opposite signs but the same y-intercept, that leaves **C** as the only correct answer choice.

63. **B** *Standard AI1 2.0*

You have to find the value of x when $4x^2 - \sqrt{81} = 55$. $\sqrt{81}$ is equivalent to 9, so the equation simplifies to $4x^2 - 9 = 55$. Add 9 to both sides of the equation, and you'll be left with $4x^2 = 64$. Then you can isolate x^2 by dividing both sides of the equation by 4. $4x^2 \div 4 = 64 \div 4$, or $x^2 = 16$. From this point x is equal to the square root of 16. Both 4 and –4 solve that equation, making **B** correct. You could always put the values from the answer choices into the original equation to see if they fit. For example, try $x = 3$, then see if $4(3^2) - \sqrt{81} = 55$. It doesn't fit, so 3 is not a proper solution. That eliminates **A** and **C**.

64. **C** *Standard SDAP 3.3*

This is a tricky question! The important thing to notice about this probability question is that every time Samantha picks a card, she puts it back—in other words, the total number of cards in the deck for each pick is always 52. That means there is the same chance of picking a heart every time: $\frac{13}{52}$, which reduces to $\frac{1}{4}$. The fact that Samantha picked a heart four times in a row doesn't matter. The theoretical probability of picking another one is still $\frac{1}{4}$.

65. **A** *Standard AF 1.5*

Line $\overline{AB}$ is a horizontal line with a slope of 0. Since it always stays three units up on the y-axis, its y-coordinate is always 3. Therefore, you can use POE to eliminate **C** and **D**. (0, 4) and (1, 4) are not even points that intersect with line $\overline{AB}$. You can sketch the line whose equation is $x + 3 = y$ on the actual graph to see where it intersects. But once you notice that (0, 3) and (1, 3) are both points on $\overline{AB}$, you just have to check to see if they're points on the line whose equation is $x + 3 = y$. Plug them in to find out. $0 + 3 = 3$, so **A** works. $1 + 3 \neq 3$, so **B** is wrong.

66. **D** *Standard MR 1.1*

This question tests your ability to distinguish needed information from unnecessary information in a problem. The problem asks for the total price Albert paid for his new shirts. To solve that you need to know three things: the original price of the shirts, the sale on the shirts, and the number of shirts bought. The solution to this problem is $2 \times [30 - (30 \times 0.25)]$. You don't need to know how much Albert paid for his favorite shirt. That makes **D** correct.

67. **C** *Standard NS 1.7*

To solve this problem you simply need to figure out the increase in the price of the magazine subscription. 15% of a $20.00 subscription is $20.00 \times .15$, which is $3.00. Therefore, the increase is $3. Be careful not to pick **A**, though. $3 is just the increase in the cost of the subscription. Add that to the original price, $20.00, to get the updated price of the subscription: $20.00 + $3.00 = $23.00.

68. **D** *Standard NS 1.2*

There's only one way to figure out which expression in the answer choices is negative: Simplify each one. Try **A** first: $(-4) \times (-2) = 8$. **B:** $(-4) \div (-2) = 2$. **C:** $(-4)^2 = 16$. **D:** $(-4)^3 = -64$. Only the expression in answer choice **D** results in a negative number.

69. **A** *Standard AI1 6.0*

Any point on the *y*-intercept of a graph must have 0 for its *x*-coordinate. That means you can use POE to eliminate **D**. Remember: (2, 0) is the *x*-intercept—not the *y*-intercept. Since the *x*-coordinate must be 0, just plug in 0 for *x* in the equation to solve for *y*. $2x - 5y = 15$ then becomes $2(0) - 5y = 15$. That's $-5y = 15$. Now divide both sides of the equation by –5 to solve for *y*: $\frac{-5y}{-5} = \frac{15}{-5}$. That means $y = -3$.

Therefore, the coordinates of the *y*-intercept of the line $2x - 5y = 15$ are (0, –3). That's **A**.

70. **A** *Standard AI1 9.0*

The easiest way to figure out which ordered pair from a list of choices is the solution for the given system of equations is simply to try them out! Plug in the values for *x* and *y*; if they fit, you've got the right answer choice! Remember to try the values in both equations. (Some wrong answer choices will be correct for only one equation.) Start with **A:** If $x = -3$, check to see if $y = 4$. Does $4 = 2(-3) + 10$? Yes, $4 = -6 + 10$. Now check to see if $4 = 1 - (-3)$, which is true. It works for both equations. You could also plug $1 - x$ into the *y* spot in the first equation and then solve for *x*. This gives you $1 - x = 2x + 10$, which works out to $-3 = x$. If you then plug –3 into the second equation you would get $y = 1 - (-3) = 4$. Your *x*- and *y*- coordinates are (–3, 4), which is **A**.

71. **B** *Standard MR 3.3*

Look at the boiling points of the noble gases in the second table. The lightest noble gas, helium, has the lowest boiling point at –269°C. Each heavier noble gas's boiling point is between 20° and 60° warmer. By the time you get to radon, the boiling point should be warmer than –108°—but not by more than 20° to 60°, according to the trend. –62° is the best answer choice, so **B** is right.

72. **B** *Standard AI1 6.0*

The *x*-intercept on a graph must have 0 for its *y*-coordinate. That means you can use POE to eliminate **A** and **C**. Then, to figure out what the *x*-coordinate is, just plug 0 in for *y* and see what you get. $5x + 3y = 15$ becomes $5x + 3(0) = 15$, which is $5x = 15$. Divide both sides by 5, and you'll find that $x = 3$. That makes the coordinates (3, 0), making **B** correct.

73. **D** *Standard SDAP 1.1*

To answer this question, you must know that the mode is the most frequently occurring value in a sequence of numbers. Locate Mao's name in the chart and compare the scores listed in his row. Mao scored an 85, 88, 91, 88, and 82. Because 88 occurs the most frequently in the data set of Mao's scores, 88 is the mode.

74. **B** *Standard Al1 15.0*

The price for bowling shoes is $1.50. The price for each game is $2.50. The total cost is $11.50. You have to choose the equation in the answer choices that could show how many games Alex bowled. The variable belongs with the number of games bowled, so that eliminates **D**. (The equation in **D** multiplies the number of times shoes were rented.) The price of shoes ($1.50) should be added to the number of games bowled $\times$ the cost of games to get $11.50. That's the equation represented in **B**. The equation in **A** subtracts the cost of shoes, and the equation in **C** adds the cost of shoes to the total cost.

75. **D** *Standard Al1 10.0*

Don't get confused by the variable in this equation! You don't need to solve for x. In fact, you can ignore the smaller square altogether—it's not important at all. The formula for the area of a square is the measurement of a side squared. You know that the length of a side of the larger square is $x + 3$. Therefore, the area of the larger square is $(x + 3)^2$. $(x + 3)^2 = (x + 3)(x + 3)$. Use FOIL to combine: $(x)(x) + 3(x) + 3(x) + (3)(3)$. Simplified, that equals $x^2 + 3x + 3x + 9$. Add the $3x + 3x$ together, and you'll get the algebraic equation in answer choice **D**.

76. **D** *Standard Al1 7.0*

You already know the x-coordinate of point $(3, p)$—it's 3. Just plug that 3 into the equation for x and see what you get. The result will be the value for p. The equation becomes $p = (8)(3) - 14$. Now you know that $y = 24 - 14$. That's 10, and that's all there is to this question.

77. **D** *Standard MG 3.2*

You need to pick the answer choice that displays a reflection of trapezoid *ABCD* over the x-axis. Because the question asks for a reflection across the x-axis, not the y-axis, you should throw out **A** and **C**. (The graph in **C** actually seems to reflect the trapezoid across both axes.) That leaves you with the graphs in **B** and **D**. The graph in **B** is the exact same shape, just moved five spaces down. That's an example of a translation. The graph in **D** is the opposite shape, much like a mirror image is an opposite image. That's the proper reflection.

78. **C** *Standard Al1 5.0*

Once you've solved the math in the parentheses, $2(y + 7) - 5 = 3(4 \times 3) + 3^3$ would become $2(y + 7) - 5 = 6(12) + 3^3$. Now you've got an equation with addition, subtraction, multiplication, and an exponent. What does PEMDAS tell you to do? That's right! Once the parentheses have been solved, the next step is to solve for the exponents. In this case, you should solve for 3^3, which is equal to 27. **C** is the correct answer choice here.

79. **C** *Standard AF 4.1*

To solve $3x - 4 > 5$, add 4 to both sides of the inequality. That will leave you with $3x > 9$. At this point you can divide both sides of the inequality by 3 to isolate x. $\frac{3x}{3} > \frac{9}{3}$ reduces to $x > 3$, which is the solution listed in answer choice **C**.

80. **D**   *Standard SDAP 2.5*

1,500 dentists were surveyed to find their recommendations on chewing gum. Out of the 1,500, more than 1,400 do not recommend chewing *NixGum* if their patients don't chew gum. The claim says, "Ninety percent of dentists surveyed recommend *NixGum* for their patients who chew gum." While this is not factually incorrect, it is misleading. The sample of dentists was not too small, so **A** isn't right. And 1,350 out of 1,500 dentists is, in fact, ninety percent, so **B** and **C** are not wrong either. According to the graph, most dentists do not recommend that their patients chew gum at all. The company's claim makes it seem that their gum is actually healthy; there's no reason to think it is, from the information in this table.

81. **A**   *Standard NS 1.1*

Refer to the circle graph to estimate how many students chose green as their favorite color. The question states that 1,000 students were surveyed. The circle graph, therefore, represents the favorite color choices of 1,000 students. According to the graph, less than $\frac{1}{2}$ of the students chose green. In fact, less than $\frac{1}{4}$ of the students chose green. Because $\frac{1}{4}$ of 1,000 is 250, you can eliminate answer choices **B, C,** and **D.** Answer choice **A** is correct because 100 is $\frac{1}{10}$ of 1,000, or 10% of 1,000. By looking at the graph, it appears that out of 1,000 students, approximately 100, or $\frac{1}{10}$ of the students, chose green.

82. **B**   *Standard SDAP 1.1*

Remember that the median is the middle number in a set of data when the data is ordered from least to greatest. If there is an even number of items of data in a set, the median is the mean, or average, of the two middle numbers. In this question, you need to arrange the scores in Sasha's row from least to greatest and then find the middle value. Of the scores 6, 6, 7, and 9, the two middle numbers are 6 and 7. Because there are 4 scores, an even number, you must find the average of 6 and 7. Find the average by adding the two numbers and dividing their sum by 2. Answer choice **B**, 6.5, is the median of Sasha's scores.

83. **B**   *Standard MG 2.3*

The question asks you to find the surface area of a given cylinder. The question also provides you with the formulas to use. Just plug the measurements into the formulas and solve the problem. First of all, though, remember that a cylinder has a top and bottom base. The top and bottom bases are just circles! The formula to find the area of a circle is πr^2. Because the radius is 10 cm, the area of each circle is 314 cm². There are two circles, so multiply 314 by 2 to find the combined areas—the areas of the top and bottom bases—which is 628 cm². Now find the lateral, or side, area of the cylinder. The formula to find the lateral side is $2\pi r h$. Because the height of the cylinder is 20 cm, and the radius is 10 cm, the lateral area is (2)(3.14)(10)(20), which equals 1,256 cm². To find the surface area of the cylinder, you now need to add the area of the bases, 628 cm², with the lateral area, 1,256 cm², which equals 1,884 cm², answer choice **B**.

84. **D**   *Standard SDAP 3.3*

The number cube Marvin rolls has 6 numbers on it. If he rolls the cube once, there are 6 possible outcomes. Because Marvin rolls the cube twice, however, there are 36 possible outcomes (6 × 6), so 36 will be the denominator of the probability fraction you will create. The question asks you what the probability is that the two rolls will have a sum of 7. There will be more than one favorable outcome with a sum of 7. Try listing all possible pairs of numbers from 1 to 6 with a sum of 7 to find the total number of favorable outcomes. It might help to draw a diagram like the one in Chapter 11. Remember, you can roll a 1 with the first roll of the number cube. You can roll a 6 with the second roll of the number cube. Or, you can roll a 6 with the first roll and a 1 with the second roll. Count all possible pairs with a sum of 7. This sum will be your numerator. There are 6 favorable outcomes with a sum of 7: 1 + 6, 6 + 1, 2 + 5, 5 + 2, 3 + 4, and 4 + 3. The probability that Marvin's two rolls will have a sum of 7 is $\frac{6}{36}$, or, in its simplest form, $\frac{1}{6}$, answer choice **D**.

85. **B** *Standard NS 2.3*
Remember that when you multiply fractions with exponents, and if the bases are the same, you add the exponents and keep the same base. In this question, the bases are each $\frac{3}{4}$. So, keep the base and add the exponents: 2 + 0 = 2. The correct answer is $(\frac{3}{4})^2$, answer choice **B**.

86. **C** *Standard NS 2.5*
One way to think about absolute value is as a measure of distance. The absolute value of a number is how far that number is from 0 on the number line. Distance must be a positive quantity. Therefore, you can eliminate answer choices **A** and **B** because they are negative numbers. Also, because $\frac{1}{6}$ is a fraction, you can eliminate answer choices that are whole numbers. To find the absolute value of $\frac{1}{6}$, ask yourself how far $\frac{1}{6}$ is from zero on the number line. It is $\frac{1}{6}$ of a unit from zero on the number line, answer choice **C**.

87. **A** *Standard AF 2.1*
To answer this question, it is best to break the problem into smaller parts. First, solve the numerator; then, solve the denominator. When you have solved the numerator and the denominator, you can then divide the numerator by the denominator. To solve the numerator, you will need to multiply numbers with exponents. When multiplying numbers that have the same base but have different exponents, add the exponents and carry the base. When dividing numbers with exponents and the same base, subtract the exponents and carry the base: $\frac{x^2y^3 \times x^4y^2}{x^3y^2} = \frac{x^6y^5}{x^3y^2} = x^3y^3$.

88. **B** *Standard MG 2.2*
The question asks you to find the area of only the shaded region. First, determine the area of the entire rectangle. Then, find the area of the unshaded region (the triangle), and subtract that area from the area of the entire rectangle. This will give you the area of the shaded region. Find the area of the rectangle by multiplying the base by the height, or 6 $\times$ 10 = 60 in². Find the area of the triangle by using the formula: Area of a triangle = $\frac{1}{2}$ bh. The area of this triangle is $\frac{1}{2} \times$ 6 $\times$ 10 = 30 in². Now, subtract the area of the triangle from the area of the rectangle: 60 in² – 30 in² = 30 in², answer choice **B**.

89. **D** *Standard NS 1.3*
Note that the question asks you for a fraction that is reduced to its lowest terms. This means that no number can be divided into both the numerator and denominator. To answer the question, first convert 0.2 into the fraction $\frac{2}{10}$ and reduce it to $\frac{1}{5}$, answer choice **D**. Be careful. Although answer choice **C**, $\frac{2}{10}$, is equal to 0.2, it is not fully reduced.

90. **D** *Standard MG 3.3*

It might help you to draw a diagonal line in the diagram. A diagonal line will divide the rectangle into two triangles. The question asks you to find the diagonal distance across the soccer field, which is the length of the line you just drew. The diagram already gives you the lengths of two sides of the triangle. You need to find the missing length. Notice that the missing length is across from a right angle. When you drew the line, you formed a right triangle! The missing length is the hypotenuse. You must use the Pythagorean theorem ($c^2 = a^2 + b^2$) to find the diagonal distance across the soccer field. $100^2 + 60^2 = 13,600$. So, $c^2 = 13,600$. Now you must find the square root of 13,600 to the nearest yard. At this point, you can just take the numbers from each answer choice, and multiply them by themselves until you come to the one that equals 13,600 when squared. It is approximately 117 yards, answer choice **D**.

91. **B** *Standard NS 1.1*

Scientific notation expresses a number less than ten times a power of ten. Although the product in answer choice **A** equals 63,000,000, it is not in proper scientific notation because 63 is not less than 10. The product in answer choice **B** is also equal to 63,000,000; and 6.3 is less than 10, so this is the correct answer. The decimal point in 6.3 is moved 7 places to the right, which equals 63,000,000.

92. **C** *Standard SDAP 1.1*

Remember that a mean, or average, is computed by finding the sum of the data and then dividing the sum by the total number of items of data. The question asks you to find Olivia's mean (average) vocabulary test score. Refer to the chart to locate Olivia's name and the scores that are in her row. To find Olivia's mean score, first add 12, 15, 11, and 14. Their sum is 52. Because there are 4 test scores, you then divide 52 by 4, which is 13, answer choice **C**.

If students need to know it,
it's in our *Cracking the CAHSEE Guides!*

Cracking the CAHSEE: English-Language Arts, 3rd Edition
978-0-375-42867-8 • $16.00

Cracking the CAHSEE: Mathematics, 3rd Edition
978-0-375-42868-5 • $16.00

And don't forget the College Prep Guides:

Cracking the SAT, 2009 Edition
978-0-375-42865-2 • $19.95

Cracking the SAT with DVD, 2009 Edition
978-0-375-42857-9 • $33.95

Cracking the ACT, 2008 Edition
978-0-375-76634-3 • $19.95

Cracking the ACT with DVD, 2008 Edition
978-0-375-76635-0 • $31.95

11 Practice Tests for the SAT and PSAT, 2009 Edition
978-0-375-42860-9 • $19.95

Best 368 Colleges, 2009 Edition
978-0-375-42872-2 • $21.95

Complete Book of Colleges, 2009 Edition
978-0-375-42874-6 • $26.95

Available at your local bookstore